CLASSIC CONFLICTS

D-DAY

CLASSIC CONFLICTS

D-DAY

'OPERATION OVERLORD' FROM ITS PLANNING TO THE LIBERATION OF PARIS

PUBLISHED BY
SALAMANDER BOOKS LIMITED
LONDON

A SALAMANDER BOOK

Published by Salamander Books Ltd
8 Blenheim Court
Brewery Road
London N7 9NT

1 3 5 7 9 8 6 4 2

© Salamander Books Ltd, 1999

ISBN 1 84065 095 8

CREDITS

Designed by DW Design, London
Set by D.A.G. Publications Ltd
Printed and bound in Great Britain by
Mackays of Chatham plc, Chatham, Kent

This book was originally published as an illustrated edition

CONTENTS

THE SECOND FRONT DEBATE

In an address to students at the US Army War College in the mid-1920s, Brig. Gen. Fox Conner harshly characterized the business of fighting as part of an alliance. While serving in France as an operations officer on Gen. John J. Pershing's staff, he had witnessed the perpetual inability of the Allied and Associated powers to settle on a common strategy against the Germans or even to agree on allocation of resources. The incessant pursuit of purely national interests, in his opinion, prevented the Allies from bringing the full weight of their military and economic power efficiently to bear against their common enemy. Thus, as he pondered the problem for the benefit of the Army's future strategists, Conner concluded that, if he had to go to war again, he would prefer to go to war against an alliance, rather than against a single power.

Conner was a considerable scholar of the military art, but his strictures on the perils of alliances had already been voiced centuries before by Sun Tzu, the ancient Chinese philosopher of war, who warned against entering into alliances without being entirely certain of the war aims of the potential ally. Hastily conceived agreements, Sun Tzu suggested, could easily founder because two powers fighting a common foe might themselves have conflicting intentions. His was sound advice, for whenever two or more nations combined their efforts in war during the succeeding centuries, bitter disagreements, rather than concord, were often the rule. In fact, one of the peculiarities of alliances is that successful ones have always tended to disintegrate in discord as fast as unsuccessful ones. That certainly was the American experience of World War I, the first major occasion since the Revolution when the United States had waged war in concert with allies. As isolationism and the depression jointly spiraled through the 1930s, a residuum of suspicion was directed even against the United Kingdom. There were those, both in the Army and out, who believed American naivety had been cold-bloodedly exploited in 1917 in a war to preserve the British Empire.

The Anglo-American alliance of World War II stood in contrast to the experience of 1917–18 as perhaps the most successful coalition in the history of modern warfare. From the very beginning, the United States and the United Kingdom adopted the defeat of Germany as their common goal. Agreement on ultimate aims nonetheless did not imply agreement in detail, and the progress of the war was marked by periodic disputes. Among the most famous was the occasionally acrimonious debate between Generals Dwight D. Eisenhower and Sir Bernard L. Montgomery about the proper strategy to be employed on the European continent: the "broad front" or the "knife-like thrust." The springs of such disagreements arose from the gradually evolving leadership of the coalition. Until 1943, Britain was the dominant partner and consequently more powerfully influenced the course of the alliance. After 1943, however, the United States, by virtue of its contribution of the greater mass of manpower and economic power, became senior partner. The Second Front debate, more than any other, was emblematic of that shift in coalition leadership. It was, furthermore, the most significant difference of opinion that arose between the United States and Britain during the war. Both nations agreed that Germany had to be assaulted, but the specific agreement that the assault would be launched from England, across the English Channel, to the coast of France, was reached only after extended discussion. At its root, the Second Front debate was the question of whether the alliance would adhere to a long-term plan for a cross-channel attack, or would retain the flexibility to take advantage of the military situation at the time of attack to strike where Germany was weakest. Economic, political, and military differences, as well as differences in national styles of waging war, complicated the debate.

■ The American Position

Even before the fall of France in May 1940, the United States was slipping away from the dubious neutrality that it had proclaimed at the start of the European war. President Franklin D. Roosevelt declared a national emergency and ordered the Navy into the Atlantic, ostensibly on "neutrality patrols," but in fact to help the British by convoying ships at least part of the way across the danger zone. Against the possibility that the United States would eventually enter the war, American naval and military staffs began a series of unofficial, unrecognized, but nonetheless crucial discussions in Washington between January and March 1941. The most important single decision the military leaders reached in these American–British Conventions, or ABC talks for short, was that Germany would be the number one enemy of any future Anglo-American partnership. Such a decision was contrary to long-standing assumptions of Army and Navy war planning. Plan *Orange*, meticulously refined over more than two decades, outlined the strategy to be employed when the United States and Japan eventually went to war, as many naval and military officers assumed would eventually happen. Tension in the Pacific increased throughout 1941, and thoughtful observers of the Far East warned of Japanese aggressive designs that would almost certainly involve American interests and possessions. Despite this, American leaders agreed that any war that might begin with Japan would have to take second place; primacy of effort would go to defeating Germany.

Much of this reflected President Roosevelt's conviction that the fate of the United States was indissolubly linked with that of the United Kingdom. The continued existence of the latter was in the best interests of the United States, not only because of the commonality of language and culture, but also because Britain stood as a bulwark against any possible Axis aggression in the Americas. American armed forces in 1941 were frankly unready for global war, and it was the British fleet, guaranteeing control of the Atlantic, that provided security during the period of national mobilization that the President was attempting to hurry. The President and his principal advisors were likewise convinced that the United States should do that which was morally right, rather than just that which was politically expedient. The conclusion Roosevelt drew was that American energies should be focused in support of the British to defeat the greatest threat to the free world. That threat, he concluded, was Germany. Prime Minister Winston Churchill's delight with the agreement, however, was soon to be tempered by the American view on how it should be carried out. American plans for the impending war were conditioned by an interplay of military philosophy and economic and geographic constraints that did not affect the United Kingdom.

One aspect of European military thought that had fallen on fertile ground in the United States came from one of the most profound military thinkers of the century, Maj. Gen. J. F. C. Fuller, a highly experienced British officer whom many regarded as the foremost exponent in the world of armored warfare. Fuller's enumeration of the "principles of war" appealed greatly to Americans. A listing of the most important considerations in military operations naturally appealed to the mechanically-minded. Yet the principles of war were more than just a check-list for military commanders. They were, rather, an organized way of thinking about war, and most officers saw the "principle of the objective" as far and away the most important of all considerations. Their military ideal was a legacy of the American Civil War and the style of Gen. U. S. Grant, who tenaciously maintained contact with Gen. R. E. Lee's Army of Northern Virginia until he achieved victory. Americans preferred a short, extremely violent war, with all possible resources brought to bear in continuous combat until the enemy was defeated. The principle of attacking a clearly defined and attainable military objective, almost always the main body of the enemy's army, accorded well with the limitations under which American officers perceived they would have to fight.

Geography was equally important. Broad oceans offered the Americas great physical security from attack, but they also isolated the continent from European and Asiatic battlefields. In the event of war, as planners at the Army War College clearly foresaw during the 1920s and 1930s, the United States would have to erect and maintain a large and sophisticated logistical structure to send substantial forces across the oceans, sustain them in foreign theaters, and employ them against powerful enemies on other continents. If war came in Asia as well as in Europe, as some officers expected, the problem of allocating scarce resources would be even more acute. Those essential demands on manpower and materiel would certainly detract from the total fighting power the United States could muster. These geopolitical factors were expressed in the American planning document for World War II.

In the spring and summer of 1941, during the last months of peace for the United States, the War Department was superintending the sale of surplus war materiel to Britain and other nations arrayed against Hitler, and considering how to meet the demands imposed by the recently passed Lend-Lease Bill, under the terms of which the United States would transfer massive amounts of military equipment to the countries fighting the Axis. At the same time, the Army was involved in a limited expansion, virtually a peace-time mobilization, that threw mobilization plans out of joint. In the work of military supply and procurement, chaos reigned. In an attempt to develop a manageable production plan, the Assistant Secretary of War and President Roosevelt asked the general staff for an estimate of what would be needed to defeat the Axis if the United States became involved in the war.

Gen. George C. Marshall, Army Chief of Staff, handed that question to Albert C. Wedemeyer, an infantry major assigned to the War Plans Division of the general staff, and Wedemeyer's staff estimate, later known as the Victory Plan, succinctly delineated the steps necessary to win a European war. Wedemeyer reasoned that he could not estimate the nation's total military production requirements unless he had some idea of the size and missions of the Army in the event of war. He immediately drew on the substance of the ABC talks to define the Army's mission in the event of war. The chief task, he assumed, was the defeat of Germany, to which all other missions would be subordinate.

Military logic, as embodied in the principles of war, demanded that the Army strictly keep its eye on the objective, and not fritter its limited energies away in attractive, but indecisive, side issues. If the defeat of Germany was the objective, then the mission was to attack the heart of German power as early and as forcefully as possible. That meant massing the Army for a direct invasion of the continent of Europe at the earliest possible date. Determining that date relied on three interrelated factors: the date by which enough men could be trained and equipped for war, the date by which the necessary shipping would be available to move them to Europe and sustain them there, and the date by which the necessary military preconditions for attack could be completed.

Careful consideration of Army mobilization and training, military construction, and naval and merchant shipbuilding revealed that the Army could expect to go over to the offensive no earlier than July 1, 1943. Achieving the necessary military conditions for attack, though simple to state, was a more uncertain proposition. Wedemeyer suggested in his plan that no invasion of Europe could succeed until the navies defeated the Axis fleets and secured the Atlantic lines of communication; the Allies established air superiority over Europe; air bombardment had disrupted the German economy and industry, thus decreasing that country's war-making potential; German military forces had been weakened; and adequate bases had been established. Although he did not specify it in the Victory Plan, Wedemeyer assumed, and fellow war-planners explicitly stated, that the only useful European bases that would still be available to the United States in 1943 would be those situated in the British Isles.

Thus, before war even began for the United States, there existed a conceptual plan for the ultimate defeat of Germany. That plan relied on an invasion of the continent of Europe to strike into the heart of Germany, to the exclusion of all other military designs. Implicit in the plan were fighting and winning the Battle of the Atlantic; what became known as the combined bomber offensive that sought to destroy German industry and economic life; continued attacks on the Germans wherever they could be found, to decrease their military strength; and the creation of a major American buildup in Britain. The climactic battle, because of the practicalities of production and military preparations, could not start before July 1943, two years hence.

American war planners accordingly had to figure on deploying a large army and air force, as well as a powerful navy, to Europe; sustaining it there while maintaining long and easily attacked lines of communications across the oceans; allotting enough military power at least to contain the Japanese in the meantime; and producing enough materiel to support not only American forces, but also the armies of the Allies. This, they felt, could never be done without a master plan, adjustable in fine detail, but not in its major points. Such massive industrial production demanded careful timing, and Americans wanted a corresponding military timetable.

The choice of Britain as a base for the attack on Europe, made while Eisenhower was chief of War Plans Division in early 1942, was equally crucial. Early, planners dismissed fanciful ideas of landings in Liberia and subsequent campaigns through North Africa, across the Mediterranean, and into southern Europe. A concept to deliver American troops to Russia was scrapped because shipping routes to Murmansk or through the Persian Gulf, both for troops and for supplies, were simply too long. Attacks through Portugal, Norway, and Spain were all dismissed as too roundabout.

For a time, there was serious thought about an attack from the Mediterranean, where the British were already doing well against German forces. Despite Prime Minister Winston Churchill's later enthusiasm for the "soft underbelly" of Europe, Americans rejected the Mediterranean avenue of approach because long supply lines made it impossible to concentrate full Allied strength there, and because of the distance to the heart of Germany from North American bases when the attack had to pass through southern Europe. More serious opposition to an attack through the south of France, or through the Balkans, arose because of the extremely difficult terrain, favorable for defense, that stood between the Mediterranean shores and Germany.

The choice settled on Britain for all the reasons that made the other options impractical. The most important single consideration was that Britain lay on the shortest of all possible transatlantic routes from the United States. A perennial problem for war planners, regardless of the proposed operation, was the perpetual Allied shortage of merchant ships. The Battle of the Atlantic had consumed too many ships, both merchant and naval; losses that were made up by new construction at the cost of accumulating the tonnage needed to increase the pace of offensive operations. Many convoys had to be dedicated to feeding and supplying the British Isles, while others tried to sustain the Soviet ally, whose continued resistance was an essential element in all American war planning. Once war began, other vessels had to be diverted to maintain American and Commonwealth military strength in the Pacific, even at minimal levels. Economy of supply was therefore a foremost consideration. A short route meant a shorter travel time. An easy route facilitated large convoys. Good ports in Britain meant a shorter turnaround time for the ships. Placing the American buildup in the British Isles was the most efficient use of scarce shipping.

Secondly, the British Isles were a logical point of departure for military operations against the continent. Big enough to support the buildup, the islands were also the best place from which to use relatively short-ranged fighters of the Royal Air Force to support the landings, and an unsinkable aircraft carrier for the American Army Air Forces. The short distance across the English Channel offered for the Allies the chance to give the attacking infantry continuous and effective air support. The Royal Navy, major units of which were already concentrated around the North Sea to bottle up the German surface fleet, could most easily be used to support landings against the Channel coast. The most important, however, was the geographical fact that the most direct route into the center of Germany was the one from the French coast opposite England, and thence across northwest Europe. That route also offered the minimum in natural, and therefore defensible, obstacles. Militarily, it was the most logical choice.

For the Americans, the decision to use the United Kingdom was axiomatic. When compared with the other possible avenues of approach, it was superior in almost every way, offering the possibility of the quickest buildup and concentration of force. The intention to concentrate rapidly in Britain meant that the United States would enforce rigorous economies of manpower and materiel in the other theaters, while intensifying the campaign of aerial attack on Germany and blockade of Europe, and the naval war in the Atlantic. Industrial mobilization plans began to structure American industry to support such a plan, and the military enthusiastically began to organize itself around the requirements for just such a major attack. American planning for what became Operation *Overlord* actually began before the United States entered the war, and it was always the essence of American war policy. Literally everything the United States did was aimed at that decisive invasion of the continent, and military operations were judged in terms of how well they contributed to that end. *Overlord* was far more than just D-Day, and far more than just one important battle. It was the culmination of the entire American strategy.

■ The British Position

Geographical location and a different philosophy of waging war gave the British a different outlook on the nature, timing, and location of the Second Front against Germany. At the time of the initial staff talks, the United Kingdom had already been at war for some two years and had suffered grievous losses during the Battle of France, the Battle of Britain, and the Battle of the Atlantic. Even as the famous Eighth Army began its successful march across North Africa after the battle of El Alamein, it was clear that the British lived in a world of ever-declining resources. Certainly from 1943 onward, their forces would never be as strong tomorrow as they were today, because the limits of British and Commonwealth manpower had been reached. It was also true that the British were forever confronted with the specter of the Somme. Politically, militarily, practically, and in humanitarian terms, it was unthinkable that Britain should again suffer the enormous casualties that she had borne in the 1914–18

THE SECOND FRONT DEBATE

war. The notion of attacking carefully prepared fortifications along the French coast struck many conscientious soldiers as being potentially as costly as any of the great assaults of World War I.

British political and military leaders were therefore inclined to be extremely cautious. They certainly were in favor of an invasion of Europe but only when the time was right; when circumstances were in the Allies' favor. They could not, many held, afford to be repulsed. If the invasion failed for any of the many possible dangers inherent in such a risky operation, then, at least from the British point of view, there could be no second try. Churchill and his commanders accordingly had the tendency to define favorable circumstances very precisely.

The British were also historically a maritime power, and their entire experience in dealing with a hostile continental military power – chiefly the wars of the French Revolution and of Napoleon – inclined them to a sea power solution. The result was that many preferred to draw a blockade, a net of steel, around the Axis and gradually pull it tighter and tighter, nibbling away with the army at exposed bits of Axis military strength. At the end, following the successful naval battles of the Atlantic and the bombing campaign which British leaders agreed were necessary preconditions for the assault, Germany would be debilitated and weak. A single, powerful blow would then be enough.

The British further counseled caution because they had a more recent, more extensive, and generally more sobering understanding of amphibious operations than the American allies, whose last important landing had been during their civil war, and who, it was possible to argue, had never conducted an opposed amphibious landing at all. British planners well understood that the English Channel, however narrow at various points, was a formidable barrier that had stopped Napoleon and, more recently, the technically sophisticated Germans. More to the point was their own World War I landing at Gallipoli, which warned of the high costs of attacking a hostile shore, and appeared to show that well-organized defenses could contain even successful landings.

Carefully studied between the two world wars, Gallipoli convinced thoughtful soldiers that the defender would always be able to bring up reinforcements faster than the attacker could build up his forces on the invasion beaches, and would likewise be better able to supply and support those forces than the attacker. Amphibious landings were by nature always frontal assaults, very much like those that characterized fighting on the

Western Front; although without the advantages of extensive artillery support, the availability of reserves, and attacks launched from prepared positions. The British experience on the Western Front had been grim; how much worse, then, a frontal attack that arose from the waves? It was the lessons learned from the 1942 attack on the French port of Dieppe (Operation *Jubilee*), however, that worried invasion planners most.

British forces had launched minor raids on the French coast almost from the moment of the evacuation of the army from Dunkirk. In August 1942, Lord Louis Mountbatten's Combined Operations headquarters passed from mere raids to a deliberate, large-scale invasion of Dieppe. The intention was never to hold the beachhead, but to test military and naval cooperation; the use of combined arms in large-scale landings of infantry and armored troops; and the organization of air forces in obtaining and maintaining control of the air over invasion beaches. Mountbatten's operation was also to test a new piece of equipment, the Landing Craft, Tank (LCT), to see whether it could place tanks directly on the beaches, thus enabling assault forces to take a port by direct frontal assault.

The August 19 landings, conducted largely with soldiers of Canadian 2nd Division, although about one thousand British troops and some fifty US Rangers also took part, were an unmitigated tactical failure. German resistance was unexpectedly fierce. Within nine hours of the assault, British commanders were forced to withdraw the survivors under heavy pressure from the defenders. Almost one thousand soldiers died in the attack and around two thousand were left on the battlefield as prisoners of war. Of the 6,100 men in the assault force, only 2,500 returned to England. If Dieppe was a dry run for the eventual invasion of France, its high casualty lists made British planners' blood run cold. Ordinary German garrison troops, it turned out, and not elite formations, had repulsed the Canadian attack. One of the chief lessons of Dieppe was thus that a large naval bombardment force was essential to crack the prepared defenses of any hostile shore, and the accumulation of that force awaited the winning of critical naval battles in the Atlantic and elsewhere. Clearly, the lessons of Gallipoli still applied. There was not much subtlety to amphibious assaults, and overwhelming force was essential if there was to be any hope of success.

The consequence of all these considerations was that the British always appeared willing to explore alternate strategies and points of attack that would enable the alliance to hit the enemy where circumstances offered, rather than adhering strictly to a carefully conceived and, as they saw it, excessively rigid, plan. Senior American officers and their staff planners tended to see Churchill's perpetual willingness to entertain other objectives than the cross-channel attack as an unwillingness to conduct that operation at all. Even as the English-speaking nations marshaled their forces for their joint war against Germany, the suspicions of which Sun Tzu had written so many centuries before began whisperingly to penetrate the structure of an alliance both Churchill and Roosevelt regarded as unshakable.

■ The Progress of the Debate

When Roosevelt, Churchill, and their chiefs of staff met at the *Arcadia* Conference in Washington, DC, immediately after Pearl Harbor, they endorsed the earlier and informal agreement to defeat Germany first, while containing the Japanese. They further agreed to wear down Axis strength by tightening a ring around those nations and to use aid to the Russians, naval blockade, strategic bombing, and limited offensives at points of Allied superiority as their principal means. While American staff studies envisioned a major attack into the heart of Germany, such a proposal formed no part of the *Arcadia* agreement because it did not seem, at that moment, to be possible.

First principles occasioned no disagreement. "The only thing that ever really frightened me during the whole war," Winston Churchill wrote, "was the U-boat peril." In the early years, German submarines threatened to starve Britain out of the war. Later, winning the Battle of the Atlantic was essential to concentrating ground, naval and air forces for an invasion of the continent. By the time the United States Navy entered the battle, the Royal Canadian Navy and the Royal Navy had established convoy routes and an effective system to escort the vital merchantmen across the ocean. Despite these efforts, sinkings spiraled until the introduction of escort aircraft carriers and effective radar coverage gave the Allies the upper hand. Losses reached a crescendo in December 1943, after which German successes dropped off sharply. At the same time, the rate of construction overtook the rate of ships destroyed. As of January 1944 the Allies could say that the Battle of the Atlantic had been won. Rapidly, delivered tonnages of supplies and equipment increased. The secure line of communication across the ocean guaranteed that the invasion, once started, could be sustained with replacements, supplies, and new weapons.

The other major precondition for invasion was also attained by 1944. When the US Army Air Forces arrived in England, the Bomber Command of the Royal Air Force was already busily attacking German cities by night. Following a profound disagreement about techniques, the two air forces each followed their own doctrines: the British bombed at night and the Americans by day. While the air war over Europe did not precisely prove the strategic bombing theories, propounded between the wars by Italian general Giulio Douhet, or realize the predictions of its American prophets – German industry was still functioning at the time of the surrender in 1945 – it did have a profound impact on the ground war. Possibly the most important result of the bombing campaign over Germany was that it drew increasing numbers of Luftwaffe fighters away from the fighting fronts and dedicated them to home air defense. The day bombing campaign was decisive in this regard, for the 8th Bomber Command became the anvil on which the 8th Fighter Command, the hammer, literally pounded the life out of the German air force. As Luftwaffe losses increased, a second consequence was the German shift in production from bombers to fighters, thereby decreasing the capability of the remaining tactical air force to support the German army. The Allies had to have aerial superiority, at least over the invasion beaches, to hope for success in the amphibious landings. The combined bomber offensive achieved that goal. By D-Day, German fighter forces were largely stripped out of France, and only two German sorties appeared over the invasion beaches. The first round of the landings was therefore won in what turned out to be very costly battles that the Allied air forces fought in the skies over Germany in the long months of 1943 and early 1944.

Simultaneously, the bombing campaign enormously increased the difficulties the Germans had to overcome in keeping their war machine running. While the factories survived, and production in some cases actually increased, the bombers crippled the German transportation network and systematically attacked the fuel supplies essential not only to the armed forces, but also to the lines of communications. German army units in France, among other places, accordingly became somewhat anaemic with respect to supplies. They were also deficient in armament, and part of that may also be attributed to the bombing campaign. That German army units, both on the eastern and on the western fronts, did not have a large artillery and anti-tank reserve may in part be attributed to the voracious demands of the anti-aircraft organization within Germany for high velocity guns and skilled gunners.

Finally air power offered a partial solution to the manpower problem. In sheer numbers, the Germans in France could always muster more men than the Allies could put on the beaches at one time. The trick was to strike the Germans, as far as possible, at a place they did not expect, and to keep them from concentrating their divisions to repel the assault. Planning for the landings assumed that Allied air forces, freed from aerial combat missions because they had already won the air battle over France, could perform the tactical mission of isolating the Normandy battlefields from the Reich, destroying rail lines, bridges, and centers of communication. Particularly by the time of the landings, Allied fighter bombers, operating almost without opposition from the Luftwaffe, made it impossible for the Germans to move in daylight. Roads became deathtraps, and German mobility – together with German capacity to mass forces to deal with the invasion – was hobbled.

British and American planners correctly foresaw all of these necessities and, as time revealed the impact of the great air battles over the continent, laid plans to exploit the advantages that were gained. From the American point of view, Maj. Albert Wedemeyer's sketch of the essential military tasks to be performed before the final attack on Germany was proceeding well, and seemed to be fulfilling the terms of reference laid down in the *Arcadia* agreement. British staffs agreed that, whatever the future plans of the alliance, these battles had to be won. When the Allies met again at Casablanca in January 1943, they agreed the plan toward entering the continent of Europe in 1944, to set up a planning staff to work out the details of such an operation, and to push the buildup of forces in the United Kingdom while continuing operations in the Mediterranean. Disagreements arose from other sources, at once perceptual and practical.

The essential point is that both Allies agreed that the ultimate attack on the German-occupied continent had to be made in northwestern Europe. While, however, the Americans were anxious to make that attack as soon as possible, the British were concerned that the time should be right. In the end, the decision to launch the invasion across the English Channel was not made final until both Allies were persuaded that it made military sense. Because of their practical concerns, that time came later for the British than for the Americans who, in part conditioned by residual suspicions from the previous war, worried that the British delays portended a refusal to make such landings at all.

The Anglo-American landings in North Africa (Operation *Torch*) exacerbated the debate, because they diverted troops already earmarked for the attack Americans saw as decisive. Gen. Marshall and his staff had already devised a plan (*Bolero*) to concentrate American troops in the United Kingdom for a massive attack on France in the spring of 1943. This attack, dubbed *Roundup*, envisioned using 48 divisions, 30 of which would be American, on a six-division front between Le Havre and Boulogne, supported by a powerful air force. An attractive aspect of *Roundup* was that the Germans had only begun to fortify the coast in 1942, and the bulk of their army was critically engaged in Russia. To exploit the unlikely collapse of the German army as a result of that fighting or, more likely, to create a diversion in case the Russians found themselves in serious trouble, Marshall's staff devised a contingency plan that used only three and a half divisions, to be launched across the Channel as early as September 1942. This plan, *Sledgehammer*, was always unlikely, but still made British planners uneasy because it suggested that the Americans did not have any realistic understanding of the difficulties involved.

Regardless of the invasion plan under discussion, President Roosevelt's agreement to divert American troops to North Africa, and the subsequent agreement to use those troops in assaults on Sicily and on the coast of Italy, made it impossible to concentrate the forces and materiel to invade northwestern Europe in 1943. Americans suspected that Prime Minister Churchill intended to continue to postpone operations in northwestern Europe indefinitely, in favor of those in the Mediterranean that would serve long-range British political interests. In fact, that possibility seems to have existed only in the minds of the American joint chiefs, who had a different and more optimistic definition of favorable military conditions for the final attacks in France than did the British.

In fact, while Americans insisted that final plans for the landings in France go forward, and that a final date be set, it was the British who pointed out the critical shortage of LSTs (Landing Ship, Tank) and other landing craft to make the assault powerful enough to succeed. Until production of LSTs could catch up with demand, no assault on the coast of France could be powerful enough to counter the expected German riposte. Such a landing would, as far as Churchill and his advisors could see, be a repetition of Dieppe, where a single, well-entrenched German company had halted three battalions and the overall losses had been proportionate to those of the first day on the Somme in 1916. It is in that context that the Prime Minister's often quoted remark about French beaches being choked with the bodies of British and American youth must be understood.

Instead of wishing to cancel *Overlord*, Churchill and his military advisors argued through 1943 that the assault had to be made stronger. Finally, only after a high-level conference at Norfolk House in February 1944, in which more tank landing ships were promised from the United States and reallocated from other theaters, did the means appear more nearly to suit the demands.

Marshall and his staff in particular, and the American joint chiefs in general, rightly complained that the landings in North Africa could have no meaningful impact on the course of the war, and that the subsequent assaults on Sicily and Italy frittered away precious resources in an aimless strategy of opportunism that formed no part of a coherent plan for the defeat of Germany. To that extent, their criticism of peripheral warfare, especially when contrasted to the ideal of maintenance of the objective, was on the mark. But that point of view overlooked important practical considerations. President Roosevelt knew that it was politically important for American troops to come to grips with the Germans some time in 1942. Forces certainly had to be accumulated in the United Kingdom for the invasion of the continent, but to hold those soldiers idle there only encouraged critics – Gen. Douglas MacArthur and senior naval commanders among them – who wanted to concentrate American strength on fighting the Japanese, a war in which Americans in general had vested far more emotion. Practically, it turned out that Mediterranean operations were militarily expedient, giving the US Army time to shake down for war and to learn the difficult lessons that the British had already had three years to assimilate. Landings and warfare in the Mediterranean hardened the soldiers, brought the most capable commanders to the fore, and gave both nations experience in conducting amphibious warfare, experience that was almost certainly crucial to the subsequent success of *Overlord*.

It was in this context that the Allies agreed at the *Trident* Conference in Washington, in May 1943, to use forces already in the Mediterranean to invade Italy, but also to set May 1, 1944, as the date for the cross-channel invasion and to that end to concentrate the buildup of their forces in Britain. Later in August 1943, at the *Quadrant* Conference in Quebec City, they reaffirmed that intention. Finally, at the Tehran-Cairo Conferences of November-December 1943, the long and anxious debates ended with the appointment of Eisenhower as supreme commander for the invasion, the principal, Anglo-American effort in 1944. An impatient Generalissimo Josef Stalin was responsible, in part, for the final decisions of the conference. He had long been pressing the Western Allies to open a Second Front that would take some of the pressure off of his forces, and it was at his insistence that Roosevelt and Churchill finally named a supreme commander. If no commander were named, Stalin believed, then there was also no prospect that plans for a Second Front would be translated into reality any time in the near future.

The final date was set, as Prime Minister Churchill had earlier suggested, by the moon and the weather. The decision for *Overlord* was finally a compromise and an artful merging of the two nations' conceptions of how to wage the war. At the end, however, it was more a reflection of the realism of the British proposal at the *Arcadia* Conference of December 1941 than of the optimism that colored the American estimates of the art of the possible through 1942 and 1943.

That the alliance stood firm throughout the Second Front debate was the result of several related and indispensable facts. One key to that success was that, from the very beginning of the most preliminary discussions between the two powers, British and American leaders agreed on their common objective. A second was the utter determination of Prime Minister Churchill and President Roosevelt that the solidity of the Anglo-American alliance had absolute primacy over every other question. A third was that Gen. Dwight D. Eisenhower, military leader of the coalition and a protégé and student of Conner came to his task as supreme commander determined to make the coalition a success, and built a staff that mirrored his determination.

PREPARATION FOR OVERLORD

Almost from the fall of France in 1940, plans and preparations began for its liberation. Churchill organized or sponsored a number of "private armies" to carry out raids or encourage resistance in France and other occupied countries, and in fact the first Commando raid on German positions in France took place only 20 days after Dunkirk. The Commandos, the Special Operations Executive (SOE), and the Airborne Forces all grew from raiding forces like these, into sizeable organizations that played a major role in the British effort on D-Day. Despite debates over strategy and the perilous British strategic position until the middle of the war, it was always clear to Churchill and his military staffs that only the liberation of France could secure the defeat of Germany.

■ Operation *Bolero*

The entry of the United States into the war made it possible to draw up realistic plans for the invasion, starting with Operation *Sledgehammer*, a possible small landing at Cherbourg in 1942, and developing to Operation *Roundup*, a major invasion of the Pas de Calais planned for 1943. In July 1942, in order to provide the American forces for *Roundup*, the Allies began Operation *Bolero*, the movement of troops and weapons to Britain on a massive scale. *Bolero* continued for nearly two years as *Roundup* was postponed until 1944, and eventually modified into Operation *Overlord*. Meanwhile the British continued to train and organize their own troops for the invasion, increasingly supplemented by forces from the Common-wealth, and from Allied "governments in exile" in London, whose forces were equipped by the British and Americans.

The United States began to build up its armed forces immediately after the collapse of France, in anticipation of its involvement in the war, and thereafter its military industrial achievement was little short of phenom-enal. Although in many cases the factories themselves had to be built before they could produce the tanks or aircraft, American war production tripled in 1941, increased over four fold in 1942, and four fold again in 1943. The United States by itself out-produced Germany by four to one in tanks during the war, and more than two to one in total munitions. In addition to equipping their own forces, the Americans supplied the British with about a quarter of their weapons and equipment, paid for largely by Lend-Lease. In return, the British provided the Americans with some of their own specialist weapons, and with most of their barracks, airfields and training grounds for *Overlord*.

■ The American "Invasion"
Nothing had quite prepared the British public, however, for the scale of the American arrival. The first American troops to reach the UK landed in Belfast harbor in January 1942, and Americans were stationed in Northern Ireland throughout the war. Because of the threat of German invasion in 1940, most of the British forces had been based in southeast and eastern England. This left the western half of Britain for the arriving American armies. The final decisions to land American forces on the western invasion beaches of Normandy, and the British on the eastern beaches, had its origins in this purely practical solution to the problem of accommodating the Americans.

By spring 1944, as the plans for *Overlord* were finalized, the British civilian population was playing host to the largest invasion force ever assembled in one place, of which about half was American. To make *Bolero* possible, the United States produced over 2,500 Liberty ships of 7,000 tons each as troop transports. The British contribution included the trans-port of 425,000 men in the ocean liners *Queen Mary* and *Queen Elizabeth*, adapted to each hold 15,000 men per trip. By 1944 the Allied domination of the sea and air was so complete that the transfer of American and Canadian troops to Britain across the Atlantic was completed virtually without loss.

The Britain to which the GIs came was a gloomy and depressing country, and this had little to do with the weather. In order to defeat Germany, Britain had organized itself for war to a greater degree than any other member of the Allies, conscripting even women after 1941. Over half the working population was either in uniform or in civilian war employment, and half the national income was devoted to war expenditure. Strict rationing, an average working week of 50 hours, and some 295,000 civilian dead and injured in air raids all contributed to an air of war. weariness in a country which had little to cheer about in its fifth year at war.

A nation traditionally wary of foreigners accepted its army of friendly occupation with remarkably good grace, although some suspicion and trouble on both sides was inevitable. The arrival of American troops far from home in a remote Cornish or Scottish village usually meant a sudden increase in prices, and a corresponding shortage of alcohol and dancing partners for the local men. Compensations ranged from razor blades and candy to American charm and the music of Glenn Miller.

The United States' armed forces were still segregated, with black troops mainly used in non-combat roles. Britain had for centuries had its own small black communities, but these existed only in the major ports, while Indian, West Indian and African troops of the British Empire were usually stationed overseas, and none were intended to fight in Normandy. Most people in Britain had simply never seen black soldiers before, and probably many believed the story that American blacks were specialist night-fighting troops with artificially darkened skins. Generally, as in all their dealings with their Allies, the British accepted the American practice of segregating their troops, while reacting with angry disbelief to American behavior outside their own experience, such as the racist attitude of many white American officers or the rare cases of serious violence between white and black troops.

By D-Day, some British people seemed to be getting almost as weary of the Americans as of the war, and both governments were acting to encourage better relations and understanding between their peoples. But as with all news, the bad was being reported more readily than the good, and the predominant American memory of Britain was of friendly people.

Just as the Anglo-American alliance coped with its strains surprisingly well, so over 70,000 British girls married GIs immediately after the war and returned home with them.

By June 1944, *Bolero* had done its work. The Allied forces assembled for D-Day numbered over 1,700,000 British troops, 1,500,000 Americans, 175,000 Dominion troops (chiefly Canadians) and 44,000 from other allies. Over 1,300 warships, 1,600 merchant ships, and 4,000 landing ships and craft were available for the liberation campaign, together with 13,000 aircraft (including 5,000 fighters and 4,000 bombers) and 3,500 gliders. In terms of fighting troops, the British had three armored divisions, eight infantry divisions, two airborne divisions and ten independent brigades ready for Normandy, plus one Canadian armored division, two infantry divisions and one independent brigade. There was also a single Polish armored division and a parachute brigade, both equipped by the British. The Americans with their much greater resources had six armored divisions (out of 16 which would fight in Europe before the end of the war), 13 infantry divisions and two airborne divisions waiting in Britain, and more still training in the United States.

The tactical air forces for direct support of these armies numbered some 100 RAF or Commonwealth squadrons (1,200 aircraft) and 165 USAAF squadrons (2,000 aircraft). Simply to assemble such a force had been a colossal undertaking,

■ The High Command

At the *Arcadia* Conference of December 1941, the Americans and British established a command system enabling them to plan and fight the war jointly. This began at the top with the close personal relationship between President Roosevelt, who was also commander-in-chief of all American forces, and Prime Minister Churchill, who created the title of Minister of Defence for himself in 1940 to fulfil a similar function. Although a lawyer by profession, Roosevelt had been Secretary of the Navy in World War I, and had a good practical understanding of warfare, but tended to leave the planning to his military staffs. Churchill, whose military and naval experience stretched back to the Malakand Expedition of 1897, took a far more active role once the invasion of France had been agreed, and was only narrowly prevented from sailing with the forces on D-Day itself.

The formula established at the *Arcadia* Conference, with Roosevelt, Churchill and their staffs meeting at intervals to decide strategy, continued throughout the war. An important part of planning was that the Supreme Allied Commander for a designated theater of war must have control over all forces in it, regardless of nationality. In December 1943 Gen. Dwight D. Eisenhower was named as Supreme Allied Commander Europe, and his command as the Supreme Headquarters Allied Expeditionary Forces, or SHAEF. Given the greater American contribution to the liberation forces, there was little doubt that an American officer should be appointed, and Eisenhower was the natural choice. Born in 1890, he had served in the army since 1911 and had considerable staff experience, but had never seen combat or commanded as much as a battalion. Eisenhower had risen rapidly from brigadier-general in 1942 to full general and Supreme Allied Commander in the Mediterranean a year later through his remarkable skill in handling the complex political problems of coalition warfare. His relaxed style and ability to find a compromise often won him only grudging admiration from his subordinate commanders, but his insistence on cooperation and coordination at all levels gave him the respect of political leaders, and was to be decisive for the outcome of the liberation battle.

The appointment of subordinate commanders for Operation *Overlord* reflected the importance of integrating British and American forces; the fact that Britain was the host nation; and the need to coordinate air forces with land operations. The Deputy Supreme Allied Commander was Air Chief Marshal Sir Arthur Tedder. The same age as Eisenhower, Tedder had originally joined the Army in World War I, transferring into the Royal Flying Corps and so into the RAF. As Air Officer Commander-in-Chief Middle East Air Force in 1941, he had pioneered the use of ground attack aircraft, developing the "Tedder carpet" of bombs laid in front of the advancing troops. A sometimes prickly figure, Tedder made little secret of his belief that air power was chiefly responsible for winning the war. Despite this, he worked extremely well with Eisenhower.

Rather than place an American in charge of the British naval and air forces which were also used to defend Britain itself, Eisenhower's remaining senior commanders were also British. The Allied Naval Commander-in-Chief Expeditionary Force was Adm. Sir Bertram Ramsay. Born in 1883, Ramsay was old for his command, but had proved his considerable abilities in amphibious warfare, first as one of the principal organizers of the Dunkirk evacuation in 1940, then of the *Torch* landings in 1943, and finally as commander of the naval forces for the

Sicily landings later the same year. Command of the Allied Expeditionary Air Force (AEAF) was given to Air Chief Marshal Sir Trafford Leigh-Mallory. Born in 1892, Leigh-Mallory was a controversial choice with an erratic reputation stretching back to his command of RAF 12 Group during the Battle of Britain. His relations with Tedder in particular were often difficult, although they agreed on the importance of air power. The AEAF itself consisted of British 2nd Tactical Air Force and US 9th Air Force, which between them averaged over 3,000 sorties a day during the Battle of Normandy, but through his ATAF Headquarters in London, Leigh-Mallory could also coordinate air support from virtually the whole RAF and USAAF in Britain.

Shortly after his appointment, Eisenhower faced and overcame his first major test on the issue of command of the air. Leigh-Mallory with Tedder's support, wanted the heavy four-engined long range bomber forces in Britain, which did not come directly under Eisenhower, switched to attack the French railway system as a crucial component of AEAF strategy. The aim was to secure control of the air over France and restrict German movement on the ground; the so-called "Transportation Plan." Instead, RAF Bomber Command under Air Chief Marshal Sir Arthur Harris and United States Strategic Air Forces in Europe under Gen. Carl Spaatz (known together as "the Bomber Barons") insisted that the best support which they could give *Overlord* would be to continue their strategic attacks on German industrial cities. Their resistance was so great that Eisenhower, despite his preference for compromise, had to threaten resignation before securing control of the heavy bombers in April. They were to play a leading part in the eventual Allied victory in Normandy.

Even with SHAEF's great resources, limitations in the number of landing craft, the number of suitable beaches, and the rate of transport across the English Channel meant that only a fraction of its forces could land on D-Day itself. The initial landing forces would be from 21st Army Group, commanded by Gen. Sir Bernard Montgomery who would act as the ground forces commander directing the battle for Eisenhower, while SHAEF headquarters remained in Britain. Born in 1887, Montgomery was an immensely controversial figure who inspired extremes either of admiration or scorn from his colleagues for his arrogant manner, made even more infuriating by his consistent ability to win. Even the tolerant Eisenhower came to threaten Montgomery's dismissal on more than one occasion during the war. The placing of increasing numbers of American troops and resources under this difficult foreigner would cause considerable friction as the Battle of Normandy progressed.

From D-Day onwards, 21st Army Group would consist of US First Army under Lt. Gen. Omar Bradley, an old collegue of Eisenhower, and British Second Army under Lt. Gen. Miles Dempsey. When enough troops had crossed to Normandy, two new armies would be created and Eisenhower with SHAEF headquarters would take over the battle from Montgomery. Bradley would take command of 12th US Army Group, consisting of US First Army and US Third Army (an additional US Ninth Army was added in August), while Montgomery would remain in command only of his 21st Army Group, by then consisting of British Second Army and Canadian First Army. Meanwhile a second amphibious landing, Operation *Dragoon*, was to take place in the south of France in August with forces of 6th Army Group under Lt. Gen. Jacob Devers, composed of US Seventh Army and French First Army. The SHAEF liberation forces under Eisenhower would finally number seven armies, four of which would be American. Although *Overlord* would start with a predominantly British high command, gradually the Americans with their much greater resources would take over.

■ Montgomery's Master Plan

Both during and after the war, Montgomery claimed that all his battles were fought according to a precise "master plan" drawn up beforehand, from which he never deviated, and which the enemy was never able to affect. This attitude earned Montgomery many critics, particularly Tedder and Bradley who regarded him as a highly suspect figure, and led to much argument after the war. The first military plans for *Overlord* and Normandy were drawn up between March and July 1943 by a joint Anglo-American staff in London under the British Lt. Gen. Frederick Morgan, known as COSSAC (Chief of Staff to the Supreme Allied Commander). Although in theory the Allies could land anywhere from Norway to the south of France, Morgan and his staff rapidly narrowed the choice of landing beaches down to two areas, the shortest route across the Straits of Dover to the Pas de Calais or a landing in the Bay of the Seine in Normandy. Regarding the Pas de Calais landing as too obvious, and likely to meet the heaviest German defences, Morgan chose Normandy.

When SHAEF took over from COSSAC in January 1944, Montgomery inherited and modified Morgan's plan. With more troops and landing craft available than COSSAC had expected, Montgomery extended the landing area from three beaches to five, including a site on the Cotentin Peninsula.

Montgomery's plan called for five divisions (instead of COSSAC's three) to land with the first wave on a 61-mile (98km) front, supported by four more divisions and divisional airborne landings on both flanks. The Americans would take the. westernmost beaches, codenamed *Utah* and *Omaha*, and the British and Canadians the eastern beaches, code-named *Gold, Juno*, and *Sword*. As with every major military operation there were two key dates. For planning purposes everything had to be ready for Y-Day, or "ready day," set for June 1. But the operation would not actually start until D-Day, a date shortly after Y-Day to be chosen by Eisenhower. Every military operation had its own "D-Day," but this would become the most famous one of all.

Montgomery rightly guessed that the Germans would put their greatest effort into stopping the invasion on the beaches on D-Day itself, rather than allowing the Allies to get ashore. Once D-Day was successfully over, Montgomery's plan depended on Ramsay's sea-borne supply-line to reinforce his position in Normandy, for which the early capture of a major port and harbor was vital. The lesson of Dieppe was that a port could not easily be captured on D-Day from the sea, and the plan was to supply 21st Army Group over the Normandy beaches for the first few days before securing the nearby port of Cherbourg. While building up its own forces and supplies, 21st Army Group would rely on Leigh-Mallory's AEAF to control the air and prevent the Germans reinforcing their line by attacking troops and transports moving towards Normandy. The most important factors restricting the choice to Normandy or the Pas de Calais was that both lay within fighter range of southern England, and that the sea lanes could be easily protected.

In broad terms, Montgomery's "master plan" depended on surviving D-Day, holding enough territory to prevent his forces being pushed into the sea, winning the buildup battle, and so breaking out of the beachhead. But at planning conferences for SHAEF and 21st Army Group commanders in April and May, Montgomery outlined his expectations for the battle in greater detail. Coming straight off the beaches, British Second Army would capture the regional capital of Caen, the only major city in the landing area, on D-Day itself, and carry on deep inland. At the same time, US First Army would move across the Cotentin and capture Cherbourg as a supply port within a week. Montgomery anticipated a fairly steady Allied advance as the Germans retreated before him, giving up most of Normandy. From a strong position between Caen and Falaise, Montgomery would then threaten a direct advance eastward towards the River Seine with his British forces. There is little doubt (except for that created by Montgomery himself after the war) that he would have carried out this threat if the Germans had failed to defend against it, but it was largely a feint to draw the bulk of German forces in against the British.

Montgomery's preferred option, instead, was for the whole of the 21st Army Group to pivot on Falaise as the Americans pushed southwards out of Normandy as far as St. Malo and Rennes by the end of June. At this point there would be a pause, as with enough troops ashore and space to deploy them, Eisenhower would take over the battle from Montgomery. With 6th Army Group arriving from the south but much hard fighting still to come, the Allies expected to reach the River Seine at Paris about three months after D-Day.

For planning purposes, in April and May Montgomery's staff drew up a series of maps showing phase lines and options on how he expected the battle to develop. Although no battle ever runs according to a timetable (or a "master plan") it was quite clear after the invasion that what was happening bore little resemblance to these detailed plans. Montgomery's insistence that everything was going perfectly, and that his "master plan" was still intact, only served to increase suspicion of him during the battle, and to tarnish his reputation afterwards. By the time France was liberated, many were arguing that the battle had been won in spite of Montgomery, and not because of him.

■ The Free French

On June 6, 1940, as the French armies collapsed under the German attack, Maj. Gen. Charles de Gaulle was called from command of his armored division to become Under-Secretary for National Defense and War. Twelve days later, as the French government also collapsed, de Gaulle fled to London, where he announced his intention to fight on, denouncing the armistice with Germany and the Pétain government, and appointing himself as leader of a National Committee of Liberation. By November 1942, when the Germans occupied Vichy France, de Gaulle's position as leader of the Free French – renamed the Fighting French in August 1943 – was reasonably secure, but his utterly uncompromising approach meant that for the rest of the war his relations with the British and Americans were difficult. The central problem, as the date of the invasion drew closer, was that de Gaulle claimed the right to assume the government of France upon liberation, whereas the Americans and British insisted on some form of election being held before recognizing that government. To de Gaulle, this was insulting and presumptuous, as was the Allies' issuing of "liberation money " to their troops without his authorization. A private understanding with Eisenhower helped ease the situation.

In 1944 most of de Gaulle's forces were in Italy or being prepared for the *Dragoon* landings as the French First Army, but it was obviously polit-ically important for French troops to take part on D-Day. The French cruisers *Montcalm* and *Georges Leygues* and the destroyer *La Combattante* formed part of Adm. Ramsay's command on D-Day, while 2nd Tactical Air Force included five RAF Fighting French squadrons. Two French, parachute battalions were serving with the British Special Air Service Brigade (SAS), and dropped three nine-man combat teams into Brittany on the night before D-Day. In order to have French troops land with the first wave on D-Day itself, a token force of 176 French commandos from No. 10 (Inter-Allied) Commando under Commandant Phillippe de Vais-seau Kieffer was transferred to No. 4 Commando to land at *Sword* Beach. De Gaulle also provided 2nd French Armored Division (armed and equipped by the Americans) as part of the SHAEF forces intended for Normandy, with the specific role of liberating Paris. Its commander, Maj. Gen. Jacques-Philippe Leclerc, had escaped from a German prisoner of war camp in 1940 to join de Gaulle. Described as "a modern d'Artagnan," he was actually the Vicomte de Hautecloque, but had taken the name "Leclerc" to protect his family, still living in France.

As part of the D-Day plans, attempts were made to coordinate the various French resistance groups, known as the "Secret Army." Although the main function of the Resistance was to provide information for the landings, some groups were also given specific sabotage targets to slow the Germans down. In December 1943 the British SOE and the American Office of Strategic Services (OSS) created a single Special Forces Head-quarters as part of SHAEF, and in May 1944 de Gaulle's chief of staff, Gen. Joseph Pierre Koenig, was appointed commander of the French Forces of the Interior (FFI) under which all resistance groups were placed, giving them some official status as soldiers rather than irregulars (or, as the Germans insisted, "terrorists"). The various factions of the Resistance were by no means all automatically loyal to de Gaulle, who in turn was prepared to take British and American arms and supplies for his own resistance groups, but not to recognise the work of the SOE and OSS. Neither de Gaulle nor Koenig was involved in the strategic planning for *Overlord*, and in April the British government blocked the movement of all diplomats or diplomatic correspondence into or out of the United Kingdom, making exception only for the Americans and Russians. As a result, de Gaulle – increasingly angry over the Anglo-American refusal to recognize his government – refused to take part in joint radio broadcasts with the other allied leaders on D-Day, insisting on his own broadcast in which he mentioned only French Forces.

■ Ruperts, Whales and Great Panjandrums

For centuries before the Allied landings in 1944, the approved way to take a sea fortress had been to land elsewhere and capture it from the landward side, as the Americans planned to do with Cherbourg. But for D-Day itself the Allies would have to assault a heavily defended position, the German Atlantic Wall, from the seaward side. Dieppe had shown the need for special equipment in order to overcome beach defenses, clear minefields, and press inland rapidly. For D-Day a host of inventions was tried out with greater or lesser success, from specialist landing craft to folding bicycles. Among the most simple was the soldier's "invasion wader," a cumbersome garment meant to keep the wearer dry from the landing craft to firm ground. For their assault on the sheer cliffs of the Pointe du Hoc, the US Rangers developed rocket-propelled grappling hooks and ropes, and borrowed extension ladders from the London Fire Brigade. The airborne forces produced a variety of gadgets, including the British-designed but American-manufactured "Eureka" radar beacon, carried by paratroop pathfinders and activated to guide aircraft approaching the drop zone. Far cheaper, and of doubtful value, was the metal toy "cricket" issued to American airborne troops as a recognition aid for their night drop into Normandy. In the fighting, the signal of a cricket clicking turned out to be too similar to the sound of a rifle being cocked. The most bizarre, if most engaging, airborne contribution to surprise on D-Day was *Rupert*, quarter-sized dummy parachutists dropped in their thousands across northern France to coincide with the real airborne drop.

From past experience, the Allies knew that landing infantry from the sea was comparatively straightforward, but to overcome enemy strongpoints they would need to get tanks and artillery ashore and inland quickly, past beach defenses, over soft sand and sea walls. A variety of specialist vehicles were built, put through trials and either adopted or discarded. A British specialist design unit, Department MD1 (sometimes known as "Winston Churchill's Toyshop"), which had already provided the PIAT anti-tank weapon, developed the "beehive" demolition charge for clearing obstacles in large numbers for D-Day, together with a bridge-laying tank known as the "Great Eastern." Among other methods of clearing beach obstacles tested by the British was "The Great Panjandrum" a giant rocket-driven catherine wheel which was meant to roll along the beach exploding mines, but which proved a signal failure. However, the "tankdozer" or armored bulldozer, and the flail tank or Crab to explode mines were both successes, and were employed on D-Day. Other successful tank designs adopted for D-Day by the British included the "bobbin" tank, the flame-thrower tank or Crocodile, the fascine tank, the Churchill ARK (armoured ramp carrier) and the AVRE (Armoured Vehicle Royal Engineers) with a 290mm petard mortar, known along with the other specialist armor as "Hobart's Funnies" with reference to Maj. Gen. Percy Hobart, the former pioneer of armored warfare entrusted with their development. In the British forces, this specialist armor was grouped together in the 79th Armoured Division.

The most successful specialist tank used on D-Day was a joint Anglo-American development, the swimming or amphibious Sherman tank fitted with its own propellers for use at sea, Known as the DD-Sherman (for "Duplex Drive") these were to be launched from landing craft and swim into the beach ahead of the first lines of infantry. Each DD-Sherman was fitted with a "flotation screen," a large canvas skirt which hid most of the tank when erected and was meant to keep the sea out, and special exhaust vents to prevent water flooding the engine. They worked well, but could easily swamp in heavy seas.

At the other end of the scale from the two-cent "cricket," Allied planning for Normandy included one project described as "probably the greatest military engineering achievement since the Persian crossing of the Dardanelles by a bridge of boats in 480BC." In order to provide a safe anchorage until the capture of Cherbourg, two giant prefabricated harbors were built in Britain under the codename *Mulberry*, to be towed across the English Channel on D+1 and assembled over the next two weeks. From July 1943 onwards, 37,000 British laborers worked on the two *Mulberry* harbors, one for the British and one for the Americans, and more than a million tons of concrete, ballast and steel were used in their construction, including the blockships sunk to provide breakwaters for them. Although their aircraft photographed the components of *Mulberry* being built in British harbors and estuaries, the Germans failed to work out its purpose. Floating breakwaters called "bombardons" protected an inner ring of giant concrete boxes known as *Phoenix*, towed across and then sunk in position, with a final line of blockships called *Corncob* to form *Gooseberry* or safe anchorages, and the great *Whales* or floating piers at which the ships were to dock, with flexible floating metal roadways leading to the shore. Other *Gooseberry* anchorages were to be formed off the remaining invasion beaches by *Corncob* blockships. The great advantage of *Mulberry* was that it gave the Allies an insurance policy against failing to take a port soon after D-Day.

■ Operation *Fortitude*

Throughout the war, one great Allied area of superiority over Germany was in political and military intelligence. The Germans had their successes, but although they were often highly proficient at gathering information, they seldom made the best use of it. German policies towards occupied countries, and even resistance to Hitler in Germany itself, made it much easier for the Allies to establish spy networks in Europe than for the Germans to build up such networks in Britain.

The most carefully guarded intelligence success on the Allied side during the war was the *Ultra* secret, which played a major part in providing the Allies with a picture of German defenses in Normandy. Before the war the Germans had adopted for encoding secret radio signals a typewriter-like machine named *Enigma*, based on a set of coded wheels which was meant to produce unbreakable ciphers. Building on work already done by the Poles before 1939, British mathematicians and crypt-analysts based at Bletchley Park, Buckinghamshire, built what amounted to a primitive computer to break the *Enigma* ciphers, and in the months before D-Day used German radio traffic together with more conventional intelligence methods to create a very accurate picture of their dispositions in Normandy. Expecting the D-Day landings to take place in the Pas de Calais, the Germans placed their strongest forces there – 17 divisions of Fifteenth Army compared to 11 divisions of Seventh Army defending Normandy – and gave the Pas de Calais section of the Atlantic Wall the highest priority. A large part of the Allied success depended on Seventh Army not being reinforced before D-Day, and on Fifteenth Army remaining in position even after the first landings.

"In wartime," Churchill observed in October 1943, "truth is so precious that she should always be attended by a bodyguard of lies." Anglo-American strategic planning throughout the war was governed by the principle that every plan should be accompanied by a plausible deception plan, to face the Germans with a choice of possible threats against which to defend. For D-Day the overall deception and disinformation plan was codenamed Operation *Bodyguard*. Central to this was Operation *Fortitude*, an elaborate attempt to convince the Germans that the forces for *Overlord* were almost double their real size by the use of dummy encampments, faked radio signals, cover names and special detachments of troops. The Germans were particularly impressed by confirmation of troop movements and locations coming from their network of agents in Britain, built up painstakingly since 1940. However, in an operation almost as well-guarded as *Ultra*, British counter-intelligence had by 1943 tracked down and caught every German agent in the country. Several of these agents were kept under British control to transmit false information back to Germany as part of *Fortitude*, run by the top secret "Twenty Committee" (from the Roman numerals XX or double-cross), which told the Germans only what the British wanted them to believe. The deception was so complete that some German reports showed two Australian divisions in southern England, when the nearest was actually in Burma.

Some of the forces for *Fortitude* were completely fictitious, like the American infantry division in Iceland reported to the Germans by Twenty Committee agents. But most had some kind of real existence, and many were fighting formations intended for another purpose. Troops training in Scotland were exaggerated by *Fortitude North* into the non-existent British Fourth Army poised to invade Norway, a threat which kept 27 German divisions waiting in Scandinavia almost until July. Even more impressive was *Fortitude South*, which created in southern England the US 1st Army Group or FUSAG to rival 21st Army Group and threaten the Pas de Calais, as the Germans expected. Allied cover plans encouraged the Germans to believe that command of FUSAG had been given to the Allied general they most feared, Lt. Gen. George S. Patton. In fact Patton was marked to command US Third Army, but even after D-Day the threat of FUSAG kept most of Fifteenth Army in the Pas de Calais, waiting for an invasion that never came. When Third Army did appear in Normandy, Twenty Committee agents passed to the Germans the story that Patton had been demoted from command of FUSAG after a blazing row with Eisenhower, and had been replaced by the head of US Army Ground Forces, Lt. Gen. Lesley McNair.

In an enterprise like *Overlord*, involving millions of men and women and months of detailed planning, complete security was at the same time vital and almost impossible to achieve. If the Germans could establish the date and place of D-Day then they could meet the invasion on the beaches with overwhelming force. A separate codename, Operation *Neptune*, was used to cover all Allied plans regarding information from embarkation to invasion, and a new security classification of *Bigot*, higher even than Top Secret, invented to cover it. Security scares in the last few days before D-Day ranged from the gruesome to the bizarre. More than one officer was sent home or demoted in April and May for indiscreet talk. When ten *Bigot* officers were lost in a German E-Boat attack on an American training exercise off Slapton Sands in Devon in April, divers had to search the sea bed to make sure that all their corpses were recovered. A major scare developed when a package burst open in an Army mail sorting office in Chicago, revealing a set of *Overlord* plans accidentally addressed by Sgt. Thomas Kane, working at SHAEF Headquarters, to his sister. Strangest of all, the compilers of the *Daily Telegraph* crossword puzzle, Sidney Dawe and Melville Jones, found themselves under investigation after several D-Day codenames, including *Overlord* itself, appeared in their puzzles during May and early June.

The result of *Fortitude* was that, although accepting the possibility of a landing in Normandy, most German assessments favored the Pas de Calais, and a landing in good weather. Through German penetration of French Resistance groups, Fifteenth Army knew some of the coded messages used to alert the Secret Army to the D-Day landings, and went on alert on June 5 in response. But the message was not passed on to the unsuspecting Seventh Army, nor to Rommel who was at home in Germany for his wife's birthday. Despite the immense preparations involved in *Overlord*, the surprise on D-Day would be complete.

THE GERMAN DEFENCES

■ "Fortress Europe"

By the time the first Allied ships appeared off the coast of Normandy at dawn on June 6, 1944, and before a single Allied soldier had set foot on land, the German defenders had already lost three battles over "Fortress Europe": for many months British and American aircraft had not only ruled the airspace over England and the Channel, but also dominated the skies over the mainland of western Europe; German surface vessels and U-boats had also failed even to interfere significantly with the vast flow of men and materiel from America to the UK, let alone bring it to a halt; last but not least, all attempts to obtain accurate intelligence about Allied intentions and options had proved fruitless. The Germans remained ignorant of the place, the time and the strength of the attack on "Hitler's Europe" until the actual moment of the landing.

Despite these important Allied successes, the Germans nevertheless attempted to arm themselves against the expected attack. First and foremost it was of critical importance as to how cooperation could be ensured with the countries of western and northern Europe, on whose territory a defensive network was to be established. Whether the French, Belgians, Dutch, Danes and later the Norwegians cooperated with the occupying forces, maintained a passive stance, or actively aided the

Resistance, would inevitably have a significant effect on the efficiency of the defensive buildup.

Although the Germans never intended to treat the peoples of western Europe as harshly as those in the east and southeast of the continent, they still failed by a long way to establish a forward-looking policy of partnership. This failure was caused both by their ideology and their lack of a cosmopolitan outlook: they established in the occupied countries only puppet governments, whose collaboration was assured, but which consequently enjoyed little popular support, left them in ignorance about their future role in a "German League of Nations" or the "New European Order": instead they set up an efficient régime of suppression everywhere and from the very beginning devoted their efforts to exploiting the manpower and material resources of the occupied countries to the full.

All these factors drove many people into an attitude of resignation, and not a few into active resistance, even though they may initially have nurtured positive expectations towards the Germans. With the waning military strength of the German Reich, their sympathies turned increasingly towards the Allies. The governments of collaboration, such as the Vichy régime in France for example, gradually lost credibility, and de Gaulle's "Comité Français de Libération Nationale" (French Committee of National Liberation) began to gather support in its native country. De Gaulle's uncompromising attitude towards the reclamation of French sovereignty and the expulsion of the invader came to represent a credible prospect for more and more French people. Similar movements were under way in the other occupied countries of western and northern Europe. Of the concept of a common European imperium, somewhat in the style of the Holy Roman Empire as the Nazi leaders now and then liked to portray it, no trace was evident by the time of the Allied landings.

■ Collaboration and Resistance

Small wonder then that under these conditions, the German commanders in western Europe had from the start to discount any possibility of direct military participation by the occupied countries against an Allied invasion. The population and their representatives were only to comply with certain instructions to facilitate German defensive measures in the event of a landing: not to block up transport routes behind the front by unnecessary travel or movement; to hand over any vehicles or other logistic material required; and to hold the Resistance movements in check with their police forces. They would continue, however, to work hard for the occupying power: in the German-controlled armaments and supply industry, in administration and in the security forces, and above all on the still-unfinished fortifications on the coast and in the ports. In the event of a major British and American landing, the Commander-in-Chief West, Field Marshal von Rundstedt, was looking for the same "loyal" behavior from the French as during Operation *Jubilee* at Dieppe in 1942.

Even if German relations with the populations of the occupied countries were not overly friendly, they at least succeeded, by means of a series of flexible measures, in avoiding a repeat of the situation in the "real bandit countries" – by which they meant mainly the Soviet Union and Yugoslavia. The Chief of General Staff at C-in-C West, Gen. Blumentritt, estimated that 10 percent of the population might undertake active resistance following a landing – and the Germans could live with that.

In addition, the Germans in the west were in a position to carry out their defensive preparations in countries which possessed an excellent infrastructure (roads, railways, rivers, canals, workshops, and depots). Allied bombers together with the Resistance, however succeeded in destroying much of this network by D-Day. Thus at the end of May thousands of supply trains were stuck in Belgium and eastern France, unable to proceed further westwards because of the shattered railway system.

This was the situation as the Germans found it (or brought about themselves) in the occupied countries. The main question remained – when, in what strength and above all where would the Allies land? German leaders had been asking themselves this question off and on ever since the cancellation of Operation *Sealion*, the plan to invade England following the defeat of France in the summer of 1940. By mid-May 1941, according to officers of the Naval War Staff, Britain was already in a position to mount raids and small landings, and exactly a year later the Army High Command estimated the strength of enemy forces in the UK at 44 divisions. The C-in-C West was prompted by these and similar indications to alert his units as early as February 1943 to the Possibility of a landing: "The signs and the available information give growing evidence that we must very soon face the long-expected major landing by the Anglo-Americans."

In contrast to the Allies, the Germans had no central commanding authority where all information could be collated in the event of a landing. There existed instead a glorious profusion of intelligence agencies of all kinds, who not only worked solely for their own benefit, but also competed viciously against each other: besides the legendary "Abwehr" of Adm. Canaris, the "Foreign Armies West" department of the Army High Command was also responsible for intelligence-gathering. Similar departments with the same job were operated by the Foreign Office, C-in-C West, the Navy, the Luftwaffe and Himmler's Reich Central Security Office. The Reich SS Leader even succeeded in February 1944 in wrestling the "Abwehr" from the Armed Forces High Command. This process continued until June 1944, with a consequent fatal effect on intelligence-gathering and evaluation.

■ Invasion Targets

This plethora of secret service agencies and their lack of cooperation inevitably meant that information obtained was never collated thoroughly enough to evaluate exactly how true it was. It is no wonder therefore that in May 1944 the Germans believed Allied reports that there were approximately 80 divisions in Britain, making up five armies (British Second and Fifth, Canadian First and US First and Ninth) in two army groups, who were capable of launching 20 divisions across the Channel simultaneously. The defenders were also convinced at an early date that the main attack must come at the Pas de Calais, since the Allies would without doubt want to advance by the shortest route on the Ruhr. At the same time their vast potential would enable them to carry out diversionary operations practically anywhere along the coastline of Europe, from Norway to the Balkans. Hitler, the Wehrmacht Operations Staff, von Rundstedt and Rommel (the commander of Army Group B) all persisted in this basic evaluation of the situation until well after the actual landing. It was only Naval Group West and Air Fleet (Luftflotte) 3 in Paris who preserved any doubts in this respect. At the beginning of 1944, the officers of the Navy could not believe that the Americans and British would attack across the narrowest part of the Channel - just where the Germans might expect them to. They also regarded with some scepticism the copious reports of an American group of forces (FUSAG) in southeastern England, since according to their intelligence there was no shipping assembled there for them. How were these FUSAG troops to get across the Channel? In their view a more likely landing site was between the Somme estuary and Cherbourg.

In May 1944, Luftflotte 3 also came to this conclusion, following the Allied bombing of the Seine and Loire bridges. When the Luftwaffe officers reported their findings to superior authority, Allied intelligence managed to intercept and decode the transmission. Although it caused some anxious moments at SHAEF, this was not the case in the German camp. Hitler, the Wehrmacht Operations Staff, von Rundstedt and Rommel, luckily for the Allies, all ignored it. They continued to anticipate an invasion further to the northeast where, according to experience, the enemy would land in the vicinity of large ports. Huge concrete caissons (sections of *Mulberry*) had of course been observed in British harbors, but they were thought to be merely embarkation aids.

In addition to the site of the landing, the date and the time of the start of the invasion were naturally of critical importance for the defenders, if they wanted to avoid keeping their units on the coast at a permanent, wearying state of alert. According to the Germans, the invasion would have to be mounted after the winter storms, most probably in May, the earliest time by which at least five consecutive days of good weather could be guaranteed. The practice landing operations of the Allies in England and the recently completed operations along the Italian coast, however, also gave various indications of the nature and date of the coming invasion. The Germans thus knew they must expect a heavy air bombardment of their defenses and the early deployment of airborne forces and armored units, together with large-scale shelling from the enemy navy off the coast. All this would take place in the early dawn of the first day, about two to three hours after the low water.

If, with this background information, one studies the exact tables of Naval Group West, showing tides, phases of the moon and first and last light, the amazing conclusion becomes inescapable: in the area between Le Havre and Cherbourg – where many Navy officers indeed expected the landing to occur – the optimal conditions for a landing, should May slip by quietly, would prevail only during the period from June 5–7. Similar favorable conditions would not recur until the 19th of the month – and even then without the moonlit nights so important to the Allied air forces. Yet Hitler, Jodl (Chief of the Wehrmacht Operations Staff), von Rundstedt and even Rommel still remained unmoved by this evidence. They steadfastly maintained the same attitude towards the enemy that they had held for years. It was only Hitler himself who briefly adopted the idea that Normandy offered good conditions for an airborne landing. The strengthening of defenses against this eventuality however made little difference to the overall German defense plan.

■ German Dispositions

The Allied strength in Britain as calculated by the Germans naturally forced them to maintain a presence along the entire coastline. It was impossible to set up a focal point for the defenses, since subsidiary operations at least could be mounted anywhere. The potential advantage of an "inner line," the rapid movement of German divisions from one coast to another, would also be nullified in Gen. Jodl's view by the large number of Allied troops surrounding Europe on all sides. Furthermore, Hitler and his generals still had to devote the major proportion of their military resources to the Eastern Front, to face the powerful onslaught of the Red Army. In summer 1943 fresh forces were needed for the fighting in Italy. The Germans were also compelled to send many divisions to combat the uprisings in Yugoslavia and Greece. Taken together, these demands far outstripped the capabilities of Hitler's Germany. The German leader and his advisors therefore resolved to seek a strategic solution.

Until the late autumn of 1943 they still looked to the east for their salvation, hoping to achieve the first decisive victory there. With the aid of the huge potential released by a defeated Soviet Union, and with their rear no longer threatened, they would then do their utmost to put fear into the hearts of the British and Americans. The Navy and the Luftwaffe would then get the lion's share of production of modern armaments instead of the Army. This plan however came to nothing as the fighting in the east became ever more bitter and prolonged.

Between October and November 1943 German strategy nevertheless underwent a fundamental change in emphasis. Hitler now ordained the struggle against the Red Army as no longer decisive to winning the war. The Germans might have to give up some territory, but they would be able to stop well before the borders of the Reich. In the west however matters were coming to a head. Should the Allies gain a foothold anywhere on the west coast of Europe, Germany would have lost the war. In Hitler's view, an attempted invasion by the Allies would also represent a golden opportunity for the Reich. For if they could inflict a defeat on the British and Americans they would be incapable, for psychological reasons alone, of mounting another invasion in the foreseeable future. Then, Hitler's imagination ran on, following a decisive victory in the west, it would be possible to concentrate all his forces in the east and finally crush the Soviet Union. Everything thus depended on ensuring that all available resources were devoted to defeating the Allies in the west.

■ The Strategic Alternatives

Yet how was this to be achieved? There were basically two alternatives: the Germans must either try to defeat a landing during its very execution, entailing the defeat of the combined sea and air operations, or force the issue on the ground following the actual invasion. At first it seemed that the German leadership would decide on the former option, as Hitler himself declared in May 1943 that, "The Atlantic is my western perimeter, and even if I must fight a defensive battle there, that's still better than having to defend myself on the coast of Europe." In this he agreed with Grand-Adm. Doenitz, who was still convinced a sea power such as England could only properly be defeated at sea. Despite the great slaughter of the U-boats in the spring of 1943, Doenitz repeatedly tried to persuade Hitler to continue the war at sea. Although the Navy had been unable to discover the causes behind the loss of so many U-boats, Doenitz resumed the tonnage war against the Allied convoys in autumn 1943, only to be heavily defeated once again.

In the meantime matters had been firmly settled in favor of the second option – defeating the Allies on the European mainland. Doenitz's plan could anyway only have worked with the cooperation of a strong Luftwaffe. Unfortunately Goering, the Supreme Commander of the Luftwaffe lacked not only the means, but also the conceptual vision for such a campaign. The Army too was still very reserved about the concept of a combined defense: "The soldier is somehow anxious and nervous about having water in front of his own positions. He wants to get away from the coast," commented the Navy in August 1944, not entirely without justification.

It is hardly surprising then that Hitler's Order No. 51 of November 1943 allocated only minor operational tasks to the Luftwaffe and the Navy in the west. Essentially, they were only to act if a landing took place. Hardly any facet now remained of the idea of a comprehensive strategy to engage the enemy before he reached the coast. The only such means still available was the intended bombardment of England by the V-weapons. Their introduction was planned for June 1944. With these weapons Hitler and his generals hoped to destroy the morale of the British population; delaying the invasion plans, if not putting an end to them entirely. Otherwise the main burden of the defense would fall on the Army.

■ The Atlantic Wall

Since there was also a shortage of manpower here, the German leadership made every effort to make good this lack with fortifications. Plans had been drawn up as early as the end of 1941 for an Atlantic Wall, which would consist of a vast number of fortified positions, bunkers, artillery pieces, anti-aircraft defenses, obstacles and barriers in the immediate vicinity of the coast. Following the model of similar installations already built in Norway, hundreds of thousands of foreign and German workers were employed in the ensuing months and years, under the control of the Organization Todt, in fortifying first the Franco-Belgian coastline, an later all sectors of the coast along the Channel. From November 1942, following the landing of Allied troops in North Africa, fortifications also sprang up in the south of France. According to von Rundstedt and his staff, the sea was to serve as "the best anti tank ditch" before the Atlantic Wall.

The German rate of construction was impressive: by the day of the invasion they had completed 12,247 of the 15,000 fortifications originally planned (with 943 more on the Mediterranean coast), built 500,000 beach obstacles, and laid 6.5 million mines. This was largely thanks to the energetic Field Marshal Rommel, who had made every possible effort to turn the coast into a fearful obstacle to the Allies. There was only one small problem however: like the other German leaders, Rommel's eyes were fixed on a landing at the Pas de Calais area, and the greatest resources were therefore devoted to the area held by Fifteenth Army. Where the Allies actually did land, opposite Seventh Army, the defenses were less thoroughly prepared. Although Army Headquarters had 74,000 Todt workers and 3,765 vehicles at its disposal, only about half the planned program had been completed by May 1944. There were many problems, particularly with the naval guns which were to have ranged far out to sea. Of the planned second line 12.5–18.5 miles (20–30km) inland only a small part had been completed. Furthermore the lion's share of the available material and manpower had been swallowed up in fortifying the ports of Cherbourg, St. Malo, Brest, Lorient and St. Nazaire, since the Germans assumed the Allies would land in the immediate vicinity of large ports.

Von Rundstedt and his staff knew of course that the chain of fortifications comprising the Atlantic Wall could only be as strong as its weakest link. He therefore made it clear to his commanders in the coastal fortifications again in February 1944: "There must be no retreat in the west!" In the event of an invasion, they would have to stand firm until motorized reserves arrived to throw the Allies back into the sea. Yet the German leaders, and especially Hitler himself, were not 100 percent convinced by their own plans, otherwise they would not, as early as autumn 1943, have reconnoitred a retrenchment line running from the River Somme via the Rivers Marne and Saone to the Swiss border. This was naturally carried out in strict secrecy, and only a few handpicked staff officers were told of it. After all, nobody wanted to demoralize the Army prematurely.

Still it is astounding that an army created for, and practised in mobility should suddenly decide to plant itself behind a wall. One reason for this may have been that the majority of the divisions under C-in-C West's control were "static," i.e. non-motorized divisions. His main objective up to November 1943 had been to form new mobile units. These divisions however were removed from the control of the C-in-C West as soon as they were brought up to strength in men and equipment. Hitler's Order No. 51 of the same month forbade any further transfers from the west to the south or east because of the new strategy. In reality however, many motorized units still left the west after this time because they were so urgently needed on other fronts.

Against this background it is easy to see why arguments raged for months in the German camp over the few Panzer divisions available. Were they in fact the real linch-pin of the German defense system in the west? Should these divisions be positioned directly behind the Atlantic Wall, to be able to react rapidly to an Allied landing, as Rommel demanded for example, or should they be retained at more central points? After much wrangling a compromise was reached: some Panzer divisions were moved closer to the coast, while others formed a central reserve around Paris. This seemed to be the ideal solution, for now an enemy landing could be opposed immediately, and the reserve deployed when the main Allied thrust had been clearly identified.

Two factors soon become evident: the Germans were clearly hoping for a decisive result in the battle for the Allied bridgehead, since they knew from experience that the Allies would be at their weakest during this initial phase of the invasion. The "Panzer controversy", however, reveals that it was only Army officers who remained involved in the defense plan. They addressed themselves chiefly to the problem of what was to be done after an enemy landing. The crucial question of where and when the Allied attack would begin, however, received much less attention. It remained a purely hypothetical question as to whether the vast resources invested in the Atlantic Wall might not better serve the Luftwaffe and the Navy. Apart from the technical and organizational feasibility of such a redirection of effort, it must be remembered that Hitler and the majority of his senior officers still persisted in the tradition of being exclusively a land power. They thus developed a "fortress" mentality, out of which they seemed unable to escape.

■ Clash of Responsibilities

The defensive preparations in the west were considerably hindered by the complicated and intermingled areas of responsibility which prevailed there. The title C-in-C West represented a pious wish rather than reflecting the real situation. In contrast to Eisenhower's comprehensive powers, von Rundstedt had direct control of only a part of the armed forces in the west. It was understandable and tolerable that the flying units of Luftflotte 3 should still come under the command of the head of the Luftwaffe. When, on the other hand, paratroop units and Luftwaffe field divisions – nominally part of the Luftwaffe – were withdrawn from the direct control of the C-in-C West, this naturally caused friction. A similar situation existed with the Naval security units and the coastal batteries. The fortress commandant in a port city was always an Army officer, and organized the defense with land operations in mind – a state of affairs which often came into conflict with the ideas of the Navy. Superior authorities such as the Armed Forces High Command or Navy High Command were often forced to intervene and settle the arguments which thus arose.

Waffen-SS and reserve units were also only von Rundstedt's to dispose of under certain conditions. He was often frustrated to find that only by chance had his staff come to learn of major manpower and equipment changes within such divisions. Military commanders in the west also had their own chain of command, which bypassed C-in-C West and ran direct to Army High Command in Berlin.

All of this could have been justified with the argument that different operational tasks required a different command structure. What remained completely incomprehensible however was the confused network o responsibilities within the Army itself. Even there the C-in-C West was not assured of complete powers of command. His most potent weapon, the motorized divisions, were partly removed from his control, in that they formed part of the Army High Command reserve. It was precisely this fact which was to have such dire consequences for the initial German reaction to the landings. The 2nd Panzer Division for example was by no means untypical, when thrown in at the crucial point of the assault, in having to give an ear to four different command authorities: in the order of battle it formed part of Panzer Group West, tactically it belonged to the I SS Panzer Corps, territorially it was under the control of the military commander for Belgium and Northern France, and for supply purposes it was still in Fifteenth Army. Nor was this by any means an exceptional case.

Even such an experienced officer as Gen. Blumentritt, the Chief of the General Staff at C-in-C West, was apt to get hot under the collar, and he gave vent to his feelings in a letter to Jodl in January 1944: "Everything here is in a complete mess, tangled and confused at every possible point."

Blumentritt may thereby have been thinking of the prolonged argument between Field Marshals von Rundstedt and Rommel, which had been going on since the end of 1943. Rommel's Army Group B Staff had originally been languishing in Italy. Perhaps Hitler saw in this a suitable opportunity to use the "Desert Fox" in the west, since nobody knew the western Allies as well as Rommel. His staff were therefore transferred to France in the New Year, in order to improve the defensive fortifications along the coast – technically a job which fell within the responsibility of the armies under C-in-C West. Rommel, who had a direct line to Hitler, then also managed to arrange things so that all troops from Holland to St. Nazaire (Army Commander Netherlands, Fifteenth Army, and Seventh Army) were placed under his command from January 15, 1944. Not satisfied with this, his hunger for power also soon gave him the veto on the use of motorized units, and he also tried to bring parts of the First and Nineteenth Armies in Southern France under his control. Von Rundstedt, seeing his own influence diminishing day by day, finally sent a note to the Armed Forces High Command in the spring of 1944, which he rounded off by saying that should his authority be restricted any further, there would seem to be little point to his continued service in the west. This had the desired effect. The dispute was terminated forthwith at the beginning of May with a victory for von Rundstedt: C-in-C West was placed in control not only of Rommel's Group B, but also of the newly-formed army Group G (First and Nineteenth Armies) and Panzer Group West. This was only a formal arrangement, however, since the restrictions on his authority mentioned above still remained in effect. In other words, the situation now, after months of frustrating arguments, was virtually the same as at the end of 1943. To illustrate this in a little more detail: when C-in-C West laid out the new organisation for his command authorities on May 12, 1944, it took eight pages just to list his main areas of responsibility.

One may well enquire into the exact reasons for such a situation. In the author's opinion the following should be borne in mind: firstly the system of divided responsibility was deeply rooted in the traditions of German leadership, the tendency running through civil and military, private and public institutions ever since the foundation of the German Empire in 1871, irrespective of the ruling political system. Bismarck's "Lesser German Empire" did not grow organically, but was a conglomeration of varying mentalities and interests, which naturally gave rise to much rivalry. Nor did this situation change at all in the 20th century.

Secondly, Hitler was very careful to observe the principle of power sharing. Nobody was allowed to become powerful enough to threaten him. In this the German dictator was simply following the established tradition. This naturally proved to be a breeding ground for petty jealousies, self-seeking servility, and obsession with prestige at all levels in the power structure. In relation to military matters one often has the impression that, for many high-ranking officers, the thing closest to their heart was not the military objective, but rather their careers or the reputation of their branch of the service or military unit. This was not an unknown motive in the Allied camp, and one has only to think of Patton, Montgomery and MacArthur in this respect. Amongst the German leadership, however, this situation and attitude was rather more the rule than the exception.

■ The Order of Battle

At the time of the landing, von Rundstedt's staff disposed altogether over 60 divisions. This represented an increase of 10 major units since mid-1943. What might at first sight seem an imposing array can easily be put into better perspective on closer examination. Over the same period, the proportion of still-incomplete divisions increased correspondingly. About 20 "static" units, and many of the Panzer divisions had only arrived in France and Belgium during the course of spring 1944. Their equipment and manpower states were particularly problematical for the C-in-C West, as was the transfer to the Eastern Front in March 1944 of the II SS Panzer corps and its two combat-ready units. Even later, when all indications pointed to an imminent invasion, the German leadership continued to withdraw motorized units from the west, some units stationed northwest of Orléans leaving C-in-C West's control as late as June 4. The would have been particularly useful only two days later when they could have been employed in attacking Allied troops in Normandy. These events only go to show that Hitler's vision of an enemy airborne landing in the Normandy region was nothing more than a passing fancy.

Yet although motorized units were still leaving the west up to the last moment, the Germans were still able to field about 1,600 tanks, all at least equal to those of the Allies in firepower and mobility.

Most of the 10 motorized units in the region were stationed close to the Channel, mainly in the central area between Holland and the Seine. South of the Seine, however, there was only the 21st Panzer Division around Caen and two further units (12th SS Panzer and Panzer Lehr) at least 62 miles (100km) from the Normandy coast. Here, where the Allies would soon land, the LXXXIV Army Corps would have to put up the best defense it could with six divisions and numerous independent anti-tank, tank, air landing, artillery and "Ost" battalions (battalions composed of eastern European nationalities).

■ **Shortages of Materiel**

The one factor which most reduced the combat readiness of the units in the west was the increasing shortage of fuel supplies. Allied bombing of the German fuel industry had had far-reaching consequences: training programmes had had to be curtailed, depots reduced in size and number, and transport in general slowed down. In many cases the Germans now had to make do with bicycles and horse transport.

The manpower state in the German camp was also gradually wearing thin. The huge losses, particularly in the east, increasingly forced Hitler and his followers to use foreign workers in the factories in order to release German workers for the Army. At the end of November 1943 the Army High Command initiated a so-called "combing out" drive to round up all surplus manpower from all walks of life for service at the front. C-in-C West even formed a special staff for this purpose in February 1944 under the command of a general. The result was pitiful. Despite the severest penalties for evasion, by April only 6,500 soldiers had been enlisted in the west (according to Jodl the available manpower in the region was 1,870,000, together with 310,000 in Norway and 170,000 in Denmark). Yet in Paris alone at this time there were 50,000 Germans engaged in innumerable occupations.

This abortive effort demonstrated once more how complicated and involved the command structure in the west had become. Nobody could even judge any more whether an organization had too many or too few personnel. It is little wonder therefore that the manpower needs of von Rundstedt's divisions underwent little improvement. In the SS divisions, more than 50 percent of the troops were often under 20 years of age, while the "static" divisions were made up with many over-age soldiers. The manpower shortage was considerably exacerbated by the Allied bombing of important transport and armaments centers in the occupied west. The Germans were forced to devote an ever-increasing number of men to repairing the damage caused. So far as the equipment of his units was concerned, von Rundstedt's divisions did not always receive the most up-to-date equipment from the factories, and often had to make do with obsolete, captured equipment to make up the numbers. This often tried the technical know-how of the operators and severely complicated supply requirements.

The flying units of Luftflotte 3 and IX Air Corps had to contend with similar problems. At the end of May 1944, Luftflotte 3 had just over 900 aircraft on inventory, of which only 650 were operational (with a further 145 aircraft in Norway). The IX Air Corps, whose bombers had carried out sporadic attacks on British embarkation ports in the weeks before the landing, albeit without causing significant damage, reported only 100 combat-ready aircraft by the end of May. In the event of an invasion the Germans planned to transfer approximately 1,000 aircraft to the west from all parts of occupied Europe. Even with this number – should the transfer actually to take place – the Germans would still find themselves in a hopelessly inferior position. Although the Minister for Armaments, Albert Speer, had again succeeded in considerably increasing aircraft production in 1944, this output far outstripped the availability of pilots. It was for this reason for example that in May 1944, out of a total of 2,155 aircraft losses by the Luftwaffe, 847 were accidents not involving enemy action.

The Navy in the west also faced a similar sorry outlook. After most of the large surface units had been brought back to harbor in Norway or Germany, only 3 destroyers, 5 torpedo boats, 34 motor gunboats, 163 minehunters and 34 U-boats were left in the west. Due to the weakness of the Luftwaffe even these units were unable to venture outside the anti-aircraft protection of their harbors during daylight hours.

Yet Doenitz ordered these warships to be employed regardless of potential losses. According to the Grand-Admiral, they had only one job in the event of a landing: "Attack and sink." At the end of March 1944, Doenitz proposed using the U-boats in a style reminiscent of the Japanese kamikaze mentality: "The U-boat which causes losses to the enemy during a landing has fulfilled its ultimate aim and justified its existence, even if it remains there." As it turned out, most of the U-boats intended for this purpose never had the opportunity, for Doenitz had ordered them back out into the mid-Atlantic at the end of May, when the threat of an invasion seemed to have receded.

The only effective weapon remaining to the Navy in the west to combat a landing seemed to be the use of mines. Naval Group West wanted to mine the whole sea around the Isle of Wight with the aid of the Luftwaffe. The latter however refused to have anything to do with this plan, leaving the Navy with the sole remaining option of laying so called "lightning barrages" along the coast at the last minute. In order for this to be feasible however, the enemy approach across the Channel would have to be detected in good time. The head of Naval Group West, Adm. Krancke, hoped to be able to do this with his few remaining patrol boats which patrolled the coastline, weather permitting, each night.

■ **The Troops' Morale**
The precarious situation of Hitler's Germany could not be kept secret from the ordinary soldier forever, in spite of all the Nazi propaganda which was showered on him. Allied air superiority over Germany and in the west was enough on its own to show the overwhelming materiel superiority already enjoyed by the Allies. The confidence in victory and the spirit of the earlier years were gone, as is revealed by the tenor of many soldiers' letters home. The troops could also notice the colder atmosphere in the occupied territories, where a passive attitude, changing to disdain and outright disobedience were encountered more frequently. Whether the fight against supposed or actual Resistance members, in which an ever-growing number of Wehrmacht troops were employed, served to raise morale, must remain undecided. In any event, the German measures against Allied "commando troops" (teams of national or Allied troops engaged in reconnaissance or sabotage) seemed likely to put their own side in the wrong: they must be granted no quarter, even if they surrendered without a fight, were the orders from above. Such orders were of course to

be acknowledged, but the written record of the orders was to be immediately destroyed. Many soldiers may have asked themselves how this was to be reconciled with the idea of the "ethical and moral superiority" and the "nobility" of German aims, as their leaders characterized them.

It appeared to be difficult, for many reasons, to turn the soldier in the west into such a fanatical fighter as his comrades on the Eastern Front. The long sojourn away from an active front had led here to typical "instances of malingering." Many troops adopted an increasingly careless and sloppy attitude: they lost their weapons and other equipment, became involved with local women and, especially in France, fell victim to a fascination with the country and the people. Rigorous punishments imposed by military courts and superior officers had little effect on these tendencies.

Another battle fought almost in vain, was that over the attitude towards the Allies in the coming conflict. In contrast to the Eastern Front, where many men believed they were engaged in a crusade against Bolshevism and the "sub-human" Slavs, the British and Americans were viewed much less negatively. The Army High Command summed up the feelings of many soldiers in the west by saying that they held the regrettable but appropriate "assumption of facing a more humane opponent." One event from the end of 1943 may serve as a good example of this attitude: an Allied "terror flier" parachuted from his shot-down aircraft over France and was soon taken prisoner by a troop of German soldiers. The NCO in charge offered the pilot a cigarette, in full view of some French civilians. Von Rundstedt practically foamed at the mouth with anger when he heard of this and ordered shortly afterwards that any similar cases of "completely misplaced sentimentality" must in future be punished. No less a figure than Goebbels, the Reich Propaganda Minister, strove to reverse this attitude and attacked the bombing of German cities as an uncultured act of barbarity.

Senior officers again emphasized that in the event of a landing, it would be a fight "to the death." Jodl made the following prognosis: "Then we shall see who fights harder and dies easier, the German soldier faced with the destruction of his homeland, or the Americans and English, who don't even know any longer what they are fighting for in Europe." At the end of 1943 he even invoked history in front of senior military men and officials in the hope of encouraging the more lethargic types: "We will be victorious, because we must be victorious, for otherwise there would be no sense anymore to world history."

It was on the "wonder weapons" that the Germans, at home and the front, now pinned their remaining hopes. Many letters home from the front show that they continued to have faith that these weapons would change the course of the war at the eleventh hour.

In view of the Allied superiority, this applied especially to the troops in the west. Where a cohesive group of soldiers with previous combat experience could be found, or where a unit with a tradition or a reputation still existed, the Allies could certainly count on stiff opposition. This was the case for most of the motorized divisions and also some of the infantry and paratroop divisions. Other units, however, bad been cobbled together out of diverse groups from all branches of the service, of differing age groups and often varying degrees of fitness. Amongst this latter category were many of the "static", security and reserve divisions, from whom a lot less heroism could be expected.

■ Before the Invasion

At the highest level, the mood amongst Hitler and his generals shortly before the invasion was one of confidence. The Führer could hardly wait for the landings since he was completely convinced of a forthcoming victory of German arms, whilst Rommel above all gave a very optimistic impression. In his view he had done everything humanly possible in the right place to prepare a warm reception for the Allies.

A week before the landing at the latest, it must have been absolutely clear to SHAEF that they would achieve strategic surprise, for there were no indications at all that the enemy had changed his long standing idea of a main thrust aimed at the Pas de Calais. Even if the Germans were to learn the true Allied intentions now, it would be far too late for them to undertake any significant regroupings.

The question still remained as to whether the British and Americans could also achieve tactical surprise on the day of the invasion. At one moment it seemed they would not, when an error of potentially huge proportions occurred at Supreme Headquarters. When Eisenhower postponed the landing from June 5 to 6 due to bad weather, SHAEF ordered all ships already at sea back to the nearest harbor, One convoy of 135 vessels however failed to receive the order, and steamed on alone towards the Normandy coast. The Allies did not succeed in contacting and stopping the convoy until it was 25 nautical miles (46km) south of the Isle of Wight. Luckily for the invasion forces the Germans failed to suspect anything. Sea and air reconnaissance in the Normandy area had been suspended due to the bad weather, a quite understandable step, for after several weeks of the most favorable weather conditions, the Allies would certainly not want to land now, in weather fit for neither man nor beast. At least so thought many senior officers in C-in-C West's area, and turned their minds to other things: they went to play war games in Rennes, took a few days' holiday or visited their French lady friends.

However, the weather forecast of the meteorologist at C-in-C West for June 5 was not so negative as this behavior might suggest. After a front of bad weather, went the report, periods of better weather could be expected on the following day. Strangely enough, this forecast was exactly the same as that of the Allies.

There had however already been much clearer signs of an impending invasion: in the middle of May, the German Security Service in France had reported that the "Secret Army" had gone to the highest state of alert and that consequently an invasion could be expected between the 20th of the month and June 10. On the first day of the same month, the Naval Intelligence Service noticed a further indicator of the approaching attack: the Allies had already changed the key code settings for their radio traffic after only 30 days, something which they normally only did after three months. They were also clearly trying to knock out by bombing all of the defenders' radio monitoring posts along the coast. Finally, on June 1 and 3 the German authorities received, quite openly, the clearest indication of all that the invasion was imminent: the BBC had been repeatedly broadcasting to the Resistance movements the first part of a stanza from one of Verlaine's poems which ran: "Les sanglots longs des violons de l'automne." If this was to be followed by the second part, the German Secret Service knew that the landing would follow within 48 hours. The British promptly broadcast the second part: "blessent mon coeur d'une langueur monotone," at 21:15, June 5. A short while earlier the C-in-C West had given the following evaluation of the situation: "There are no definite signs that the invasion is imminent," since the result of Allied air attacks on the coastal fortifications certainly could not have come up to enemy expectations. Naval Group West expressed the same conclusion a day earlier, on June 4: the Allies, as they thought, had only enough landing craft for just over 10 divisions. They would therefore need more time to assemble the shipping capacity for the 20 divisions estimated as necessary by the Germans.

On the basis of these judgements, the C-in-C West still took no concrete steps against a possible landing on the evening of June 5. In any case, the BBC had sent out many such alert messages in the past, without the expected invasion happening. The officers at C-in-C West simply assumed that this latest message was the signal for the start of widespread acts of sabotage.

The situation began to change however shortly after midnight when airborne landings were reported on the Orne and the Cotentin peninsula. LXXXIV Army Corps in Normandy now initiated Alert State II (highest alert): they were shortly followed by Fifteenth Army. Naval Group West and Luftflotte 3 also followed suit. Even now the High Command in the west did not think they were facing a major landing, and therefore deemed sea reconnaissance by surface vessels as unnecessary. The weather conditions and tides were hardly favorable anyway.

When a few ships were sighted off Port-en-Bessin towards 03:00 on the morning of June 6, Adm. Krancke nevertheless ordered sea reconnaissance by surface vessels. An hour and a half later the first torpedo boats put out from Le Havre.

Around 06:45 the situation seemed to have calmed down a little, when the Chief of Staff of Seventh Army reported that, contrary to earlier estimations, there was no evidence of any seaborne landing. At that moment in fact the coastal fortifications were already under fire from Allied warships. Nevertheless, the Seventh Army Headquarters, according to the Chief of Staff, were quite capable of handling the situation without any assistance.

At that very moment, landing craft were approaching the coast under the cover of naval and aerial bombardment. The invasion had begun and the Allies had succeeded in achieving complete tactical surprise.

OPERATION NEPTUNE

When daylight began to pierce the darkness on the morning of June 6, D-Day, German observers on France's Normandy coast saw spread out before them as far as the eye could see an armada of over 5,300 naval vessels, from the largest battleship to the smallest patrol boat. This invasion flotilla, the most powerful ever assembled, with warships, amphibious ships, auxiliaries, and landing craft from Great Britain, the United States, France, Canada, Poland, Norway, Greece, and the Netherlands, was poised to start the liberation of Europe.

Over two years before that momentous day, British and American military staffs had begun preparations for the invasion of the continent. The London-based staff of Lt. Gen. Frederick E. Morgan, the Chief of Staff to the Supreme Allied Commander (COSSAC), had begun planning for a landing in western Europe back in early 1943. Morgan's group developed the so-called "COSSAC" Plan for the invasion of France, from May 1943 on code-named *Overlord*. The naval aspect of that enormous undertaking would later be called *Neptune*.

The COSSAC plan called for an amphibious assault along a relatively narrow 30-mile (48km) front, with three infantry divisions seizing the beachhead and two others reinforcing them. Morgan unveiled the plan to

Allied leaders at the first Quebec Conference in August 1943 and soon afterwards the US-British Combined Chiefs of Staff approved it in principle. Although the COSSAC planners would have preferred a stronger effort, they did not have the clout to get for *Overlord* the additional air, naval, and ground forces they felt essential. That year the Americans were focused on the war in the Pacific and the campaign against the U-boat menace in the Atlantic, while the British, especially Prime Minister Churchill, were seriously considering alternative campaigns in Norway and the Mediterranean.

The appointments of Generals Eisenhower and Montgomery to *Overlord* at the end of 1943 finished the COSSAC plan. Neither was happy about its limited scope, either in number of divisions deployed or its narrow beachhead. By January 1944 the COSSAC plan was being completely revised to include an attack by five infantry divisions abreast on a 61-mile (98km) beach front. Unlike Morgan, these officers, who had the strong support of Roosevelt and Churchill, were able re-emphasize the prior understanding that *Overlord* had first call on Allied resources worldwide.

An officer who shared the views of Eisenhower and Montgomery on the broad front approach was Adm. Sir Bertram Ramsay, selected by the British Admiralty to serve as Naval Commander Allied Expeditionary Force, Ramsay was an easygoing naval officer who possessed a brilliant intellect and the ability to address a problem clearly. This veteran of World War I, and more recent amphibious operations at Dunkirk and in the Mediterranean, was charged with planning and overseeing the naval aspects of the invasion program.

■ Planning *Neptune*

During the first half of 1944, Allied leaders, including Ramsay and Rear Adm. Alan G. Kirk, the ranking American naval officer in *Neptune*, feverishly worked to acquire additional assault divisions and a host of additional landing ships and craft, escorts, minesweepers, and logistic support vessels. The change to the strategic plan meant that embarkation ports and training grounds had to be set aside in southern England already chock-a-block with troops. motor transport, and supplies. Furthermore, the new invasion plan made it clear that the Allies would not have the wherewithal to support a simultaneous and complementary landing in the south of France, code-named *Anvil*, or to launch the Normandy assault in May, as originally planned. Eisenhower postponed *Anvil* to August and rescheduled the cross-channel operation for June 5, 1944.

It was soon clear that the Royal Navy could not by itself meet the new operational requirements for *Neptune*. The British felt compelled to maintain a strong Home Fleet in Scotland in case Hitler's pocket battleships, cruisers, and other major combatants based in Germany sortied into the North Sea or moved south into the English Channel to contest the Allied landing. The British also feared a foray by the German battleship *Tirpitz* deployed in Norway against Allied convoys steaming through Arctic waters to the Soviet Union. As a result, the British kept in reserve three fleet carriers, three modern battleships (which they also chose not to risk to the mines off the French coast), and 16 other major units. British intelligence, however, over-estimated the operational ability of the German surface fleet, whose warships and bases had been the target of Allied bombers for many months and would have been hard pressed to mount a serious attack against the Allies in any area.

The British took drastic steps to provide the additional sailors, warships, and other vessels needed for *Neptune*. The Royal Navy laid up 49 old combatants and decommissioned a minelaying squadron so that their crews could man more combat-effective ships and craft. The British even transferred soldiers and airmen to the sea service. Finally, the Admiralty recalled ships from the Mediterranean theater, halted the dispatch of units to the Eastern Fleet in the Indian Ocean, and reduced the number of Atlantic convoy escorts.

Despite these measures, Eisenhower's naval staff was concerned they still lacked enough amphibious vessels and bombardment ships to carry out the expanded *Neptune* plan. Hence, they called on the US Navy to make up the deficit. This led to one of the few acrimonious exchanges between the British and the Americans during the preparations for *Neptune*. The British felt the Americans were employing too many amphibious vessels in their Pacific operations to the detriment of the European theater. Adm. Ernest J. King, the flinty C-in-C US Fleet and Chief of Naval Operations, disagreed, contending that he had been generous with the allocation to the European theater of Landing Ships, Tank (LST) Landing Craft, Infantry (LCI) Landing Craft, Tank (LCT) and other amphibious vessels.

The crux of the problem was that there were just not enough amphibious types in service to handle all of the Allies' global requirements. The high losses in the Atlantic and the Caribbean to German U-boats during 1942 had mandated increased building in US shipyards of convoy escort ships rather than landing ships and craft. The postponement of a 1943 landing in Europe also diverted amphibious vessels to other theaters.

The whole issue became moot when the British shifted LSTs and LCIs from the Mediterranean and increased the troop and vehicle load capacities of their vessels, as the Americans had done. What is more, Adm. King began to send newly constructed amphibious vessels directly from the shipyards to England. Consequently, the Allied naval force had a sufficient number of amphibious vessels on D-Day.

The short-tempered but brilliant King also objected to the dispatch of major US warships to European waters. He felt that the British had an adequate number of these combatants to handle bombardment and naval gunfire support duties. He was persuaded otherwise when Rear Adm. John L. Hall, slated to head one of the two American amphibious task forces, strongly expressed his concern for the success of the operation. Finally in April 1944, King deployed to England three old battleships (*Arkansas, Nevada* and *Texas*) and a squadron of destroyers. Still, as the American naval historian Samuel Elliot Morison has correctly observed, "the Royal Navy supplied the lion's share of gunfire support ships" and, he might have added, the majority of the other ships and craft involved in *Neptune.*

The Royal Navy (which included units of the Royal Canadian Navy) would put to sea on June 5 with a total of three battleships, 17 cruisers, 65 destroyers, 360 coastal craft, and 447 frigates, destroyer escorts, corvettes, minesweepers, and similar vessels. The US Navy contribution included three battleships, three cruisers, 34 destroyers, 111 coastal craft, and 49 frigates, destroyer escorts, minesweepers and patrol craft. Another 49 French, Polish, Greek, Dutch, and Norwegian-manned warships and combat craft would sail in the invasion fleet. The amphibious landing ships and craft totalled 4,126 vessels (3,261 British and 865 US).

All of the Allied leaders associated with *Neptune* were conscious of the British amphibious disasters at Gallipoli in World War I and at Dieppe in 1942, while the American knew that even though their recent landing at Tarawa Atoll in the Pacific by US Marines in November 1943 had succeeded, the cost in lives had been much too great. These military professionals knew that an amphibious landing operation, involving coordinated air, sea, and ground operations, was one of the most complex of military evolutions to achieve successfully.

To avoid a catastrophe in France, Allied soldiers, sailors, and airmen underwent thorough and continuous training. Rear Adm. John Wilkes, great grandson of Commodore Charles Wilkes, the 19th-century American explorer of the Pacific, was charged with preparing US forces for their part in *Neptune*. Beginning in December 1943, the energetic admiral put the Americans through demanding training exercises at Slapton Sands and Torquay in Devon. Full-scale rehearsals took place in which the troop units and ships that were slated to fight together also trained together. Much of this training occurred in late April and early May. The Germans helped make this training real. On April 28, nine fast German E-boats burst in on a night exercise in Lyme Bay off the Devon coast and sank two of the precious LSTs before escaping in the confusion. That night off southern England, 600 American soldiers and sailors died, most of them by drowning. Despite this tragedy, the rigorous training régime prepared US and British amphibious forces well.

Furthermore, Allied maintenance and repair units were especially successful in keeping the ships and craft of the amphibious flotilla operational. On June 1, 99.3 percent of the US and 97.7 percent of the British amphibious vessels were seaworthy and prepared for action.

The Allied navies also emphasized training for the gunfire support mission. Separate teams of naval officers were assigned to the landing forces to help ensure naval gunfire accuracy. The British called these teams Forward Observers Bombardment and the Americans referred to them as Shore Fire Control Parties. These groups, which would go ashore with airborne and amphibious assault troops, trained intensively with the gun directors of their primary support ship. They were trained to call in fire from other Allied ships as well. British and US Navy aircrew of Royal Air Force Spitfires and Mustangs and Royal Navy Seafires trained with the fire directors of the bombardment ships to adjust fire from the air.

The success of the Normandy invasion hinged not only on sound and thorough training but on the preparations for the logistic support of the mammoth enterprise. Allied forces had to seize a beachhead and hold it against determined German counterattacks. But they also needed strength to break out into the interior of France. Thus, the flow of troops, tanks, guns, vehicles, food and fuel into the beachhead had to be heavy and uninterrupted. The Allied capture of Cherbourg, the only major port of the Cotentin Peninsula, would alleviate some of their logistic problems. But this could not be expected to happen early in the campaign ashore, and if the Germans feared losing Cherbourg, they would undoubtedly sabotage the port to render it unusable.

Consequently, the British developed two artificial harbors, code-named *Mulberry*, that would be emplaced off the invasion beaches. The design and construction of these pier and pontoon structures, which Morison characterized as a "tribute to British brains and energy," was handled by the British Admiralty and War Office. Through prodigious effort, British defense plants, shipyards, engineering firms, government agencies, and other sectors of the British warmaking establishment completed both *Mulberries* in time for D-Day. The Royal Navy was assigned the task of assembling the *Mulberry* components in four areas off Portland, Poole, Selsey and Dungeness; towing them across the Channel with over 150 US and British tugboats, and forming them into beachhead breakwaters and harbors. Within several days of the landing, the Allies hoped to have both Mulberries functioning, one off the British beaches and one off the American. Each *Mulberry* was designed to berth seven deep-draught ships, 20 coastal craft, 400 tugs and auxiliary vessels, and 1,000 smaller craft, and handle 7,000 tons of supplies daily.

Allied naval planners, who understood the devastating power of spring storms in the Channel, also felt it prudent to develop five beachhead shelters, known as *Gooseberries*, for landing craft and other smaller vessels. The *Gooseberries* would be formed by the sinking of blockships, called *Corncobs*, just offshore. Once Adm. Ramsay approved the concept, the Allies gathered 69 surplus British and US ships in Scotland.

Other preparations involved operations in proximity to the enemy. Throughout early 1944, the Allies launched small boat forces on missions all along the French coast, not only to deceive the Germans about the true invasion site, but to gather essential intelligence for the landing. For instance, in January the Royal Navy deployed several trawlers and motor launches and midget submarine *X-20*, all under the command of Lt. Cdr. H.N.C. Willmott, off the proposed American beaches on the Normandy coast. Two British soldiers swam ashore from the submarine and after collecting vital information on the beach sand, shingle, and gradients returned safely to the boat.

Perhaps the most important information available to the Allies, however, was gleaned by codebreakers from intercepted enemy radio traffic. American intelligence units hit a bonanza when they picked up a series of transmissions from Berlin to Tokyo made by Gen. Oshima Hiroshi, Japanese Ambassador to Germany. Having just completed a personal inspection of Hitler's Atlantic Wall, Oshima sent his superiors detailed reports of German defenses.

Armed with intelligence such as this, in April 1944, Adm. Ramsay issued his final plan for *Neptune*. The mission of Allied naval forces was to transport the Allied Expeditionary Force across the sea, help secure and defend a beachhead on the continent, and develop logistic facilities to sustain the advance into France of 26–30 infantry and armored divisions. The admiral stressed that the naval operation was a "combined British and American undertaking by all services of both nations."

Eisenhower had not only assigned Ramsay overall responsibility for the naval forces connected with *Overlord* but with control in battle of those naval forces deployed off the invasion coast. The admiral's chief combat commands comprised two task forces. The Western Task Force was led by calm, self confident Adm. Kirk, a veteran of the Sicily landings and commander of the US Atlantic Fleet's amphibious forces. His contingent included two infantry divisions of Lt. Gen. Omar N. Bradley's US First Army, which would storm the *Utah* and *Omaha* beaches on the western flank of the invasion. Kirk's chief subordinates were Rear Adm. Don P. Moon (Force U) and Rear Adm. John L. "Jimmie" Hall (Force O), who would direct the assaults at *Utah* and *Omaha*. The Eastern Task Force, under British Rear Adm. Sir Philip Vian, would land one Canadian and two British divisions of Lt. Gen. Miles C. Dempsey's British Second Army on 30 miles (50km) of coast between the River Orne and Port-en-Bessin. Responsible for the naval assault forces at the *Gold, Juno* and *Sword* beaches were Commodore Cyril E. Douglas-Pennant (Force G); Commodore Geoffrey N. Oliver (Force J); and Rear Adm. Arthur G. Talbot (Force S).

Force B, led by Commodore C.D. Edgar, and Force L, commanded by British Rear Adm. William E. Parry, had the critical responsibility of landing the seven support divisions on the second tide of D-Day, together with the assembly of the *Mulberry* artificial ports and *Gooseberry* boat shelters.

For the most part, British and American naval commanders directed the forces of their respective nations, but ships and craft from every national contingent steamed in each of the task forces. Thus British destroyers, French cruisers, and a Dutch gunboat operated in Adm. Kirk's command while US coastal craft, two Greek corvettes, and a Polish cruiser fought with Adm. Vian's forces.

■ Preparing the Ground

Allied superiority at sea and in the air over it made the Normandy invasion possible. The British and American navies and air forces were so successful against Grand-Adm. Doenitz's U-boats in 1943 that his fleet was unable to prevent the Allied buildup in Britain and early in 1944 was clearly on the defensive in the Atlantic Ocean. The battleships and cruisers of the German Navy, which once dared to operate from French ports and even to steam brazenly through the narrow English Channel, had either been sunk or penned into their ports.

Even for the less-easily detected German combatants such as destroyers, E-boats, and minelayers, it became foolhardy, except on moonless nights, to venture into the Channel.

The same applied to the Luftwaffe, whose fighters were already fully committed defending vital industrial plants, transportation links, and military resources ashore from the depredations of the Allied bomber fleets. In short, by June 1944, the Allies owned the Channel between England and France and the air over it.

To keep the enemy on the defensive, beginning on April 17, British minelayers, motor launches motor torpedo boats, and aircraft laid almost 7,000 mines off the enemy's principal naval bases at Boulogne, Le Havre, Cherbourg and Brest and along much of the Breton coastline. This operation was not without cost. German torpedo boats sank an escorting ship, the Canadian destroyer *Athabascan*, and a British motor torpedo boat (MTB) ran afoul of an enemy mine.

In spite of these Allied measures, the Germans still had lethal forces that they could throw into battle to defeat an Allied landing The Allies expected their foe to spare no man or machine in their defense of the Atlantic Wall. The most immediate threat to the invasion armada would come from 50 U-boats based in Brittany and approximately 100 fast attack craft (E-boats and R-boats) and midget submarines concentrated in the French Atlantic ports. The Allies would also have to contend with German sea mines.

Protection of the invasion fleet's flanks in the waters between Cornwall and Brittany on the west and the Dover–Calais narrows on the east was provided by 24 destroyers and frigates and approximately 22 flotillas of motor torpedo boats, motor and steam gun boats, and motor launches.

The Allies took measures to combat the enemy's naval threats. The RAF Coastal Command reinforced its air groups patrolling the waters between Ireland and the Brittany Peninsula and off Scotland. There were so many aircraft in 19 Group, responsible for the western approaches to Normandy, that each segment of the broad patrol area was overflown every half-hour, day and night. Most of the U-boats, if they escaped attack, would be forced to proceed submerged and this would exhaust their batteries long before they reached the cross-channel invasion routes.

The Coastal Command units off Scotland drew first blood in the campaign against the U-boats. On May 16, Doenitz ordered many of the boats operating in Norway to deploy to the Bay of Biscay off France. For the next 18 days the submarines ran the gauntlet set up by the British in the North Atlantic. Coastal Command aircraft sank 7 of the 22 U-boats they spotted.

Other Allied air forces prepared to cover the passage of the naval armada across the Channel and to protect the vulnerable transport and glider aircraft ferrying the three US and British airborne divisions to Normandy. For this task, the Allies deployed almost 2,000 fighter aircraft organized in 171 squadrons. These units would be controlled from fighter direction stations located in England, on board three LSTs in the Channel, and eventually ashore in Normandy. Swarms of fighters would also fly covering missions high above and all around the invasion site and maintain this presence, day and night, throughout *Neptune*.

To avoid Allied sailors mistaking paratroop-laden transports for German fighters and bombers and shooting them down, which occurred too frequently during the invasion of Sicily, the command established air corridors that would skirt the invasion armada to the east. In addition, sailors were schooled in aircraft recognition.

For the invasion armada to converge on assembly points off southern England, form into groups, and proceed through established lanes to the French coast without ships going off course or straying into German or Allied minefields, it was essential that there be navigation aids all along the route. These aids included motor launches and floating beacons situated at critical points.

The destruction of enemy coastal guns and beach defenses would begin with strikes by Allied bombers in the early hours of D-Day and reach a crescendo in the hour before the assault. Furthermore, each of the five assault forces was assigned a group of bombarding ships and these groups would concentrate their fire on the 24 enemy batteries emplaced around the landing beaches.

Each of the larger bombarding ships was assigned an enemy coastal gun site, normally containing four guns, as her first priority. The German batteries usually armed with the long-range, anti-ship 4.9-inch and 6.1-inch guns were protected by seven feet (2m) of reinforced concrete. Wheeled artillery pieces, smaller guns which could shift their fire from naval vessels to troops on the beach, were positioned both in concrete casemates and in the open.

In late May thousands of warships, amphibious landing ships, transports, and auxiliary ships and craft, and hundreds of thousands of Allied troops converged on the ports, rivers, and open roadsteads of southern England. Armored vehicles and trucks boarded ships directly from the beach by way of newly built hard stands, appropriately called "hards." The British and American infantry assault divisions, and the naval forces that would enable the Allied host to cross the treacherous Channel, assembled in England in the same order in which they would storm the Normandy coast. The US 4th Infantry Division, slated to assault *Utah* Beach on the Cotentin Peninsula, gathered on the Devon coast at Salcombe, Dartmouth, and Brixham. To the east in Dorset at Portland, Weymouth and Poole was the US 1st Infantry Division, which would seize *Omaha* Beach. Continuing on to the east in Hampshire was the British 50th (Northumbrian) Infantry Division at Southampton, the Canadian 3rd Infantry Division around Southampton and Portsmouth, and the British 3rd Infantry Division near Portsmouth and at Shoreham and Newhaven. The last three divisions would storm ashore on *Gold*, *Juno*, and *Sword* Beaches.

The reinforcing or follow-on divisions and their naval escorts were located on the wings of the Allied invasion assembly, with the US 29th Infantry Division to the west on the Devon and Cornish coasts at Plymouth and Falmouth and the British 7th Armoured and 51st (Highland) Divisions around the Thames Estuary at Tilbury and Felixstowe. The battleships and other heavy units of the bombardment groups swayed at anchor in Belfast, Northern Ireland and in Scotland's Clyde Estuary.

One of the keys to a successful amphibious operation is to select the day and time of day when the weather and the tides are optimum. To increase the chances of surprise and to provide the invading forces with concealment from enemy guns, Allied army leaders advocated a night landing. Naval officers, however, made it clear that a landing during daylight hours was absolutely essential to ensure accurate naval gunfire support and to coordinate launching and reloading of landing craft. Moreover, Allied underwater demolition teams and beach engineers needed light to clear lanes to the beach through the German obstacles.

Allied planners wanted the assault to begin three or four hours before high tide and be preceded by a moonlit night that would ease the navigation problems of the thousands of vessels and aircraft making the Channel, and help the airborne troops maintain some order as they dropped behind the beach defenses. There were only three or four days each month in the spring when all these conditions prevailed in the Channel between England and Normandy. Taking all these factors into consideration, on May 23, General Eisenhower established D-Day as June 5. Two days later, this critical information was passed to naval commanders when Adm. Ramsay ordered them to open their sealed operation orders. Simultaneously, he prohibited the crews of the invasion flotilla from sending out mail, using the telephone, or wiring telegrams. Then, on May 28, all crews and troops were "sealed" in their ships.

A few security breaches occurred anyway. Several communication transmissions connected D-Day with June 5, and tugs were inadvertently issued charts of the Bay of the Seine. Despite these lapses the Germans remained unaware of the invasion date.

On June 1, Adm. Ramsay, from his "battle headquarters" at Southwick House near Portsmouth, took command of Allied naval forces. The following evening two British midget submarines, *X-20* and *X-23* (markers for Forces J and S), proceeded out to sea from Portsmouth, and the bombardment ships sortied from the Clyde. In the words of Stephen W. Roskill, the British naval historian, "like the giant flywheel of a power plant its first movement was barely perceptible, but with every revolution it gained further momentum until it was running smoothly at the speed for which it had been designed."

On Sunday, June 4, however, convinced by his meteorologists that the weather would be too rough the following day, Gen. Eisenhower postponed the operation for 24 hours. Convoys that had already set sail had to return to their anchorages; all except one large US convoy that received the recall message when approaching French waters.

Time was running out for Gen. Eisenhower. If the invasion could not be launched on June 6, tide and moonlight conditions would not be suitable for another two weeks. The troops, many seasick, could not be confined too long on board crowded ships. To let them disembark would compromise security. Finally, at 04:15 on June 5, the Supreme Commander Allied Expeditionary Force started the monumental enterprise with the simple words, "OK, we'll go."

That same morning Adm. Ramsay boarded a motor-torpedo boat which proceeded to a vantage point off the coast of southern England. The most powerful invasion fleet the world had ever seen began steaming past him en route to the hostile shore of occupied France. Allied minesweepers cleared coastal waters along the coast of southern England and four channels leading to a general assembly area, nicknamed "Piccadilly Circus", eight miles (12km) southeast of the Isle of Wight. From this staging point, five miles (8km) in radius, the Allied naval units established five marked channels, altogether known as "the Spout," south toward France. The Germans had laid a mine barrier to the west of Dieppe and south of the 50th parallel, through which the Allied minesweepers cleared and marked ten channels with lighted buoys, each channel being 400 to 1,200yards (360–1,080m) wide. The Western Task Force was allotted four lanes and the Eastern Task Force six.

Once the invasion convoys crossed into the assault area off Normandy, the minesweepers swept ahead of the task forces to clear areas from which warships would bombard coastal targets and amphibious ships would lower away landing craft for the run-in to the beach. During the operations, German mines damaged two British ships, the destroyer *Wrestler* and an LST. By skilfully clearing passages through the German minefield, however, Allied minesweepers made it possible for the thousands of other vessels in the armada to reach the far shore safely.

Equally important to the success of *Neptune* were the hundreds of buoy-laying vessels, salvage and rescue vessels, colliers, water tankers, telephone cable-laying vessels, despatch boats, smoke-making trawlers, and landing craft repair vessels.

Aside from mines, the elements, including a sea with large, foam-crested waves and a 16- to 20-knot wind from the west, posed the greatest hazard to the Allied naval force. A small number of light craft, most of which were being towed across the Channel, sank before reaching the far shore.

The heavy seas that caused thousands of seasick soldiers to long for landfall also induced the German command to suspend the daily surface ship patrols of the Channel. In addition, Allied bombers destroyed the enemy's radar stations at Cape Barfleur and elsewhere on the invasion coast. The Allies also jammed enemy radars. No one in the armada compromised radio security. Finally, Allied forces staged feints and other ruses to divert enemy attention from Normandy. As a result, the Allies achieved complete strategic and tactical surprise. The Germans learned of the Allied presence only when their few remaining coastal radars picked up surface contacts around 03:00 on the morning of June 6.

■ The American Landings

Thanks to thorough planning, intensive training, skillful execution, and just plain good luck, the great majority of Allied ships and craft arrived off Normandy on time and at their appointed stations.

The selection of June 6, when the sun rose at 06:00 and high tide occurred between 09:45 and 12:45, meant the time of landing (H-Hour) on the invasion beaches would be as follows: *Utah* and *Omaha*, 06:30; *Gold* 07:25; *Juno* 07:35–07:45; *Sword* 07:25.

Beginning around 02:00, British and US minesweepers began their dangerous work in the transport areas, the fire support areas, and the approach lanes to *Utah* Beach. Right behind them came the ships of the bombardment group, which anchored in their assigned areas, 11,000 yards (9,900m) offshore for battleships and cruisers and 5,000 yards (4,500m) offshore for destroyers.

At 04:05, under the gaze of Adm. Moon in US transport *Bayfield*, troops began to scramble down cargo-net ladders into craft that rose and fell in the strong swell. Even though the *Utah* landing force would have to navigate 11 miles (17km) of ocean to reach the shore, Pointe de Barfleur and Pointe du Hoc extended out into the Channel on either side of the beach approaches, moderating the sea state. Consequently, Moon's landing craft were able to stay in formation as they headed for the shore. In addition, patrol craft (PC) and control landing craft equipped with radars and radios were on hand to guide the force to the beach. Landing craft with mounted artillery pieces and multiple five-inch rocket tubes accompanied the assault landing craft to provide them with direct fire support.

Benefiting from the element of surprise, at 05:30, naval forces landed a detachment of Army troops on the St. Marcouf Islands located only four miles (6km) offshore in the middle of the landing zone. The soldiers quickly took control of the position, which soon served as an anti-aircraft artillery site. Meanwhile, a German battery had opened up on US destroyers *Fitch* and *Corry*. To silence the German guns, Rear Adm. Morton Deyo, commander of the bombardment force at *Utah*, ordered his units to open fire. The thunderous salvoes disoriented the Germans, whose response was desultory and ineffective. US battleship *Nevada*, a veteran of Pearl Harbor, and US cruisers *Quincy* and *Tuscaloosa* lofted hundreds of shells at the German coastal gun redoubts near the center of the invasion beach. Later in the day they fired their shells far inland, knocking out German tanks, artillery, and troops that menaced the US 101st Airborne Division. British monitor *Erebus* and cruisers *Hawkins* and *Black Prince* worked over the enemy defenses on the flanks. Ironically, the latter cruiser operated off the port of St. Vaast-la-Hougue, where English King Edward III and his son, the "Black Prince," landed in 1346 at the head of an invasion army. British light cruiser *Enterprise*, Dutch gunboat *Soemba*, and eight destroyers poured their fire directly into enemy defenses, especially in front of St. Martin-de-Varreville. The naval bombardment at *Utah* was especially accurate and within a short period of time the Allies had silenced German counter-battery fire and reduced other defensive positions to rubble.

Not for the first or last time in modern warfare, however, enemy mines exacted a toll of men and ships. German mines that Allied minesweepers failed to detect embedded in an offshore sandbank exploded and sank the destroyer *Corry*. During the first ten days of the operation, these lethal enemy weapons sank in the *Utah* area another destroyer, a destroyer escort, two minesweepers, a patrol craft, and five landing craft. Mines also damaged another 25 vessels.

As the first waves of the landing force approached the objective, LCTs prepared to release into the water 32 DD amphibious tanks. These armored vehicles, intended to provide the infantry with direct fire support were equipped with special canvas skirts, or "bloomers," designed to keep them afloat on the approach to the shore. Lt. (j.g.) John B. Richer, USNR, the commanding officer of control vessel *PC-1176*, realized that the water was much too rough for the planned launch 5,000 yards (4,500m) offshore. He directed the commanders of the LCTs to carry the tanks into the relatively calm waters just off the beach. As a result of Richer's clear appraisal of the situation and bold action, not one of the precious amphibious tanks fell prey to the treacherous seas, as happened elsewhere on D-Day.

Meanwhile, other naval forces rapidly cleared lanes through enemy beach obstacles, which were not extensive and which the Germans had not mined. Then, at 05:42, one craft hit a mine and sank. Because of the loss of this and other guide vessels, strong cross-beach currents, and battle smoke over the *Utah* area, the first waves veered off toward the south-east. Thus, when the combat infantrymen of the 4th US division debouched from their craft at exactly 06:30, they were a little over one mile (1.6km) from the beach they had planned to storm. Fortunately for the attacking American soldiers, the beach they actually landed on was much less heavily defended than their original objective.

The first-wave troops at *Utah*, supported ably by the DD tanks, quickly established positions ashore.

The men of 11 Navy underwater demolition teams (UDT) landed with the second wave and began clearing beach obstacles. By the end of the day, they had destroyed or removed steel and concrete structures from 1,600 yards (1,440m) of *Utah* Beach. Despite minor setbacks, the assault at *Utah* of 27 assault waves went especially well and by 18:00 Adm. Moon's task force had landed over 21,000 troops, 1,700 vehicles, and 1,700 tons of supplies.

Omaha, the target of the US 1st Infantry Division and the second beach to be stormed by the assault formations of Adm. Kirk's Western Task Force, proved to be the Allies' greatest D-Day challenge. The pre-invasion air bombardment of beach defenses was not especially effective at *Omaha*, Moreover, Kirk decided that his bombardment group would open up on the German coastal guns in his sector only 40 minutes before H-Hour, which contrasted with the two hours the British had allotted for their preparatory bombardments. As a result, there was not sufficient time to neutralize all the big German weapons trained on the landing area. Compounding the difficulties, Allied intelligence of the enemy's defenses at *Omaha* was inadequate. As an illustration, the 14-inch guns of US battleship *Texas* fired 250 rounds into the German coastal gun site on top of Pointe du Hoc before US Army Rangers discovered it empty of the enemy's big guns. *Arkansas*, the other American battleship off *Omaha*, French cruisers *Georges Leygues* and *Montcalm*, and British cruiser *Glasgow* leveled their guns against enemy defenses in the vicinity of Port-en-Bessin and St. Laurent but with limited success.

Furthermore, as at *Utah*, the landing ships at *Omaha* lowered their smaller craft into the water some 11 miles (17km) off the beach, in contrast to the British, who established their lowering points four miles (6km) closer in. Adm. Kirk was concerned that if he moved his transports any closer, they would fall prey to the German long-range coastal guns. As a result of this decision, however, it took the American landing craft almost three hours to close with the shore. And, in the waters off-shore, not protected by the geography as at *Utah*, many landing craft fell out of formation. Landing waves became intermixed. In contrast to *Utah*, the LCTs on the left flank at *Omaha* launched their DD tanks into the sea about 5,000 yards (4,500m) offshore. The result was catastrophic. Twenty-seven tanks, most with their crews, foundered and sank in the heavy seas. Only five reached the relative safety of the beach. On the right flank, however, Lt. D. L. Rockwell, USNR, correctly assessed the danger and decided not to disembark his 32 tanks until the transporting LCTs touched sand.

The rough waters off *Omaha* took a heavy toll of Allied assault craft, including DUKWs laden with critical artillery pieces and boats specially designed to destroy offshore obstacles and clear lanes through to the beach. Seizing the initiative, several American commanders used their vessels to smash through the barriers and open passages to the beach. Some vessels got through, but others were damaged or sunk in such attempts. Many more were forced to mill around outside the defensive belts searching for a cleared lane to the beach.

Working mightily to create openings in the obstacle belts were 16 joint teams of Navy UDTs and Army combat engineers. Although German fire wiped out two of the teams, almost to a man, their comrades managed to detonate explosive charges and blow eight channels through the defensive works. The rising tide eventually forced the demolition men to suspend their efforts.

Witnessing the distress of the Army units on the beach, Capt. Harry Sanders, Commander Destroyer Squadron 18, ordered his ships to close with the shore to support the troops. Risking grounding and counter-battery fire, eight "tin cans" moved to within 800 yards (720m) of land and poured hundreds of rounds into German pill boxes and mortar positions, troop units caught in the open, and emplacements blocking the key exits from the beaches. US destroyer *Emmens* knocked down part of the Colleville church tower from which enemy spotters were adjusting fire on to the beach.

By 11:00 the crisis at *Omaha* had passed. Heroic army officers, sergeants, and even individual soldiers rallied the knots of men around them and stormed through the beach exits and over the bluffs which dominated the beach. Soon tanks, artillery, troops, and supplies began to pour ashore. The bravery and determination of American soldiers was key to the victory at *Omaha*, but the contribution of the small boat commanders, demolition men, and battleship, cruiser, and destroyer sailors was equally vital. At the end of that momentous day, Maj. Gen. Leonard T. Gerow, commanding general of V Corps then pushing inland from *Omaha*, sent a message to Adm. Kirk's flagship, the cruiser *Augusta* in which he simply said, "Thank God for the United States Navy."

■ The British Landings

The drama at *Gold, Juno,* and *Sword* beaches began around 05:00, when the British five-man midget submarines *X-20* and *X-23* surfaced, after remaining submerged for three days, and flashed green lights seaward to mark the parameters of Adm. Vian's Eastern Task Force landing sites. Soon afterward, as the naval force approached its objective, German Adm. Krancke, Commander Naval Group West, dispatched against it from Le Havre three torpedo boats: *T-28, Jaguar,* and *Möwe.* The vessels loosed a spread of torpedoes at the Allied fleet, sinking the Norwegian destroyer *Svenner,* and escaped through a smoke screen.

The approach to *Gold* beach was to be no easy matter. There, the Germans had emplaced 2,500 obstacles, consisting of 900 tons of steel and concrete, on a coastal front of three miles (5km). It proved virtually impossible to clear lanes through these barriers until the tide went out. For much of the morning, Germans holed up in the village strongpoints directed a withering fire on to the beach, which added to the troubles of the assault units. Many landing craft, especially those transporting No. 47 Royal Marine Commando, were damaged or destroyed. As a result of this difficulty and strong German ground opposition, it took two days and 200 casualties before the commandos could seize their D-Day objective, Port-en-Bessin, which the Allies had hoped to develop as a logistics hub.

Critical assistance to Commodore Douglas-Pennant's *Gold* assault forces came from the bombardment group, composed of British cruisers *Ajax, Argonaut, Emerald,* and *Orion,* Dutch gunboat *Flores,* and 13 destroyers. In fairly short order the Allied formation eliminated opposition from enemy coastal gun emplacements in the vicinity of Arromanches. The

Gold ships put a number of 6-inch rounds right through the embrasures the Longues position, destroying both guns there. By nightfall on June 6, Task Force G had successfully landed all three brigades of the British 50th Infantry Division.

At *Juno* beach to the east, naval forces experienced some difficulty getting the units of the 3rd Canadian Infantry Division to shore. Allied leaders had scheduled the landing on the right flank of *Juno* 20 minutes later than on the left flank. Staff planners figured that the landing craft would need higher water to traverse what aerial photographs suggested were underwater rocks, but which actually turned out to be floating seaweed. Another ten minutes was lost to difficulties during the passage of Task Force J from England. When the units approached the beach, they discovered that the water was too high for demolition personnel to clear lanes through the beach obstacles. Consequently, landing craft had to disembark their troops among the obstacles or smash through them. Vessels transporting No. 48 Royal Marine Commando had an especially tough time breaching the obstacles and a number of the wooden-hulled vessels were sunk or badly damaged.

Meanwhile, cruisers, destroyers, and rocket ships off *Juno* pumped hundreds of rounds into German gun positions, redoubts, communication trenches, and other defenses.

Like his decisive American colleagues on the other beaches, the British commander of the landing craft carrying the first-wave DD tanks at *Juno* ordered his landing craft commanders to deposit the armored vehicles safely on the beach.

By that evening, Task Force J had successfully landed the Canadians and preparations were being made to deploy ashore the follow-on formation, the British 7th Armoured Division and the British 51st (Highland) Division.

Like the eastern flank DDs at *Omaha*, the DDs at *Sword* had a tough time navigating the rolling seas. Forty DD amphibian tanks and a number of mine clearance tanks were launched 5,000 yards (4,500m) offshore and eight of them promptly went down. Following the DDs came the infantry landing craft, whose crews skilfully traversed the extensive German beach obstacles. Leading the assault at *Sword*, the eastern-most landing beach, were two LCIs loaded with 176 French marines of No. 4 Commando. The first troops of the British 3rd Infantry Division hit the beach just after H-Hour. An entire brigade was established ashore only 18 minutes later than scheduled. However, German opposition steadily mounted on the beach and succeeding landing craft found the going rougher. German guns and mortars zeroed in on landing craft and mined beach obstacles sank or damaged many others. Some vessels got stuck in the sand as the tide ebbed.

Assisting the landing craft flotilla and the troops ashore were two British battleships, *Warspite*, a veteran of the Battle of Jutland in World War I, and *Ramillies*, together with British monitor *Roberts*. These ships neutralized the heavily casemated German guns enfilading the landing site from the east. In addition, five cruisers knocked out enemy guns positioned directly behind the beach. Guns encased in concrete were especially difficult to disable, but the *Sword* bombardment force scored a direct hit on one of two such protected weapons in the Houlgate battery. Because of this naval gunfire support and hard fighting by the infantry brigade ashore, Rear Adm. Talbot's Task Force S was able to land the division's other two brigades in the afternoon. Marring the day's otherwise exemplary performance, anti-aircraft gunners afloat and ashore mistook Allied aircraft overhead as German and shot down several fighters and transport planes.

In addition to troops, on D-Day the Eastern Task Force put on the beach 900 tanks and other armored vehicles, 240 field guns, 280 anti-tank guns, 80 light anti-aircraft guns, 4,500 vehicles, and 4,300 tons of ammunition and supplies.

When he surveyed the scene from his flagship *Scylla*, off *Juno* that evening, Adm. Vian could be pleased that all had gone reasonably well.

A little less than 17 hours after the first American infantryman debouched from an assault vessel onto *Utah* beach, the combined navies of the Allied Expeditionary Force had landed close to 133,000 soldiers in Normandy.

■ The German Navy Responds

With the beachhead won, the Allies now had to hold it in the face of German counter-attacks not only on land but at sea and in the air. But the transport ships and craft that carried the Allied combat divisions and logistical support forces from England to France during the weeks after D-Day were protected by an almost impervious shield of naval and air forces. Try as they might, German surface units, aircraft, and submarines did little to impede the invasion.

On D-Day the German naval command ordered submarine flotillas in Brittany, Norway, and mid-Atlantic to move against the force. A formidable contingent of 16 German U-boats sortied from Brest and La Pallice bound for attack positions south and west of the Isle of Wight. Another 19 submarines formed a defense to contest any Allied move against that strategic peninsula. Even as this occurred, Allied air and sea patrol units were on the hunt for U-boats. Within hours, British aircraft sank *U-955*, damaged five other boats, and forced the remainder to run submerged, limiting their combat effectiveness. British Sunderland, Liberator, and Mosquito aircraft sent another five enemy vessels to the bottom during the next three days. These losses forced the German naval command to recall to Brittany all but the most capable units, those six equipped with the sophisticated "schnorkel" breathing system. Another five schnorkel boats were dispatched from Norway on June 9. Canadian and British aerial attackers soon sent two of these boats to the bottom. On June 24 and 25, the RAF's Coastal Command and the Royal Navy's surface forces combined to sink no fewer than three German submarines on the western approaches to the invasion convoy routes.

The German U-boat fleet scored only a few successes during June. On the 15th, *U-767* and *U-764* each torpedoed a British frigate in the Channel and *U-621* sank a US LST at the western edge of Adm. Kirk's landing area off Normandy. Then, on the 29th off the southern English coast, *U-984* torpedoed and sank three Liberty ships bound for France. These victories were a small return for the many brave submariners and boats sacrificed by the German high command in its fruitless attempt to halt the invasion.

German surface units fared little better than the U-boats. British fighters caught three German destroyers bound for Cherbourg off Brittany on June 6 and strafed them so savagely that the enemy force had to put in at Brest. Joined by another destroyer, on June 8 the formation sortied for another attempt to reach Normandy. This time the aircraft that spotted them called in a flotilla of eight British, Canadian, and Polish destroyers guarding the western approaches to the Channel. The battle was joined at 01:25 on June 9 when the Allied force opened fire at 5,000 yards (4,500m), evaded torpedoes and closed with the enemy. The bold Allied dash disrupted the enemy formation and sent the German destroyers fleeing in two directions. The Canadian destroyers *Haida* and *Huron*, gave chase to the German destroyers *Z-24* and *T-24* and heavily damaged *Z-24* before both of the hunted ships reached safety of Brest. Meanwhile, the British and Polish units chased down and sank *ZH-1*. Finally, the Allied force converged on *Z-32*, set her afire, and forced her to beach. While this latter action was taking place, US destroyers and MTBs encountered a number of German E-boats off Barfleur and drove them away from the invasion forces.

On June 13, British Beaufighter aircraft pounced on a group of E-boats and R-boats of Le Touquet, sinking four of the enemy units. The following night, 325 British Lancaster bombers devastated the German flotilla at Le Havre, destroying 11 E-boats in their concrete shelters and sinking two torpedo boats and 40 other craft in the harbor. Adm. Krancke characterized the Le Havre raid as "catastrophic" to his force. One day later, RAF Bomber Command visited similar destruction on the German light naval units at Boulogne, eliminating the surface threat to the Normandy beachhead for some time. German surface units were only able to sink two LSTs and nine smaller vessels.

The once-vaunted German Luftwaffe did little to impede the Allied invasion. During the entire month of June, German planes managed only to sink US destroyer *Meredith*, British destroyer *Boadicea*, frigate *Lawford*, and a few small craft.

Greater damage was done to the Allies by German mines laid before and after the invasion. The Americans suffered the most losses to mines early in June but toward the end of the month, British naval forces, operating closer to the enemy's air and surface minelayer bases in France proper, took a number of heavy hits. German mines sank nine warships and other vessels and damaged seven more, including Adm. Vian's flagship *Scylla*, which had to be towed back to England for repairs.

As Gen. Eisenhower and Adm. Ramsay already knew when they arrived off the invasion-beaches in British minelayer *Apollo* soon after the landing, the great Normandy enterprise would fail if the troops ashore were not reinforced, armed, and supplied on a massive scale. Until "Lightning Joe" Collins US VII Corps seized Cherbourg on June 26, the Allies had to rely totally on the few small ports in the invasion area and over the-beach supplies. The heavy seas made offloading of cargo ships difficult and hazardous during the first few days after D-Day. Over 100 LSTs and other vessels were forced to idle offshore until Adm. Vian and Adm. Kirk took bold action. They directed the LST skippers to beach their ships, even though they realized that the vessels would be caught high and dry with the ebbing tides. Despite its unorthodoxy, this approach worked. The naval leaders also reinforced the ship-to-beach logistic effort by diverting LCTs and similar craft from cross-channel transport duties. In addition, Adm. Vian quickly made use of the harbor facilities of Port-en-Bessin and Courseulles, which had not been damaged badly in the first day's fighting, And, in short order, hard-working engineering parties had emplaced the *Gooseberry* boat shelters and *Mulberry* artificial ports.

Then, in the early morning hours of June 19, a threat arose that was much greater than anything the Germans could pose. The wind from the northeast rose to gale-force strength, whipping up the sea and compelling Allied naval commanders to halt logistic traffic to and from England. They also stopped unloading and transport operations in the invasion areas. For the next three days, the wind and sea of perhaps the worst June storm in the Channel in 40 years pounded the Allied Expeditionary Force. The American *Mulberry* at St. Laurent was damaged beyond repair. Hundreds of landing craft, small boats, and other light vessels were sunk or smashed on the shore and 800 craft were grounded. The force of the storm dragged ships' anchors across the bottom and caused cables to part, Sections of partially completed breakwaters broke loose and battered hapless vessels in their path.

Allied forces were bruised but not beaten by the fierce Channel gale. Small boat captains and crews often braved the weather to deliver ammunition and other vital supplies ashore. When this was not possible, the naval units made use of the *Gooseberry* boat shelters, which proved a godsend, to ride out the worst of the weather. Seamen of many nations kept their ships afloat, protected precious cargoes from damage, and prepared to resume operations. So, when the wind finally died down and the sun shone through the clouds on the evening of June 22, the combined naval force regrouped and resumed the buildup of the Allied armies.

When Adms. Kirk and Vian turned over their commands and returned to England in late June and early July it marked the end of Operation *Neptune*, the largest and most complex amphibious landing in military history. Cooperation among the Allied naval, air, and ground forces in the monumental effort was extraordinary. In the words of the British official history of the Normandy invasion, "where *Neptune* will long, and perhaps for ever, remain unique is as a feat of inter-service organization. Never before had so many soldiers, sailors and airmen been assembled and trained to achieve a joint purpose."

D–DAY

■ American First Army Plan
On February 1, 1944, the *Neptune* Initial Joint Plan revised COSSAC's original *Overlord* plan by adding a landing beach on the eastern face of the Cotentin Peninsula, thus putting Cherbourg, a key invasion objective in closer reach. Lt. Gen. Bradley's First Army was ordered to assault and develop two beachheads astride the Carentan estuary between Vierville-sur-Mer and Colleville-sur-Mer. In the west, on First Army's right flank, the VII Corps would assault *Utah* Beach at the base of the Cotentin Peninsula. After cutting across the peninsula's neck, it would take Cherbourg whose port was the logistical lifeline that would make a substantial Allied buildup possible. East of the estuary on the Calvados coast, V Corps would attack *Omaha* beach between Carentan and Bayeux, and move south to cover British Second Army's advance.

The Cotentin would not be an easy place to start an invasion. The new landing area designated *Utah* Beach was small, with its dunes rising onto ground flooded by the Germans. If the exits were blocked, the invaders would be trapped.

The flooded areas covered most of the terrain inland to less than two miles (3km) from the shore; the ground rose steadily to an elevation of about 45 yards (50m). This high ground dominating the landing areas was part of the bocage country, territory covered with a complex latticework of man-made hedged fields. The open fields and frequent orchards could be acres large, but the hedgerows posed tactical problems. These hedges were often reinforced by extensive dirt embankments and interspersed with trees. Narrow dirt tracks dominated by hedges whose over-arching greenery could reach a dozen feet (3.6m), canalized military movement, and made any paths fire lanes for anti-tank or automatic weapons. The hedges themselves were impenetrable to vehicles and often so for soldiers.

Intelligence showed a strong defensive crust with reserves located near critical points. Rommel intended to destroy the invasion at the water's edge. Allied intelligence identified two divisions in the peninsula belonging to General der Artillerie Erich Marcks's LXXXIV Corps. The 709th Coastal Division's two regiments held the 50 miles (80 km) of eastern beaches facing the Calvados coast. The 243rd Infantry Division held Cherbourg and the peninsula's western coast.

■ The American Air Assault

The February airborne plan tasked the 101st Airborne Division to seize the western exits to *Utah* Beach, help expedite VII Corps' moves to cut the peninsula, and then swing northwards to Cherbourg. When additional aircraft gave the Americans a second drop division, the 82nd Airborne planned its drop west of the Douve River, to seize St. Sauveur-le-Vicomte and control the roads from the coast.

Hitler's intuition saw a threat to Cherbourg. Rommel did too, personally traversing the peninsula energizing local commanders to improve defenses in every potential Allied landing area. Rommel saw the Cotentin as a prime airborne objective. His response soon dotted numerous fields. "Rommelsspargel" "Rommel's Asparagus," were poles roughly a foot (.3m) in diameter and six feet (1.8m) high placed vertically in fields to disrupt parachute drop zones or to block glider landing zones. Rommel wanted 1,000 per square kilometer (about 3,000 per square mile) with wire linking the stakes, which would be topped by mines or artillery shells rigged to detonate when the wires were hit.

Hitler sent the 91st Airlanding Division to occupy the Cotentin's center. As Seventh Army's reserve, it backstopped the beach defenses as a counterattack force. Additionally, the 6th Parachute Regiment and a Panzer battalion were added south of Carentan, both threatening the planned American landings.

At May's end, with the 91st's presence confirmed and thousands of Rommelsspargel appearing on air photos of the 82nd's drop zones, the airborne plan appeared to be compromised. Gen. Bradley felt the airborne was essential for the *Utah* landing and Montgomery agreed. Air commander Sir Trafford Leigh-Mallory predicted catastrophic losses recommending cancelling the drops behind *Utah*. Eisenhower disagreed. The American air drops would go ahead.

The 82nd's drop zones moved east astride the Merderet River, with Ste. Mère-Eglise the east end of the objective area. The 101st's drop was compressed, easing its D-Day mission to assist the VII Corps.

The 101st would get the invasion off the beaches. The division would capture the four exits and causeways leading from the beach, and the lock and bridges controlling the water obstacles and traverses throughout the invasion area. Its three parachute infantry regiments (PIRs), one airborne field artillery battalion, and one airborne engineer company planned to begin their drops between 01:15 and 01:30 on D-Day. Small fields and Rommelsspargel limited the use of gliders in darkness; but two glider lifts would come in at 04:00 and 21:00.

The 82nd's drops would begin a few minutes later, with two PIRs west of the Merderet and one northwest of its objective at Ste. Mère-Eglise. Its gliders were scheduled for three group landings, one after the 101st's 04:00 lift, one following the 21:00 lift, and one in twilight at 23:00.

All American aircraft approached from the west, dropping the pathfinder troops about 00:15 hours and the main body one hour later. The drops were scattered. Pilots evading anti-aircraft fire flew erratic courses or dived below prescribed drop altitudes. Many mis-identified drop zones. Some pathfinders were mis-dropped and, with only minutes to light their drop zones, opted to bring in the arriving lifts where they were. The 101st estimated that about 1,500 of its 6,600 paratroopers fell outside the division's battle area.

By 01:30, the German Seventh Army had received reports of airborne drops stretching from Caen to the Cherbourg Peninsula. But, with most of its troops sticking to their defenses and hesitant to root out the invaders, no coherent pattern appeared. As dawn approached, the German commander estimated that the paratroop plan was "to tie off the Cotentin Peninsula at its narrowest point."

In the north, the 502nd PIR and a supporting artillery battalion planned to land on Drop Zone (DZ) "A" just west of the high ground

81

between its objectives, exits 3 and 4 at St. Martin-de-Varreville. Every plane load missed the DZ, scattering troopers to the north and south or onto Drop Zone "C." One battalion was so scattered that it was not heard from on D-Day. The 502nd's 3rd Battalion, landed near the 82nd's objective, Ste. Mère-Eglise, and had to reform and fight its way towards its objective. Finding the northern causeway's exits undefended, a small group under Lt. Col. Robert G. Cole ambushed fleeing Germans late in the morning and by 13:00 had established contact with the 4th Division's 8th Infantry moving in from the landing areas.

Meanwhile, the 2nd Battalion which was also scattered gathered enough men to move towards the German battery positions behind exit 4 and to establish road blocks throughout area. Exit 4 was clear but skirmishes were frequent throughout the day with elements of A Company attacking the small village of Foucarville.

Exits 1 and 2 in the south were assigned to the two battalions of the 506th PIR and one from the 501st landing in DZ "C" in the division's center. Two battalions of the 501st Regiment and the remaining battalion of the 506th would land north of Carentan and east of the Douve River and marshes in DZ "D" to capture the la Barquette lock and the nearby bridges, while destroying the rail bridge northwest of Carentan to seal the southern part of *Utah's* landing area.

The southern exit forces were luckier than those in the north. More than half of the 506th dropped east of its DZ but gathered forces and began moving on exit 1 with orders to ignore the second objective.

Simultaneously, 101st commander Maj. Gen. Maxwell D. Taylor, lacking reports from any of his units, also ordered a battalion from the division reserve to move towards exit 1 and accompanied the force himself. The division reserve commanded by Lt. Col. Julian J. Ewell captured Pouppeville by noon, establishing a road block while awaiting the landing force, which soon arrived making the first airborne and seaborne linkup. The battalion originally sent to capture the exit fought several engagements en route and arrived after Ewell's battalion's success. With all four beach exits under control, Taylor focused his attention on capturing the southern bridgehead.

DZ "D"'s force was likewise scattered. The lock fell without a fight, but the scramble to capture and destroy the bridges reflected the haphazard attempts of mixed forces, assembled from individuals separated by misplaced drops, the darkness, and the bocage.

The only real opposition met in the German 709th Division's sector was towards the Douve River at St. Côme-du-Mont and at Carentan then held by one of the division's battalions and the 6th Parachute Regiment. By nightfall on D-Day, 101st's southern line consisted of groups from three companies, not the planned full regimental defense of three battalions.

The 101st glider Landing Zone (LZ) "E" was southwest of DZ "C." Rommel's asparagus and the hedgerows restricted the 52 gliders taking in troops from the 327th Glider Infantry, some anti-tank guns, and supplies in their pre-dawn landing. The first glider crashed, killing Assistant Division Commander, Brig. Gen. Donald F. Pratt, D-Day's senior Allied casualty. About 30 troopers were killed, injured or missing in mishaps when most of the gliders missed their LZs. A second lift of 32 gliders landed at 21:00 but due to Leigh-Mallory's protests, and a lack of glider pilots, most of the 101st's glider troops arrived by sea on *Utah* Beach.

By day's end, the 101st Airborne had suffered at least 1,200 casualties and could account for slightly more than a third of its total strength, but its missions of clearing the beach exits and protecting the invasion were accomplished.

The 82nd Airborne's three drop zones placed the division on the edge of the German 91st Division's concentration area in a distorted triangular configuration astride the Merderet River west and northwest of Ste. Mère-Eglise. Even more badly scattered than the 101st, Maj. Gen. Matthew B. Ridgway's division lost the use of two of its regiments in its D-Day missions. The division successfully captured Ste. Mère-Eglise due to a fortuitously good drop of the 505th PIR. Taken in a hasty attack in darkness using grenades and knives but little gunfire, Ste. Mère was the first town liberated by the Allies. The enemy reacted immediately. Soon German forces appeared from different directions all to be held up and driven off.

The 507th and 508th Regiments whose missions were to hold the west banks of the Merderet, found no lighted DZs. Their pathfinders found German positions in the fields and marked no landing areas. The resulting confusion and the individual decisions of scores of transport pilots put troopers all over the division sector, dropping many into flooded fields and swamps. Surprised by the flooded areas and laden with equipment, many drowned in waist-deep water. Much of the divisions equipment was lost in the swamps, and with few troops to hold a wide perimeter, the division was forced into a small bridgehead between the two roads running west of Ste. Mère-Eglise and the Merderet with two small pockets at the opposite end of the swamp. The airborne was holding its own, but no contact was made with either the 101st division to the east or the invading forces moving inland from the sea.

The 82nd's 04:00 lift used 52 gliders carrying guns from an airborne anti-aircraft battalion plus forward parties for signals, artillery, and the division headquarters landing on DZ "O." Additional elements followed, with 76 gliders landing on LZ "W" after 21:00 and a further 100 at 23:00. Nearly 300 pilots and troopers were casualties due to flak or crashes. The 82nd suffered about 1,200 D-Day casualties, and by nightfall reported that it had less than 40 percent of its infantry under division control.

While the 82nd formed the outer perimeter of VII Corps' landing, Gen. Dollman commanding the German Seventh Army ordered concentric attacks from the 91st and the 709th Divisions west of the Merderet and the 6th Parachute Regiment south in Carentan. Totally uncoordinated, none of these attacks gained ground. By nightfall, one German division commander lay dead from an ambush, while the other commanders and the corps headquarters generally felt the same "fog of war" that descended over the entire airborne battlefield.

■ *Utah:* H-Hour 06:30

Utah is located in the Dunes of Varreville. The designated assault zones *"Tare Green"* and *"Uncle Red"* were about 1,000 and 1,300 yards (900-1,170m) wide respectively. Located astride exit 3 and stretching north toward exit 4, Maj. Gen. J. Lawton Collins's VII Corps assault would use the 4th Infantry Division's 8th Infantry Regiment, landing with two battalions abreast. Reinforced by the DD tanks of the 70th Tank Battalion, the attack would begin with four rifle companies in the first wave with two tank companies floating ashore under their own power.

But the 4th Division's soldiers were not the first in the corps to land. Both airborne divisions were attached to the corps on landing, and from the main body, the dismounted troopers of the 4th and 24th Cavalry Squadrons landed at H − 2 hours, 04:30, on the heavily mined islands of St. Marcouf, whose shores were thought to hide guns which would imperil the transport area.

German radars missed the invasion's buildup, but coastal guns began firing about 20 minutes before the fleet's preparation bombardment, starting at 05:50. Within minutes, 276 B-26 Marauder aircraft dropped more than 4,400 bombs on seven designated target areas. Most missed, with at least one third of the bombs falling into the sea between the high and low water marks. A fire support group including rocket-equipped vessels drenched the beach just prior to landing while the landing craft began their final run-in.

The 8th Infantry's first troops touched down at 06:30, missing the planned assault areas. Both primary control vessels for the red and green beaches struck mines and sank and with a single control vessel left, the amphibious tanks led the assault in after leaving their carrying craft about 3,000 yards (2,700m) from the beach instead of the 5,000 yards (4,500m) as planned,

The first wave had 20 landing craft each carrying 30-man assault platoons and was followed immediately by a second wave of 32 craft, which included combat engineers and naval demolition teams to begin obstacle clearing. At H + 15 minutes a third wave was scheduled to arrive with dozer tanks and then followed by a fourth, landing two engineer battalions.

Though formed according to plan, the landing force soon faced an unforeseen situation. With strong currents and perhaps confused by smoke and haze, the boat groups veered south making landfall astride exit 2, on *Victor* Beach about 2,000 yards (1,800m) south of their planned beachheads.

First ashore was the 2nd Battalion, 8th Infantry, followed within minutes by the 1st Battalion. Of the 32 dual-drive tanks, some 28 made the beach 15 minutes after the first wave. Simultaneously, Lt. Col. Cole's paratroopers arrived at exit 3, awaiting the planned landing there.

The 4th Division's Assistant Division Commander, Brig. Gen. Theodore Roosevelt, Jr., landing with a first wave assault company, imme-diately recognized that the initial waves were put ashore on the wrong beach. Amid occasional mortar bursts and without waiting for his forces to finish disembarking, Roosevelt moved ahead reconnoitering the dunes and locating the critical causeway leading inland.

Roosevelt decided that the rest of the division's units would follow the 8th Infantry at exit 2. His orders were concise, "We're going to start the war from right here."

The mislanding was a boon; unknown to the planners, the exit 2 area was both less obstructed and less heavily defended than the planned landing site.

The division's plan called for the 8th Infantry to move east to link up with the 101st and then to move southeastward onto the high ground north of Carentan.

Successively at H + 85 minutes and at H + 4 hours, the 22nd and 12th Regiments would land, the 22nd to move northwest clearing the beaches and the high ground overlooking it to the northwest. The 12th would move directly inland wheeling on to the 22nd's left flank. Both regiments would, in effect, relieve the 101st Airborne from the responsibility for the invasions northern flank. They would also be in position to advance on Cherbourg.

Roosevelt's decision sent the 8th Infantry inland to immediately reduce the complex of beach fortifications and move towards their original inland objectives. Single companies assaulted the forts blocking the beach exits while other troops cleared individual houses in the area. Exits 1 through 3 were cleared within three hours, but troops moving inland were forced to wade through areas flooded to waist level to reach exit 4 and to move on objectives to the north. By noon, the 4th Division with its supporting 70th Tank Battalion, pressed inland and linked with the 101st at Pouppeville.

By nightfall, the 8th Infantry alone had achieved its D-Day objectives. The 12th and 22nd Regiments failed to make their deep swing to the northwest, while a pocket of Germans controlled a two-mile (3km) finger on the ridge north of les Forges, at the edge of the 101st and 82nd divisional boundaries. But all four exits were clear, the 4th and 101st were linked, and though neither yet realized it, the 82nd and 4th Divisions were a mile (1.6km) apart, a mile unoccupied by Germans. The 4th Division's casualties totaled fewer than 20 dead and 200 wounded. The *Utah* gamble of an extended beachhead and a two division airborne drop inland now verged on success.

■ *Omaha* Beach: H-Hour. 06:30

Omaha was the westernmost assault beach under the original COSSAC plan. Located between Port-en-Bessin and the River Vire, its sectors stretched over 7,000 yards (6,300m), and was the largest of *Overlord's* assault areas, Maj. Gen. Leonard T. Gerow's US V Corps planned to land two regimental combat teams abreast, one from each of the corps' assault divisions.

Assault Force "O" included the 1st Infantry division (Maj. Gen. Clarence R. Huebner) headquarters, its own 16th and 18th Infantry Regiments, and the 115th and 116 Infantry Regiments drawn from the 29th Infantry Division. Attached were artillery, tanks, the Special Engineer Brigade, and the Provisional Ranger Force of two battalions (the 5th and 2nd). Together, there were over 34,000 men and 3,300 vehicles.

The beach was backed by high bluffs, which merge into high cliffs at each end of the landing area. The area behind the sand exposed by the withdrawing sea was heavy shale with seawalls in the western area. Five draws provided small exit corridors off the beach and onto the high ground behind, three with dirt tracks, one with a paved road, and one merely a steep draw leading to a rough road. These were seen by both sides as key to a possible landing. At the end of three of these were villages whose stone buildings made natural defense strongpoints.

The *Omaha* sector had 12 strongpoints, and beginning in April the Germans began fortifying the area with three bands of obstacles. Starting with huge gate-like obstacles some 250yards (225m) from shore a second band consisted of posts or logs driven seaward and mined about 225 yards (200m) from the water's edge, and the final belt consisting of mined, triple-pronged hedgehogs, each 5½ feet high (1.5m) and some 130 yards (117m) from shore. The tidal sands were free of mines, but the trek inland and the approaches to the draws were heavily booby-trapped.

The German 352nd Division took over this area in May, and was a complete surprise to V Corps who still expected to find a reinforced battalion in the sector and not the two regiments that they encountered holding the bluffs and the ground behind.

Huebner planned to land two battalions from the attached 116th Infantry on the right, and two battalions from his own division's 16th Regiment on the left. Their D-Day objective was the ridge line parallel to the main coastal road ranging from two to three miles (3-5km) inland.

Additionally, the 116th was responsible for seizing Pointe du Hoc's coastal battery with two attached Ranger battalions. This battery located to the west, about four miles (6km) from *Omaha*'s right flank, and about seven (11km) from *Utah*'s left, was a significant component of the German coastal defense. Its six French-made 155mm guns, two thought to be casemated, could reach 25,000 yards (22km) and hit both corps transports and landing craft.

Three companies from the 2nd Rangers would scale the 85–100 foot (25–30m) cliffs and assault the guns, while another company landing with the 116th moved on the position from inland.

Omaha's violence contrasted with *Utah's* relatively bloodless success. At H – 50, two companies of DD tanks launched 6,000 yards (5,400m) from the beach. Heavy seas sank 27 tanks, drowning many crewmen; three of the five making the beach were actually put ashore by a craft whose ramp malfunctioned. Heavy seas also swamped ten landing craft making the 11-mile (17km) run to the beach, DUKWs ferrying artillery to the beach also foundered, losing most of the guns of two battalions and a separate cannon company. Additional guns were lost when landing craft struck mines.

Starting without hope of tank or artillery support, the infantry suffered more severely. Lateral currents dragged units hundreds of yards from their objectives, landing them on a strange beach out of sight of rehearsed objectives and in front of heavy enemy opposition. Though the Germans claimed that the preparatory bombardment exploded entire inshore mine-fields, beach defenses were neither destroyed nor suppressed. The defense rapidly recovered and brought its weapons to bear.

Heavy machine gun and mortar fire greeted inbound boats whose equipment-burdened soldiers were often dumped in waist-to-neck deep water, causing many to discard equipment or drown. The scrambled landing bunched units in two areas, two companies in front of the D-3 draw (les Moulins) and four companies astride the E-3 draw near Colleville. Right flank companies landed on the wrong beaches; one company's boats were pulled so far from their objective that they circled offshore for 90 minutes.

The Ranger company and company of the 116th at the right beach exit lost more than half of their men to mortar fire and small arms before making the seawall. The 29th's landing force decided to bring its DD tanks all the way into the beach rather than floating them in, but artillery fire rapidly destroyed eight of the 16 tanks before their tracks hit dry sand. Further to the east, two full tank companies made the beach in their landing craft to find their assigned infantry teams either missing in the tangled landings or withering away under heavy fire.

Subsequent waves piled onto a confused mass of men pinned to the beach. With leaders downed by fire, others rose to take their places. With the German defense pinning the invaders to the seawall or behind obsta-cles, the naval demolitions and Special Brigade troops were unable to clear obstacles, soon adding 40 percent of their number to the rising casualty list. With a tide rising four feet (1.2m) and shrinking the dry beach 80 yards (72m) each hour, obstacles were soon covered with water compounding the danger to shorebound boats. Wounded too weak to crawl faster than the advancing water drowned.

After nearly an hour and a half of what appeared to be impending disaster, the flow of battle started to change. Several destroyers risked grounding and fired on visible enemy activity from close inshore. The surviving tanks moved forward giving supporting fire as groups of men attempted to crack the defense by climbing the bluffs and attacking the defense line that blocked the exits.

The 2nd Ranger Battalion's three companies (D, E and F) landed at Pointe du Hoc at 07:10 40 minutes late – victims of currents and rough seas. While the Rangers scaled the cliffs with one company to the west and two companies to the east of the promontory, the destroyers USS *Satterlee* and HMS *Talybont* provided effective suppressive fire from close inshore. Once atop the cliffs, small groups rushed the casemates finding them empty with the actual battery hidden farther inland, unmanned and unguarded. After destroying the guns, the Rangers endured heavy counterattacks and were besieged for two days while V Corps expanded its beachhead.

While the Rangers were overrunning the Pointe, V Corps and Gen. Bradley were receiving observer reports from a liaison boat circling offshore. Through the smoke, enemy fire was seen to be hitting troops who were pinned on the beach. Bradley later was said to have considered pulling troops off and relanding them at *Utah*, which was probably an impossibility.

But what couldn't be seen were the four thin penetrations made in the defense, two in each regiment's sector. A score of nameless leaders emerged to form small groups to move forward and reduce defenses.

After they individually landed some time after H + 1, Gen. Cota and Col. Canham of the 29th Division, and Col. Taylor of the 16th Infantry, each started tying together independent group actions, galvanizing the pinned-down troops who were already beginning to fight back.

Waterlogged radios and the nature of the terrain made coordinating attacks impossible, but the picture developed identically in each of the footholds gained. The independent fire of the destroyers had inflicted significant losses on the defenders whose thinning ranks focused more heavily on blocking key exits. Once assaulting troops cleared the fireswept beaches, they found that stretches of the dominating bluffs were undefended.

Gaining these heights, the assault groups began moving inland to become entangled in hedgerows.

Even with troops moving inland, the situation was tenuous. The beach area remained under fire, and follow-on waves were restricted to narrow columns by uncleared obstacles. By mid-morning, large landing craft ignored obstacles, ramming their way to the beach while destroyers moved closer to continue firing on targets. By midday, the battle devolved into three independent battles for the villages of Vierville, St. Laurent, and Colleville, the villages controlling the east-west road and the keys to capturing the ridgeline, which determined if the landing force could survive serious counterattacks.

■ Nightfall

By D-Day evening, First Army held firm beachheads. On *Utah*, the 4th Division and a reinforcing regiment were ashore and linked with the 101st Airborne. Although the planned northern edge of the bridgehead still had to be taken and the 82nd Airborne was yet to be contacted, VII Corps was in a good position to move inland, receive reinforcements, and begin its fight for the peninsula and Cherbourg. The predicted airborne disaster failed to materialize.

V Corps on *Omaha* recovered from what appeared to be impending disaster during the first hours and held the major exits, the three villages, and a broken line that was a mile and a half (2.5km) at its deepest point. The right flank units and the Rangers at Pointe du Hoc held isolated pockets. Reinforcements, particularly in artillery and armor, were needed before any move inland could be attempted. V Corps estimated its losses at about 2,400 in killed, wounded and missing.

■ The British Second Army Plan

British Second Army's landing area, with Caen as its main objective, stretched for nearly 25 miles (40km) from the seaside village of Port-en-Bessin (a little beyond Bayeux and next to the American landing beach at *Omaha*) eastwards along the coast to the flooded estuary of the River Dives at Cabourg, Between the offshore shoals, three sandy beaches, each about two miles (3km) long, offered suitable landing points, separated by between five and ten miles (8-16km) from each other. The British invasion would start with 6th Airborne Division dropping northeast of Caen before dawn, followed by amphibious landings by XXX Corps, led by

50th (Northumbrian) Division at *Gold* Beach with Bayeux as its objective, and by I Corps with 3rd Canadian Division at *Juno* Beach, and 3rd Division (usually known as 3rd British Division to distinguish it from the Canadians) at *Sword* Beach directly north of Caen. 6th Airborne Division would come under I Corps once contact was made.

The landing beaches themselves were gently shelving sand, fronted by little holiday villages which the Germans had turned into strongpoints. Other gun positions, obstacles and minefields of the Atlantic Wall stretched from the water's edge to between 400 and 800 yards (360-720m) inland. Away from the beaches, the ground rose up into farm country of rolling ridges which reached down to the sea as cliffs at the western edge of *Gold*, separating it from *Omaha* by about ten miles. The River Orne, flowing with the Canal de Caen through the city of Caen and into the sea at Ouistreham just east of *Sword*, was the only major water obstacle on the British sector, except for the flooding of the Dives to the east.

The value of Caen and Bayeux to the British was obvious. Any town or city made a good defensive position, costly and time-consuming to capture. If the Germans could hold the old medieval town of Bayeux (once William the Conqueror's capital as Duke of Normandy) they could prevent a firm link-up between the British and the Americans from *Omaha* Beach, and deny them the use of the roads leading into the heart of Normandy. Even more important, the British planned to build their *Mulberry* harbor at Arromanches, just west of *Gold*, and to use Bayeux as their main administration and supply centre. The same argument applied with even greater force to Caen, a city of 50,000 inhabitants with its own aerodrome at Carpiquet, and the most important Allied objective on D-Day. If they could hold Caen, the Germans could use the city as a defensive block to hold up the whole 21st Army Group advance.

For this reason, Montgomery placed great stress on his British and Canadian forces getting rapidly inland. For D-Day the first three divisions to land were reorganized into four assault brigades each, by the addition of extra armor, engineers and specialist troops, including two brigades of commandos. If everything went well, Montgomery hoped for British Second Army to capture the whole of its landing area from the Germans on D-Day, including Caen and Bayeux and the road linking them, to join up with the Americans, and to get armored forces well inland as far as Villers-Bocage and even Falaise. Against that, the worst fate which could befall the landings was to be destroyed on the beaches without ever getting inland at all.

▮ The British Air Assault

The plan called for 6th Airborne Division to drop between the rivers Orne and Dives, so as to cover the flank of the landings at *Sword* Beach. Unlike his American counterparts, the flamboyant Maj. Gen. Richard ("Windy") Gale of 6th Airborne Division planned to use his men like airborne commandos, in small parties to take specific objectives. "What you get by stealth and guts," he told them, "you must hold by skill and determination." In order to secure their objectives before the first amphibious landings, the airborne forces would land by night, relying on darkness to hide their numbers and confuse the Germans. Night landings carried a high risk of failure, and Gale depended on the training of his men to carry his plan through.

On June 6, at a few minutes after midnight, high over the Normandy coast, the British liberation of France began as the first of Gale's men, 181 assault troops in six gliders under Maj. John Howard of 2nd Oxfordshire and Buckinghamshire Light Infantry (the "Ox and Bucks"), cast off their tow ropes and began the silent glide down to land. Their target was the bridges at Bénouville over the Canal de Caen and the Orne, the only bridges between Caen and the sea, guarded by about fifty German troops and wired for demolition. Gale wanted these bridges intact, as the link between his division and the commandos landing at *Sword.*

At 00:16, Howard's lead glider skidded to a halt only yards from the Canal de Caen Bridge, probably the first Allied troops to land in Normandy on D-Day, followed seconds later by two other gliders. Bombing of the area by the RAF had already started, and the bridge's defenders hardly noticed the dark shapes of the gliders until Howard's men burst from them, guns blazing. In 10 minutes it was all over, and for the loss of two men dead and five wounded the British had captured the bridge intact. Although it was wired for demolition, the Germans had not yet placed the explosives. At the same time two more of Howard's gliders, coming down by the Orne Bridge, discovered that its defenders had fled. The sixth glider missed the target altogether, landing beside a bridge over the Dives.

While the glider troops dug themselves in around the bridges, the main airborne drop had already begun, and within an hour the first paratroopers of 5th Parachute Brigade arrived. Throughout the night there were sharp fire fights as Germans drove up out of the dark, only to find the bridges blocked. By morning the defenders had fought off more than one attack by tanks, and the battle swung back and forth as more airborne troops joined in. Finally, at just after noon, the men on the bridges heard the distinctive sound of bagpipes, heralding the arrival of reinforcements from 1st Special Service (Commando) Brigade under Lord Lovat, coming from *Sword* Beach. In honour of the "Pegasus" divisional insignia of British airborne troops, the Canal de Caen Bridge was later renamed Pegasus Bridge.

Gale's other main target for the night was a well-defended German gun battery position at Merville, across the Orne estuary from *Sword*. The silencing of this battery was entrusted to Lt. Col. Terence Otway of 9th Parachute Regiment, who devised an elaborate plan involving the bombing of the German battery by the RAF, support from Canadian para-troops with special equipment, the storming of the battery by his own battalion accompanied by a simultaneous glider landing, and a final bombardment from British warships just as dawn broke. In the confusion of the night this plan broke down completely. The RAF bombers missed the battery, nearly killing Otway's advance party instead. Only just over 150 men reached the rendezvous in time for the attack, and little of the special equipment arrived. Clearing their way through a minefield protecting the battery, the paratroops launched their attack at 04:30. Just as they did so, two of the expected gliders flew over the battery, missed it entirely, and crashed nearby. To this accompaniment, Otway's men stormed the battery casemates, driving the Germans back and taking 30 prisoners, but in the smoke and darkness underground failed to realize that they had only damaged, and not disabled, the four 100mm guns. With dawn coming up and nearly half his men killed, wounded or missing, Otway pulled his force back from the battery, having achieved his objective of silencing it for D-Day.

Throughout the night, the paratroops and gliders continued to land, roughly half of them where the plan intended and the rest scattered between the Dives and the sea. Small parties of men, largely from 3rd Parachute Brigade, succeeded in destroying the five bridges over the Dives next to their landing area, so sealing off the landing from serious German interference. Others became lost and were taken prisoner, or fought with equally lost German patrols, Soon after dawn, Gale, who had established his headquarters near Pegasus Bridge, could feel confident that his division had achieved its objectives, and with daylight the main glider force of 6th Airlanding Brigade could start its landings. Any Germans trying to reach *Sword* Beach across Pegasus Bridge would find their way securely blocked.

◼ *Gold* Beach: H-Hour: 07:25

Dawn over Normandy came almost exactly at 06:00, three hours after the start of the main RAF bomber attack on the Atlantic Wall positions in the landing area. As the light improved, the gathering flotilla of warships offshore joined in the bombardment. Expecting hard resistance from the village strong-points facing them on the beaches, the British delayed the start of their landings until almost an hour after the Americans, choosing assembly areas only seven miles (11km) offshore for a shorter final assault by their landing craft. The first troops of the 50th Division were expected to land at 07:25, a few minutes behind the DD tanks, and press inland to Bayeux, followed by commandos who would swing westward overland to Port-en-Bessin, linking up with the Americans.

The bad weather on D-Day seriously affected this plan. German gun emplacements on the cliffs near Arromanches were not properly destroyed by bombing or naval gunfire, the tide was running high, and a fierce current and force five wind meant that the DD tanks were almost certain to sink. Rather than launching at sea, their crews brought them into the beach still in their landing craft, 5 minutes behind the first infantry. *Gold* was wide enough to land two brigade groups side by side, 231st Brigade at the little villages of le Hamel and 69th at la Rivière. At le Hamel, 1st Hampshire Regiment hit the beach unsupported by armor, as the tanks which got ashore either bogged down or were crippled by German fire, to find that the wire was not cut. Wading chest deep through the water, the men were briefly pinned down, but with help from one surviving flail tank and an AVRE were eventually able to press forward. The Hampshires were surprised to find that many of the "German" defenders in their pillboxes were unwilling Asiatic conscripts from the southern Soviet republics, put into the front lines by the Germans.

To the east, the Victoria Cross was won by CSM Stanley Hollis of 6th Green Howards. As Hollis's company advanced off the beach at Mont Fleury it passed two German pillboxes which the company commander ordered to be checked. In the words of Hollis's citation, "When they were 20 yards [18m] from the pillbox, a machine gun opened fire from the slit and CSM Hollis instantly rushed straight at the pillbox, recharged his magazine, threw a grenade in through the door and fired his Sten gun into it, killing two Germans and making the remainder prisoner. He then cleared several Germans from a neighbouring trench." As the company advanced past Crépon later in the day it was fired upon by a field gun and machine guns. Taking cover with his men in a nearby house, Hollis used a PIAT to destroy the gun and pulled back, only to find that two of his men had remained in the house. "In full view of the enemy who were continually firing at him he went forward alone using a Bren gun to distract their attention from the other men," so allowing them to escape. Hollis's Victoria Cross was the only one won in Normandy on June 6.

While the battle to drive the last of the Germans out of their emplacements continued, the beach was laboriously cleared of mines and obstacles, with much assistance from Hobart's Funnies. By midday the division was ashore, and ready to move off the beach complete with its remaining brigades, 151st and 56th, while the next division (the famous "Desert Rats" of 7th Armoured Division) prepared to land. Meanwhile, despite losing many of their assault craft on the approach, No. 47 Royal Marine Commando had moved off the beach along a clifftop route to Port-en-Bessin to link up with the Americans, but had not quite reached the village by nightfall.

Clearing its way through the Atlantic Wall, 50th Division did not quite achieve the objectives set for D-Day, pushing to within a mile (1.6km) of Bayeux while linking up with the Canadians from *Juno* and almost reaching the Caen-Bayeux road. By nightfall the division had three brigades in line and ready to advance next day, while 231st Brigade secured Arromanches for the arrival of *Mulberry*. The division's big anxiety, and part of the reason for the slow advance towards Bayeux, was that its western flank was hanging in the air. There was no sign of the Americans from *Omaha*.

■ *Juno* Beach: H-Hour (delayed): 07:45, 07:55

Like *Gold*, *Juno* beach was wide enough to land two brigades side by side, Canadian 7th Brigade at Courseulles and 8th Brigade at Bernières. The Canadian landing was deliberately delayed in the plan, to give the rising tide time to cover underwater shoals near the landing area revealed by air reconnaissance (it was later discovered that many of these "rocks" were floating seaweed). The tide, the rough weather and the high wind delayed the approach of the landing craft still further, and both brigades touched down ten minutes later than planned, the troops at Courseulles at 07:45, and those at Bernières at 07:55, the last of the first wave to land. As at *Gold*, the sea was far too rough to risk launching the DD tanks ahead of the infantry. Most came in by landing craft, but a few were launched from close to the shore, and reached the beach ahead of the infantry at Courseulles as planned. But the rising tide covered more of the beach obstacles, and the current pushed landing craft out of position. "The heavy seas meant that people who should have been in front were behind," remembered one sapper, "and we ourselves were twenty minutes late." The Regina Rifles had to endure 20 minutes on their landing beach before the first armor arrived. It was nearly 08:15 before the last troops of the two brigades finally struggled ashore. Just 30 minutes later, No. 48 Royal Marine Commando of 4th Special Service (Commando) Brigade came ashore and moved off eastwards along the coast to link up with the forces from *Sword*.

3rd Canadian Division's objective for D-Day was the Caen-Bayeux road and Carpiquet aerodrome, forming a link between the two British lodgments. As on the other beaches, on *Juno* the Canadians found that the extra firepower from the DD tanks or the Funnies often made all the difference between overcoming a German strongpoint or being held up. Between the beach obstacles and German fire, mainly from mortars onto the beach, the landing craft had a difficult passage. One Canadian naval officer recalled that he was just disembarking the troops from his landing craft when "a wave lifted it onto an obstruction. The explosion that followed ripped the bottom out of the craft." Despite severe injuries to a boat officer, all the troops got ashore safely.

Bypassing positions that they could not take quickly, the Canadians moved inland. The French Canadian Regiment de la Chaudière of 8th Brigade recorded that "the French were very welcoming and greeted us heartily in the midst of the ruins of their houses." Some Canadians of Polish origin also found that their "German" prisoners were Poles, surprised to hear a familiar language. By mid-afternoon, the 3rd Canadian Division was ashore and its third brigade, 9th Brigade, started its advance through the remaining German defenses. To the west, the division made good progress and its leading armor reached almost to the Caen-Bayeux road. But closer to Caen the German resistance intensified. Neither the Canadians, nor the commandos who were held up at Langrune, could break through to close the gap between themselves and the men coming off *Sword* Beach. By evening the Canadian line conformed roughly to that of 50th Division to the west, a few miles short of its objectives, but still in a strong position. But to the east a gap of two miles (3.2km) still separated them from the troops from *Sword,* and the airborne forces beyond.

■ *Sword* Beach: H-Hour: 07:25

The landing of 3rd Division at *Sword* and the capture of Caen was the most important event in Montgomery's plan for D-Day. Between the offshore shoals and the estuary at Ouistreham, the beach itself at the little hamlet of la Brèche d'Hermanville was wide enough only for one brigade at a time to come ashore, the first – 8th Brigade – at 07:25 to coincide with the landing at *Gold.* While the four brigades of 3rd Division fought their way inland towards Caen, Lovat's commandos would cross the bridges at Bénouville and reinforce 6th Airborne Division, which continued to receive glider reinforcements throughout the day. Problems of landing and stiff German resistance at *Sword* meant that Lovat arrived a few minutes late, but in good time to help secure the bridges against further German counterattacks.

The terrain at la Brèche is explained by its name, which means "the breach"; a dip in the ground leading from the beach inland to the village of Hermanville. This proved irresistible to Maj. "Banger" King of the 2nd East Yorkshire Regiment, who went in with the first wave reciting "Once more unto the breach! "from Shakespeare's *Henry V,* while nearby a rescue launch played "Roll Out the Barrel" over its loudhailer. The first landings went well, with the first troops of 8th Brigade touching down one minute late, and nearly all the DD tanks and specialist armor, including the leading elements of 27th Armoured Brigade, reaching the beach safely. The strongpoints at la Brèche itself were subdued by 10:00, and while the last of the German guns and machine guns were silenced, and the barbed wire entanglements cleared away, Lovat's commandos (some of them on folding bicycles) pushed inland towards the waiting airborne troops. No. 4 Commando, including Commandant Kieffer's force, moved eastward to secure Ouistreham. Kieffer's men successfully assaulted the sea-front at Ouistreham, known as Riva-Bella, including a German strongpoint at the old casino. "All my fellow commandos," one of Kieffer's men mused, "idealists or madmen, saints or rogues, sailors or daredevils, united by a love of danger, are going back to where we started

– France." It was a small but important gesture: Gen. de Gaulle's Fighting French had returned.

The bad weather showed little sign of abating, and as the morning wore on the rising tide reduced the narrow beach to a strip of sand only 10 yards (9m) from the seafront to the water's edge. Engineers and frogmen trying to clear obstacles in the surf found themselves swept out to sea. Although infantry continued to land without much trouble, most of 3rd Division's armor and vehicles were packed close together on the beach or waiting offshore to land, and the beach remained under fire. There was, remembered one tank officer, "a terrible jam on the beach where no organization appeared to be operating and no marked exits were to be seen." With only one road off the beach, vehicles had to land at exactly the right spot.

Advancing only a short distance inland, many of the available tanks of 27th Armoured Brigade were drawn in to help the infantry fight their way past two German strongpoints, codenamed *Morris* and *Hillman* by the British, just beyond Hermanville and Colieville. A further brigade, 185th Brigade, was able to move off the beach soon after 11:00 as the spearhead of 3rd Division's drive on Caen, but only by leaving most of its tanks and heavy weapons behind, to catch up as best they could. By late afternoon the leading troops of 185th Brigade had reached the villages of Beuville and Bieville, only two miles (3km) short of Caen itself. The division's last brigade, 9th Brigade, was still assembling, having disentangled itself from the beaches.

For a moment it seemed that Caen was within the British grasp. But by mid-afternoon the leading units of 185th Brigade started to report German tanks or assault guns emerging northwards from Caen, and German infantry on the Périers ridge north of the city. These were the leading troops of 21st Panzer Division, which the British had expected to find much further south. Without much armor support of their own, the infantry halted to engage the tanks, giving up any further advance.

It was the crisis of D-Day for British Second Army. Having checked the advance, the Germans were ready to launch their big attack to throw the British back into the sea. The two-mile (3km) gap between 3rd Division and 3rd Canadian Division was still not closed, and at 19:00 21st Panzer Division launched a charge of 50 tanks into it, trying to split the British landing in two. But 3rd Division were waiting for the PzKpfw IVs with artillery, fighter-bombers, and another surprise, the "Firefly"

Sherman, fitted with a 17-pounder anti-tank gun instead of the smaller 75mm gun of normal Shermans. In exercises back in England, the commander of 27th Armoured Brigade's Staffordshire Yeomanry had analyzed the ground and the German plan. "They will form up their squadrons, give out their orders, then drive straight for their objective," he had predicted. "What they do not know is that I have three troops of Fireflies which I will station on the Hermanville ridge and leave as a backstop." Thirteen German tanks were knocked out for the loss of one British M-10 tank destroyer. It was an important lesson – the British might be slow in the advance, but they were almost unbreakable in defense.

Whether any of the German tanks actually reached the coast at Lion-sur-Mer along with their infantry is debatable. But just as the attack faltered, at 21:00 in the gathering dusk, there came one of those chance events by which battles are sometimes decided. Still trying to press forward, the German tank crews were astonished to see in the sky above them a force of over 250 British gliders, which swept over their heads like giant bats and came to land just behind them, close to Pegasus Bridge. This was the final fly-in of the day by 6th Airlanding Brigade, and by sheer coincidence it had arrived just in time to completely demoralize the German survivors, who pulled back towards Caen. The German threat to *Sword*, like the British threat to Caen, had been ended for the day.

■ Nightfall

At the end of D-Day, the British and Canadians were off all three of their beaches, through the Atlantic Wall, and inland on a front of about twenty miles (32km). The average penetration inland was about six miles (9km), barely half what had been planned. The position was not yet continuous or completely secure, but it was defensible, and the chances of the Germans pushing the invasion back into the sea as Rommel had hoped were virtually gone. In these terms, D-Day had been a major success for British Second Army. The landings had also been much lighter in casualties than had been feared in planning. As far as can be told, of 6,250 men of 6th Airborne Division who had landed, 650 were casualties by the end of the day, while nearly 25,000 men had landed at *Gold*, 21,500 at *Juno* and 29,000 at *Sword*, for the loss of 3,000 casualties evenly spread between the three beaches. Of the German forces opposing them, 716th Static Division had been virtually destroyed and 21st Panzer Division had taken serious losses.

To the east of the Orne, 6th Airborne Division was still intermingled with German troops, including arrivals from 21st Panzer Division. Not only the village of Cabourg, but the coastline almost up to the Orne estuary remained in German hands. The British would not actually reach their extreme eastern D-Day objectives until August. The link-up between 6th Airborne Division and 3rd Division still depended entirely on Pegasus Bridge, but that was strongly held. 3rd Division had failed to take Caen, far less get past it to Falaise, while the gap west of *Sword* remained open. 3rd Canadian Division had failed to reach the Caen-Bayeux road in any strength, but was securely linked up with 50th Division, which in turn had just failed to reach Bayeux. The western flank of the entire lodgment was threatened by the absence of the Americans from *Omaha*. All these were relative problems: what mattered was that the landing had succeeded.

The retreating Germans would abandon Bayeux without fighting next day, the only town in Normandy to be captured without serious fighting. But their hold on Caen meant that the British were restricted to a lodgment area only a few miles deep, from which a breakout either eastwards or southwards would be extremely hard to achieve. The fight for Caen would dictate the shape and nature of the remaining battle for Normandy, distorting Montgomery's "master plan" as it did so.

THE BUILDUP

Logistics governed all planning for *Overlord* and dominated the selection of landing beaches, initial objectives, and the size and composition of the assault force. Once the Allies were ashore, the first combat task was capturing enough space to permit the installation of depots and a supply system adequate to maintain a constantly growing expeditionary force in France. The beachhead had to be enlarged to give it greater depth, and therefore greater security, to provide the ground to conduct the logistical buildup, and only then to provide the room for maneuver essential to a breakout.

Field Marshal Erwin Rommel, who understood the Allied style of fighting as well as any German officer, privately held out little hope for the eventual outcome of the fighting in Normandy. If, he believed, the Germans allowed the "overwhelming industrial capacity of the United States" to make itself felt on the continent of Europe, then the war was certainly lost. "Tactical skill," he warned, "could only postpone the collapse ..." The only hope of success was to defeat the landings or to crush the beachhead immediately, a fact that Gen. Montgomery well understood when he correctly predicted that Rommel would use all force available, from divisions down to individual rifle companies, to make constant assaults against the Allied perimeter.

The lines were clearly drawn. It was crucial for the Germans to repel the invaders as quickly as possible, and at any cost. The Allies had to create a large enough beachhead to permit the rapid build up of forces that the *Overlord* plan called for, to outpace the countervailing German buildup, and secure what Eisenhower called the "elbow room" to maneuver for a breakout into the interior of France. Thus the supreme commander turned his attention from the initial problem of getting the assault forces ashore and focused instead on keeping them ashore and, Gallipoli and the more recent experience at Anzio clearly in his mind, preventing a stalemate from developing.

Three interlocking factors influenced Eisenhower's task. The first was that the logistical plan to support operations on the continent of Europe had to be properly developed and carried out. The second was that the nature of the terrain on which the soldiers had to fight considerably complicated the tactical problem. The third was the ability of the British, Canadian, and American soldiers to develop the beachhead in accordance with the *Overlord* plan.

■ The Logistical Plan

To support combat operations, *Overlord* planners had arranged the pre-stowage of eight days of supplies in various landing craft, small freighters, and modified Liberty ships. Following a 13-day transition period, the majority of resupply would begin to arrive in Normandy via the larger Liberty ships. By D + 41, planners intended the majority of the logistical requirements to be met by using deep-draft cargo ships berthing at ports the combat forces would by then have captured, supplemented by smaller vessels delivering materiel from England.

To accommodate those ships, planners intended using Cherbourg, Lorient and Brest, minor ports in Brittany and at the mouth of the Seine, and artificial *Mulberry* harbors to be laid off American and British invasion beaches. The *Mulberries* were initially the most important, because the Germans were expected to fight hard for the ports and demolish them if forced to withdraw. *Mulberry* A, for example, planned for *Omaha* beach, was to be emplaced by D+4 and to handle seven Liberty ships, five large coastal freighters, and seven medium coastal freighters at one time. The open beaches, counting the tonnage of beached landing craft and lightered cargo in addition to the *Mulberry* ports, were expected to handle almost 15,000 long tons (1 long ton =

2,240lb, 1,016kg) of cargo each per day by D+10, rising to almost 46,000 long tons per day by D+90.

Such large trans-shipments of war materiel demanded careful beach organization, a task assigned to several special engineer brigades. Planners had learned through the painful experience of previous amphibious operations that specially trained troops had to be on hand to clear minefields and obstacles from the beaches and beach exits, manage the landing operations of succeeding waves of troops and the delivery of supplies, and to create and operate depots within the beachhead. Traffic control, both afloat and ashore, loomed as an important challenge, as did the requirement to maintain local security after the assault troops moved inland. To accomplish all these tasks, the engineer special brigades were organized not only with engineering units to emplace, maintain, and operate the artificial harbors and pierheads, but also with transportation, port and amphibian truck companies, quartermaster service and railhead companies, and ordnance, chemical, medical, military police and signal units.

While the beaches would be the principal and initially most important focus of the lines of communications, major combat operations could be contemplated only if the Allies had the use of regular ports. The planners expected to bring a few of the smaller ports into operation quickly, Cherbourg and other of the smaller ports by D+30, and the major ports of Lorient and Brest a month after that. Looking at the situation realistically, no one expected that ports would be ready to use immediately; some reconstruction to repair war damage or intentional demolition would be necessary. For that purpose, engineer and transportation troops were detailed to bring the ports into usable condition by D+90, when deep water facilities were to take the burden of all supply operations.

The scale of the logistical requirements was imposing. In the simplest terms, an infantry division in combat required roughly 700 tons of supplies per day. Projections for early September called for 37 divisions to be ashore, consuming 26,000 tons of supplies each day. That cumulative total of 780,000 tons per month defined a hand-to-mouth existence for the armies. Before they could seriously consider extended offensive combat, reserves, particularly of ammunition and fuel had to be built up, and provision had to be made to replace combat losses in tanks and other major pieces of equipment. Logistics, as Gen. Bradley said, was "the dullest subject in the world" but obviously the "lifeblood of the Allied armies in France."

Acknowledging the many practical difficulties, Prime Minister Churchill told Eisenhower that "if by the coming winter you have established yourself with your 36 Allied divisions firmly on the Continent, and have the Cherbourg and Brittany Peninsulas in your grasp, I will proclaim this operation to the world as one of the most successful of the war." Eisenhower, more confident, predicted that the Allies would stand on the borders of Germany by the coming winter. Everything depended, however, on the speed and success of the buildup in Normandy. In June and July, the race was on to see whether the defenders or the attackers could reinforce the battle front faster.

As events unfolded, developments on the battlefield quickly reduced the carefully phased logistical plans to chaos. Neither the British or the Americans captured ports on schedule, and German demolition work, especially in Cherbourg, was much more complete than anyone thought probable. That port did not become operational until July 16, and then handled only 2,000 tons of supplies per day. It remained the most important port until well into August, by which time it could handle around 12,000 tons a day. Other ports, such as Le Havre and Rouen, unloaded substantially less. The ports of Lorient and Brest never became available, and the tenacity with which the German garrisons defended them right to the end of the war gave Gen. Bradley occasion to wonder how much more stubbornly the German soldier would fight when defending his own land. Thus the logistical plan, dependent on good ports, began to unravel and improvisation became increasingly important.

It was therefore fortunate that the special engineer brigades worked with great efficiency and developed the landing beaches into something resembling major ports. Again, the examples of the American beaches are typical. By the end of the second week after the assault (Sunday, June 18), the engineers had cleared the beaches of almost all wrecked landing craft and were well on their way to clearing the minefields behind the sea walls. They pushed additional roads inland to support the increasing number of trucks that were being landed. Trucks, both regular and amphibious, were the key factor that allowed the beach depots of supplies to be built up and moved forward. Toward the end of June, the beaches were handling nearly 100 percent of their planned tonnages each day, in addition to the continued landings of combat troops and evacuation of casualties.

The complicating factor was a storm that arose in the English Channel on June 19 and lasted through June 22. Although not a particularly powerful gale by Channel standards, it was enough to wreck *Mulberry* A and beach as many as 800 ships, wrecking around 300. The immediate result was that, while roughly 80 percent of the soldiers landed according to schedule, the cumulative volume of supply at D+15 only reached 61 percent of that which was planned. To compensate, the Allies resorted to an extremely inefficient way of delivering critical supplies, but the only one available under the circumstances. For three days, the air forces used their C-47 transports to deliver 500 tons of artillery ammunition each day to Bradley's troops, and particularly to his VII Corps, then poised for the final assault on Cherbourg. Elsewhere on the American front, Bradley drastically reduced ammunition expenditure, a step that virtually halted forward momentum in V Corps. The problem was so severe that a number of coastal freighters loaded with ammunition were beached and had holes cut in their sides to allow unloading. In the long run, the loss of *Mulberry* A and disappointments with activating captured French ports affected Allied operations all the way to the Siegfried Line. In the short term, tactical problems that kept the forces close to the beaches tended to ameliorate shortcomings of the logistics system.

■ The Normandy Battlefield

Probably no military operation had ever been planned more thoroughly, or with more thought given to possible contingencies that might arise, than the landings on the Normandy beaches. The great oversight, as almost every senior commander has subsequently confessed in his memoirs, was that no-one gave adequate thought to the problem of continuing operations once the beaches were secure, and particularly to the difficulties of fighting in the Norman terrain.

The Allies chose the battlefield chiefly on the basis of beach requirements; the choice entailed inevitable compromises, and planners perforce had to accept as given the terrain that lay behind the beaches. The Caen-Falaise plain, which opened before British Second Army, was open, rolling farm and pasture land that was both dry and firm. It was ideal for armored operations. The drawback was that, equally aware of that fact, the Germans did their best to deny it to the Allies. To fend off attacks by the armored divisions the British landed on the first day, the Germans drew toward Caen all the soldiers that could be spared elsewhere in Brittany, divisions from the south of France, and units from the Netherlands. Caen was the essential connecting link between German forces in Normandy and the Fifteenth Army in the Pas de Calais. To maintain connection between the two armies, Caen had to be held. If that connection were sundered, the German Seventh and Fifteenth Armies could operate together only if they made a long withdrawal from the coast to reestablish contact. Thus the German command concentrated the strongest divisions, and the bulk of their available armor, 7½ divisions by the end of June, at Caen and prepared for a hard fight to hold that critical city. In contrast to the 150 heavy tanks (Tigers and King Tigers) and 250 medium tanks confronting the British, the Germans sent the equivalent of only a half division of tanks – 50 medium tanks and 26 Panthers – to defend against American operations in the V and VII Corps sectors.

They could well afford to do so, for when the Americans moved off the beaches, they advanced on to ground that was ideal for a defending force weak in mobility and armor. Passing from the Caen-Falaise plain on the Allied left flank the character of the ground rapidly changed the further one moved to the west. Between the Orne and Vire rivers was a broad mass of broken terrain, the small hills, valleys, and low ridges gradually rising in elevation to the south. Further to the west, at the base of the Cotentin Peninsula, the land was low-lying and very marshy, frequently crossed by slow-moving streams and drainage ditches. Compounding the problem, the Germans had flooded broad stretches of that low country. Approaches to the interior were accordingly limited, with vehicular traffic constricted to a few easily-defended causeways and embanked roads that crossed the flooded areas.

The use to which French farmers had traditionally put the land increased American difficulties. The entire area into which the First Army was attacking was known as the bocage, a general term given to the Norman hedgerow country. Hedgerows were fences, usually half earthen and half hedge, that subdivided the land into individual fields. Those parapets around each plot of land varied from one to four or more feet (.3–1.2m) in thickness and might be anything from 3–12 feet (.9–3.6m) high. On top of the parapets grew characteristically a compacted mass of thorn, brambles, trees and vines that could increase the height of the barrier to 15 feet (4.5m) or more. The irregularly and unpredictably shaped fields, rarely more than 200 yards (180m) wide and 400 yards (360m) long, abutted each other and were linked by trails that were often sunken lanes that ran among them and gave access to openings through the hedges to allow farm traffic to enter the fields.

Such terrain gave the defenders enormous tactical advantages. Each field was, in effect, a small earthen fort, and a connected series of them constituted a fieldwork that could easily be organized for defense in depth. It was a simple matter to position anti-tank guns to cover the approaches to the fields, as American armor quickly found out to its cost. Driving tanks over the hedgerows was no better solution, however, for the tank then exposed its relatively unprotected belly as its front climbed the parapet. Dense vegetation obscured observation and fields of fire and made artillery difficult to employ with any effectiveness. The effects of artillery were also diminished by the many and very effective earthen blast walls that gave protection from individual shell bursts.

To fight in the hedgerows was to make a series of deliberate attacks on a well-prepared defensive position that, once taken, was merely the prelude to yet another well-prepared defensive position. American infantrymen learned with dismay that the bocage, to which they usually referred simply as "this goddam country," was almost 50 miles (80km) in depth.

Because the hedgerow country severely restricted maneuver, it took away the chief advantage of American tactical organization – mobility. Combat in such terrain assumed many of the aspects of a bar-room brawl. The only advantage was that, when American tanks encountered German tanks, the conditions were more nearly even, for the short combat distances of 150 to 400 yards (135–360m) neutralized the great German advantage of being able to kill at ranges out to 2,000 yards (1,800m) and put the more maneuverable Sherman within a range at which even its weaker 75mm gun could be effective. Finally, Americans found a solution to the mobility problem. Curtis G. Cullin, Jr., a sergeant in the 102nd Cavalry Reconnaissance Squadron, welded steel scrap to the tank to form a pair of scythe-like blades. Using them, the tank rammed itself into the hedgerow and then drove through the wall by main force, carrying a bit of earth and vegetation with it as camouflage and entering the field with its guns firing. Maj. Gen. Walter M. Robertson, commanding 2nd Infantry Division, showed the improvisation to Gen. Bradley, who ordered as many tanks converted as possible. Using such expedients, but also suffering many casualties, the American attack slowly gained momentum.

In the planning for *Overlord*, some staff officers believed that the bocage would give the Allies ability to hold on to their beachhead against heavy German counterattacks while the British advanced with their armor through Caen, outflanking the difficult country. Eisenhower, Bradley, and Montgomery, deeply concerned with the problems of putting a powerful enough force ashore at Normandy, gave the bocage little thought. But it turned out that the pre-invasion concerns of some senior British officers about the defensive utility of the Norman countryside were well founded. Field Marshal Sir Alan Brooke, Chief of the Imperial General Staff, and Lt. Gen. Frederick E. Morgan, as COSSAC one of the chief British *Overlord* planners, had both warned of serious difficulties to be anticipated in the hedgerows.

Unfortunately for Eisenhower, the Allied attack appeared headed for stalemate not just in the bocage, but also in the more favorable terrain around Caen. By the end of July, around D+50, his troops stood on ground they were supposed to have captured by D+5. These difficulties had not been apparent on June 6–7. After the euphoria of the successful landings, the hard fighting and slow progress behind the beaches came as a shock that could not be explained entirely by the stiffness of the German resistance and the difficulty of the terrain.

■ The Military Situation

As night fell on June 6, Eisenhower had reason to feel cautious satisfaction with the progress that had been made. British, Canadian, and American assault troops were established all along the 61-mile (97km) stretch of coast, and the additional men and supplies brought by succeeding waves of landing craft made the lodgment ever more secure. From the west, where US VII Corps had easily overcome German resistance and stood six miles (9.6km) inland, to the east, at the mouth of the River Orne, where the British I and XXX Corps also stood well inland in the approaches to Caen, the beachhead was firmly held. Even in the middle, where the most heavily fought actions occurred, US V Corps had finally cracked the German defenses and moved to the bluffs above bloody *Omaha* Beach.

Beyond the obvious need to supply the combat forces, the immediate object of the combat power that the logistical buildup could generate was twofold. First, Eisenhower wanted to base a large number of fighter-bombers in Normandy to provide quick, responsive, overwhelming tactical air support for the armies. Second, he wanted to develop operations into areas in which the Allies' great tank strength could be used to advantage. For both of those needs, the land to the south and southwest of Caen was essential, and captured the attention of armor commanders, logisticians, and airmen. The rolling, open ground there was ideal tank country that offered a direct route to the Seine and Paris. Moreover, the open fields offered adequate space to build the 27 airfields needed to support the 62 squadrons tabbed for early deployment to the continent. Then too, Caen had a small but important port facility that was necessary to sustaining an adequate rate of supply to the armies ashore.

Therefore the plan called for the British Second Army to capture the wide plains situated south of Caen; for the American V Corps to move inland abreast of the British; and for the American VII Corps to cut off the Cotentin Peninsula and seize the port of Cherbourg as quickly as possible, thereby easing the resupply problems. Intelligence estimates predicted the heaviest fighting around Caen, adjacent to large German forces positioned in the vicinity of the Pas de Calais. Eisenhower expected the Germans to maneuver those divisions to contain the Allied landings. Operating with speed and surprise, however, Caen and Cherbourg might be captured quickly, satisfying conditions for wider operations on the continent.

The divisions ashore on D-Day were the point of a powerful Allied wedge poised in England to exploit the landings, and the Allies enjoyed a considerable advantage over the German defenders. The most important fact was that the core of the German Army was deployed against the Soviets, and that the German high command had, for a long time, systematically looted divisions posted to occupy France for their best and youngest manpower and most modern equipment. Fighter squadrons of the Luftwaffe deployed in France had been recalled to the desperate air defense battles over the Reich, replacing units consumed in the steady Allied bomber offensive, or those redeployed to the Eastern Front. The number of German divisions in the west, apparently greater than that which the Allies could muster, was deceptive because those divisions were generally not at full strength, were manned in some cases by Russians or other volunteer formations, and were equipped with a hodge-podge of obsolete, obsolescent, and foreign weaponry. The task, to cite only one example, of supplying ammunition to more than 30 different types of artillery was very nearly insurmountable.

Along the coast, the German divisions defending the beaches in the Seventh Army sector occupied frontages of approximately 50 miles (80km) each, making the defensive "crust" fairly thin indeed. The first-rate divisions, including the armored divisions on which Rommel and von Rundstedt counted to smash an invasion attempt, were concentrated largely in Fifteenth Army or in the high command reserve, well back from the coast. The "Transportation Plan," the systematic Allied bombing campaign that had largely destroyed the French rail network and cut both rail and roadway bridges into Normandy, effectively isolated the German defenders both from speedy reinforcement and from adequate resupply. From the beginning of the battle, it was clear that the Germans would have to make do with what was on hand on June 6. Allied air supremacy made German maneuver behind the battlefield virtually impossible in daylight and destroyed many valuable tanks, assault guns, and artillery pieces committed to the counterattack, as well as delaying German concentration of forces. German war diaries reported that British and American fighter-bombers "strangled" every attempt at tactical maneuver. Largely because of the Allied use of air power, Eisenhower was already winning the race to reinforce the beachhead.

Allied assault troops also benefited from the concentrated firepower of an enormous battle fleet, the guns of which could range far inland to overcome the smallest resistance to the advance of Bradley's and Montgomery's troops. German accounts of the battle speak of the paralyzing effect of overwhelming bombardments that shattered the offensive spirit of the infantry and halted almost every attempted counterattack notably that of the 12th SS Panzer Division against the British on June 7. Naval artillery and air power together achieved the crucial effect of preventing the Germans from using their armored and mechanized units in large-scale and coordinated attacks on the perimeter of the beachhead. Small-scale attacks, even where they achieved a measure of success, could always be dealt with. Compounding the German dilemma was the accident that the invasion came when many commanders were away from their headquarters at a war game, and that confusion ruled in the critical first hours of the battle.

Such circumstances augured well for success, and Eisenhower had no doubts that fairly quickly his troops would secure the several essential and minimum objectives for the Normandy landings to succeed. Beyond that, he entertained hopes that Allied military operations could attain what he called "reasonable expectations" of success beyond the scope of the plan. Finally there lay the "realm of hope," of which he was optimistically thinking when he described future operations to Mr Churchill. At first, supreme commander's thinking was entirely too optimistic, and it appeared that even the minimum objectives set for *Overlord's* opening days would not be met.

The first became apparent on *Omaha* Beach, where Maj Gen. Leonard T. Gerow's US V Corps met stiffer resistance than expected, where the majority of the DD tanks were lost, and where soldiers struggled through the high surf encumbered by individual equipment loads that exceeded 60lb (27kg) for a rifleman. Despite having assigned a regiment of the experienced 1st Infantry Division to the *Omaha* assault, Gen. Bradley found that soldiers were stunned by the withering defensive fire and halted at the tide line. Finally, heroic leaders led the drive to the bluffs above the beach, but for some hours Bradley worried that he would have to evacuate his troops from *Omaha*. American VII Corps, far more successful on June 6 and driven by the dynamic Maj. Gen. J. Lawton Collins, made more impressive gains. In the event, that corps took Cherbourg on D+20, rather than on D+8 as planned, and the Germans managed a systematic destruction of the port that kept it out of action for a considerable time.

Eisenhower's greatest disappointment however, was at Caen, which Montgomery had intended to capture on June 6 as a prelude to pushing his tanks as far inland as Falaise. The Germans had repulsed what could only be described as a feeble attempt to take Caen on June 6, and likewise halted all movement toward the town on the next day. Throughout the remainder of the month of June, the Germans continued to hold the British and Canadian forces at bay, and when the Allies finally captured portions of Caen by July 10, the choice airfield sites were still out of reach. In the end, the British did not break out of Caen until after the American breakthrough at St. Lô on July 19, and the Allies never realized the potential advantage of an early armored attack in the direction of the Seine, outflanking the ideal defensive terrain of the bocage.

The conspicuous lack of progress all along the landing front, particularly in view of the truly enormous advantages the Allies enjoyed over the Germans, can be attributed only partially to difficulties imposed by terrain, weather, and unexpected delays in developing the logistical base. It was unfortunely also true that the Allied armies were neither as aggressive nor as capable as they might have been.

Since the opening of the North African campaign, senior British officers had privately derided the fighting quality of American soldiers and the generalship of their commanders. Over the intervening 18 months,

Americans who had indeed shown all of the characteristics of untried troops had become more battle-ready and at least the combat equals of any soldier in the alliance. Still, even American commanders acknowledged a lack of aggression in the infantry and a pervasive tendency to allow the artillery to fight the war as much as possible. According to some analyses, the American practice of expending materiel, rather than men arose from an institutional appreciation of the political consequences of a high casualty rate, an awareness that some believed stemmed all the way back to the Battle of Antietam, in the American Civil War.

The tactical consequence was the kind of caution that could easily produce inertia on the battlefield. When, as Gen. William Simpson, the commander of US Seventh Army, put it, commanders would "never send an infantryman in to do a job that an artillery shell can do for him," the inevitable consequence was a loss of time and momentum. Historian Russell Weigley concluded that American practice in Europe reversed the traditional formula of fire and maneuver, wherein firepower held the enemy in position while the infantry maneuvered to attack. Instead, American infantry maneuvered to locate the enemy and then used artillery fire to destroy him. While respecting the material superiority of their enemy and the general excellence of American artillery and air power, German commanders considered that Americans were timid soldiers who often missed opportunities through a want of initiative. They were not, as one German officer phrased it, "tactically at all clever." American tactics, according to Gen. Max Simon, commander of the XIII SS Corps, were "based on the idea of breaking down a wall by taking out one brick at a time."

The costs of such tactics were high, and not all American divisions, or American combat commanders, were up to it. High casualties typified hedgerow combat. The survivors became battlewise and wary, but the demands of battle gave the veterans little time or opportunity to pass on their hard-won knowledge to the constant stream of replacements. Hedgerow combat was costly. The 4th Infantry Division, as one example, suffered 6,000 casualties, or roughly half of the division's strength. The usual experience of an American infantry regiment in 1944 and 1945 was that it would replace its entire strength about every 90 days. Thus even veteran divisions might be somewhat shaky. Other divisions, particularly including the 79th and 90th Infantry, did not fare as well and continually disappointed Bradley and Eisenhower. Reliefs

Above: *From left to right, Generals Eisenhower, Patton, Bradley* *and Hodges.*
Below: *A US Army mobile field kitchen* *rolls up into an LST (Landing Ship, Tanks) during loading opera-* *tions in England, early June 1944*

Above: *American assault troops on a US Coast Guard transport,* *near the French coast.* **Below:** *An LST unloading on the* *beachhead. These vessels shuttled back and forth, day and* *night, keeping the Allied troops supplied.*

Above: *A US Coast Guard LST unloading British tanks, trucks and equipment.*

Right: *Typical of the men who faced a long and deep wade ashore are these infantrymen of the 1st Battalion, Royal Norfolk Regiment, which was part of the 185th Infantry Brigade, the second of the British 3rd Infantry Division's three brigades to land.*

Above: *Explosive charges and mines were attached to many of the German beach* *obstacles. Here they are being disarmed and removed by British specialists.* **Below:** *German prisoners carrying wounded comrades to beach areas where* *their wounds can be attended to.*

Above: *A Panther tank of the 2nd SS Panzer Regiment burns after being knocked out by troops of the US* *4th Infantry Division at Sainteny, 5 miles south-west of Caretan.* **Below:** *Troops of the 1st Battalion of the* *Welsh Guards prepare to move forward from a concealed position near Cagny on 19 July. This area was about* *the farthest south that the British managed to penetrate during Operation Goodwood.*

Above: *A Churchill Crocodile flame thrower tank (note the trailer for carrying the flame fuel) standard Churchills, Canadian M10 tank destroyers, Stuart light tanks and universal carriers during Operation Totalize.*
Below: *An M-3 Stuart light tank and US infantry, all on their way to Brittany, pass a knocked out Panther.*

Above: *In southern France, for a short time after Lyon had been liberated, there was sporadic German resistance. Here French troops and Resistance fighters (FFI) fire across the River Rhône at German snipers occupying the city hospital.*

Below: *Seen on the move towards Brest, 18 August 1944. As part of Major General Troy H. Middleton's US VIII Corps effort in northern Brittany is this 155mm Gun M1, affectionately called the 'Long Tom' for its great range and high level accuracy.*

Above: *Smoke rises over the rooftops of Paris. Hitler had ordered that Paris be held at all costs or* *reduced to rubble, but the German garrison put up only sporadic resistance and then surrendered before the* *city had suffered very much.*
Below: *General Leclerc and an aide watch French Sherman* *tanks move through the streets of Paris. His tanks were the first to reach the French capital.*

from division command were far more common in the US First Army than in the rest of 21st Army Group.

British and Canadian ground operations were similarly timid, despite the fact that Montgomery, like Bradley, decided to use veteran divisions in the assault and immediate attacks to deepen the beachhead. The 7th Armoured Division, the famous "Desert Rats" from North Africa and Italy, and the proud 51st (Highland) Division both turned in disappointing performances, appearing tired and overly cautious. It was the judgement of Lt. Gen. Brian Horrocks, the XXX Corps commander, and Maj. Gen. G. L. Verney, who took command of the 7th Armoured in Normandy, that the men were tired, unprepared for fighting in the restrictive terrain of France, and had been in battle long enough to have had dash replaced by caution. The same, they believed, was true of the veteran 51st Division, proud of its past victories but no longer, as Montgomery reported to Brooke, battle worthy. Other divisions performed similarly.

Command philosophy had something to do with it, for it was accepted in 21st Army Group that the need to keep down casualties was a pivotal consideration. Although it now appears that there were some 100,000 uncommitted infantrymen in the United Kingdom – possible evidence that Churchill still harbored doubts about the ultimate success of *Overlord* – in practical terms the British contingent of 21st Army Group was as large and as powerful on June 6, 1944, as it would ever be. There were no more reserves to be committed, and Montgomery lived in a world of ever-declining resources. While more American units were available, the British began *Overlord* at maximum strength. The concern to limit casualties inevitably had an effect on the aggression with which the divisions fought and their willingness to take chances and exploit opportunities. Instead, careful battle preparation, already a Montgomery trademark, was the hallmark of 21st Army Group operations.

Like the Americans, the British and Canadians preferred to let the artillery do the fighting wherever possible. The men did not lack courage, but did lack boldness. In general terms, as historian Carlo D'Este has concluded, Commonwealth infantrymen took a piece of terrain that invited counterattack, then used their machine guns in what was essentially a tactic of attrition little changed from the days of World War I. Because there were doctrinal problems in tank-infantry co-operation that stemmed from a British understanding of armor as an independent, exploiting force, tank units also suffered heavily in the Normandy fighting. German criticisms of the British and Canadian infantry were much like the criticisms of American infantry, assessing fighting morale as not very high, finding little willingness to engage in close combat, and observing an excessive dependence on artillery support, without which they would not advance.

Throughout the Normandy fighting, it was the Germans who impressed. Given their enormous disadvantages in manpower, fire support, lack of mobility, lack of logistical sustainment, and above all lack of air power, and considering the countervailing Allied superiority in every one of those categories, the German ability to contain the beachhead for so long was a very impressive achievement. Hitler's order that his troops stand and fight in Normandy derailed the *Overlord* plan. It also, however, resulted in the destruction of the fighting power of the German Army in the west. Despite, and in fact as a consequence of, the difficulties they faced and the slow advance they managed, the British and American forces methodically ravaged German divisions. By the end of the battle in Normandy, not only were the coastal defense divisions destroyed, but also many of the first-class armored and mechanized divisions. Three months after the landings, the Germans could muster no more than 120 of the 1,300 tanks and assault guns they had committed to battle in Normandy, and the average Panzer division could count fewer than ten tanks. Perhaps just as damaging, the Germans lost more than 15,000 vehicles of other types, further crippling their tactical mobility. It was the destruction of the Panzer divisions in the hedgerows that made it possible for the Allies, once they broke out of the beachhead, not only to catch up with the *Overlord* plan, but to exceed it, racing all the way to the German frontier by September.

It was, however, the overwhelming materiel superiority, coupled with overwhelming air superiority and artillery firepower, rather than tactical and operational acumen, that allowed the Americans and the British to prevail. That fact amply justified the *Overlord* planners' preoccupation with logistics and with the development of the continental logistical base. The Allies' often-criticized battlefield caution helped to minimize casualties, and is the more understandable in view of their clear decision to use American industrial might, not men, in what Churchill called "merely the proper application of overwhelming force." The palm for tactical adroitness in Normandy must be awarded to the Germans, but it is worth noting that tactical skill and small-unit initiative and aggression were not so much virtues as essential, in view of German military shortcomings in almost every other way.

Despite any actual or perceived problems at the tactical level, the difficult ground battles of June and July were important Allied victories that it would be wrong to discount. Hard fighting in front of Caen, on the Cotentin Peninsula, and in the morass of the bocage made reality of Eisenhower's boast to Churchill about standing on the German frontier by winter.

THE AIR BATTLE

During the spring of 1944, as part of general preparations for the invasion, Spitfires, Mosquitoes, Mustangs, and Lightnings of Allied reconnaissance units flew many hundreds of sorties over France and Belgium. Their cameras took tens of thousands of photographs which revealed details of the German coastal defensive system running from Holland to the Spanish frontier. Most of the photographs were taken from medium and high altitude, and showed the targets vertically, from above. Additionally, low-flying aircraft fitted with sideways-looking or forwards-looking oblique cameras took close-ups of important objectives. Aircraft flew high-speed runs over the beaches at low altitude, taking photographs for the coxswains of landing craft and platoon commanders to show the appearance of their objectives as seen from the seaward approaches. It was vitally important that the aerial activity should not betray the invasion area, so for each sortie flown over western Normandy three were flown over the Pas de Calais.

Also at this time, fighter-bombers set about the important task of knocking out radar stations along the French and Belgian coasts. During the ten-week period prior to the invasion, Typhoons, Spitfires, and Mosquitoes of the RAF 2nd Tactical Air Force flew nearly 2,000 sorties against radar sites. These targets were well defended, and on occasions the attackers suffered serious losses. But by June 5 the fighter-bombers would have put out of action all but 16 of the original 92 sites and left no radar fully operational overlooking the invasion area.

During this phase, medium bombers of the 2nd Tactical Air Force and the US 9th Air Force carried out systematic attacks on transportation targets. Following a carefull analysis of the railway system in northern France, Prof. Solly Zuckerman devised a clever plan of attacks that would isolate Normandy while giving the impression that the invasion would take place somewhere in the Pas de Calais area (the "Transportation Plan"). A total of 72 specific objectives were singled out for attack: 39 in western Germany and 33 in France and Belgium. The targets included railway junctions, marshaling yards and rolling stock repair shops. Fighters and fighter-bombers flew over the rail network shooting up the rolling stock with the aim of clogging the repair system with damaged units, By the beginning of June, of 2,000 steam locomotives that had been available in northern France and Belgium, 1,500 had been immobilized as a result of direct air attack or lack of maintenance.

The US 9th Air Force also delivered concentrated attacks on bridges and airfields. By June 5, of the 24 bridges over the Seine between Paris and the sea, 18 had been destroyed and three were closed for repair. Also, during the final six weeks prior to the invasion, 36 Luftwaffe airfields in France, Holland and Belgium were attacked.

■ Eve of D-Day

By the eve of D-Day the Allied air forces possessed a clear qualitative and quantitative superiority over the Luftwaffe in the west. Between them the US Army Air Force and the RAF could send into action some 2,800 heavy bombers, 1,500 medium and light bombers and 3,700 fighters and fighter-bombers, Luftflotte 3 (Air Fleet 3), which controlled all Luftwaffe units based in France, Holland and Belgium and was responsible for countering the invasion, possessed only about 140 medium bombers, 90 anti-shipping aircraft, 200 fighters and fighter-bombers and 56 nightfighters. Once the invasion began it was planned to reinforce Luftflotte 3 with a further 400 single-engined fighters from home defense units in Luftflotte Reich. Even with this transfusion of strength the Luftwaffe units in the west would still be heavily outnumbered. In the pre-invasion address delivered to his forces Gen. Eisenhower felt able to make a jaunty prediction on the outcome of the battle in the air: "Don't worry about the planes overhead. They will be ours ..."

On the afternoon of June 5 all aircraft earmarked to take part in supporting the invasion were hastily painted with distinctive black and white stripes on their wings and fuselages, to assist in identification. As darkness fell and the invasion fleets set sail, from more than a hundred airfields throughout the length and breadth of Britain there came the thunder of aero engines as planes roared into the air to fulfil their allotted tasks.

Six squadrons of RAF Mosquito night fighters maintained standing patrols over the English Channel and France to safeguard the huge armada of ships, and the streams of bombers, transport aircraft and gliders heading for Normandy. The night fighter operation was completely successful – not a single enemy aircraft was able to interfere with the enterprise. The only combat over the Channel that night was by a Mosquito of No. 409 (Canadian) Squadron, which engaged a Junkers 188 on reconnaissance off the south coast of England and claimed it "probably destroyed."

Twenty anti-submarine aircraft of RAF Coastal Command equipped to carry out night attacks – Sunderland flying boats, Wellingtons, Liberators and Halifaxes – headed for their designated patrol lines off the coast of Cornwall. The appropriately named *Cork* patrols would be flown round the clock throughout the weeks ahead and were intended to saturate a 20,000 square mile (50,000km^2) area of sea between Brittany and the Irish Coast. Any U-boat attempting to reach the invasion area from its base on the French Atlantic coast would have to run the gauntlet of air patrols cruising most of the way on the surface, for the distance was too far to cover submerged. And while it was on the surface, a U-boat was liable to suffer repeated attacks from the air.

As the U-boat hunters moved into position, aircraft from RAF Bomber Command – 551 Lancasters, 412 Halifaxes, and 49 Mosquitoes – headed out to bomb ten coastal batteries situated at strategic points along the Normandy coast. Most of the objectives were covered in cloud, so Pathfinder Mosquitoes fitted with the highly accurate *Oboe* radar attack system dropped pyrotechnic markers to point out the targets for the rest of the force.

Shortly before midnight, heavily laden transport planes staggered into the air and headed south. Three divisions of troops and their equipment were being committed in the largest airborne assault operation ever attempted. Making for the Drop Zones covering the west flank of the landings were 821 USAAF troop-carriers – C-47s and C-53s (the latter a modification of the former, equipped for glider towing), together with 104 Horsa and Waco gliders. These carried the two US airborne divisions to their Drop Zones. Meanwhile, heading for Drop Zones covering the east flank of the landings were 266 Halifaxes Stirlings, Dakotas, and Albemarles, and 98 Horsa and Hamilcar gliders, carrying the British airborne division. During the small hours of the morning the aircraft put down their troops and equipment with varying degrees of accuracy. Twenty-one US and seven British transport aircraft were lost in the operation.

In one of many unusual operations flown as part of *Overlord* shortly before dawn, a pair of Douglas Boston bombers of No. 342 (French) Squadron flew low over the sea along the west flank of the invasion fleet to lay a smoke screen to shield the columns of ships from visually aimed fire coming from German coastal batteries along the Cotentin Peninsula. At ten-minute intervals, relays of bombers arrived to renew the curtain of smoke which significantly reduced the accuracy of the enemy's long range artillery. Bostons of No. 88 Squadron RAF carried out a similar operation along the eastern flank of the invasion force. Two aircraft were lost in the course of these operations.

At 04:30 the first day fighter units arrived to relieve the Mosquito night fighters patroling the invasion area. Six Groups of P-38 Lightnings of the US 8th and 9th Air Forces flew on a rota designed to maintain two full squadrons on continuous patrol over the concentrations of ships throughout the period between dawn and dusk. The Lightning, with its unique and unmistakable twin-boom layout, was particularly suitable for the task, for it was the type least likely to be misidentified by naval gunners liable to engage any aircraft within range unless they were sure it was friendly.

To provide defense in depth, squadron-sized formations of Spitfires, Thunderbolts, and Mustangs ranged far and wide over Normandy to block the path of enemy planes making for the landing areas.

As the landing craft approached the beaches, battleships and cruisers lying off shore loosed off broadsides at the enemy shore batteries, assisted by spotter planes. One of the latter, a Seafire of No. 866 Squadron piloted by Lt. Dick Law RN, corrected the fire from the battleship HMS *Warspite* as she engaged a coastal defense battery of six 155 mm guns near Trouville. "The battleship was a magnificent sight as she lay at anchor, loosing off four-gun salvoes with her main 15-in guns," he recalled. "During one

119

of the early salvoes I was a little over-enthusiastic in positioning myself to observe the fall of the shells, with the result that some 35 seconds after *Warspite* fired my Seafire suddenly shivered and I actually saw one of the giant shells, weighing almost a ton, go sizzling close past me on its way to the target. During subsequent salvoes I made good and sure that I was well to the side of the line of fire! From time to time the German batteries returned *Warspite*'s fire; when that happened we were treated to the spectacle of a giant-sized tennis match. During one of these exchanges a salvo straddled *Warspite*, but she received only slight damage."

While Law was directing the battleship's fire, 1,077 B-17 Flying Fortresses and B-24 Liberators of the US 8th Air Force laid carpets of bombs along the shore lines where Allied troops were about to land. One of the heavy bombers was shot down by flak.

Among the US 9th Air Force units providing direct support for the initial landings was the 366th Fighter Group with some 45 fighter-bombers – P-47 Thunderbolts – each carrying two 1,000lb (400kg) bombs. The Group commander, Lt. Col. Norman Holt, later wrote: "The sky was quite gray but brightening rapidly as the definite line of the French coast moved toward us. Preparing to dive-bomb our primary targets, shore gun batteries, terse commands came from the squadron leader, 'Relic Squadron, echelon right, flights in trail.' Inching slowly over into formation, we stole a quick look down at the beach as often as we could, at the same time we looked around for any enemy aircraft which could be very troublesome during the crucial forming of the beachhead. Below us, for a three or four mile (4–6km) stretch, we could pick up innumerable water craft of all sizes, shapes and types. There seemed to be thousands of them! Battleships standing off-shore were firing broadsides over the other craft. Their firepower was helping pin down and hamper return fire from the enemy. At the shore line, landing craft were spewing out men and equipment at an astonishing rate. We could see them scattering like kids from school." After the Thunderbolts had delivered their bombs they flew inland to strafe targets of opportunity.

Allied medium bombers were also active against enemy positions, attacking from altitudes much lower than usual to ensure accurate bombing. For example, 54 A-20 Havocs of the 416th Bomb Group, 9th Air Force, descended to 1,700 feet (510m) to deliver a devastating attack on the Argentan cross-roads. The target was undefended and all of the aircraft returned safely.

Eighteen squadrons of RAF Typhoon fighter-bombers supported the landings in the British sector. As the first troops went ashore, three squadrons dive-bombed strong-points immediately in front of them. Throughout the day relays of squadrons flew "cab rank" patrols, orbiting over the beachhead waiting for their forward air controllers to call on them to attack enemy positions that were holding up the advance. If there was no suitable target near the beachhead, the Typhoons were sent south to attack targets of opportunity in the areas around Bayeux and Caen.

■ The Luftwaffe Reply

The initial Allied landings came as a complete surprise to the Luftwaffe. No German reconnaissance aircraft reported the approach of the armada, and initially there was no reaction from the defenses. Even when Luftflotte 3 had firm evidence that the landings had begun, the powerful defensive umbrella prevented it from mounting effective air attacks. During one attempt to reach the shipping, Mustangs of the 355th Fighter Group intercepted a gaggle of Junkers Ju 88 bombers and shot down nine of them and forced the remainder to jettison their bombs and run for home.

A few German fighters did succeed in reaching the landing area that morning, however. In a well-known incident a pair of Focke-Wulf Fw 190s piloted by Oberst Josef Priller, commander of Jagdgeschwader 26, and his wing man Unteroffizier Heinz Wodarciyk delivered a strafing attack on *Sword* Beach. Elsewhere, a dozen Messerschmitt Bf 109s bounced Typhoons of No. 183 Squadron as the latter were engaged in strafing a column of German Army vehicles, and shot down three before the remainder were able to fight them off. The total Luftwaffe effort during the day amounted to about a hundred sorties, mainly by fighters, fighter-bombers and fighter-reconnaissance aircraft.

The IIIrd Gruppe of Schlachtgeschwader 4, a ground attack unit with some 50 Focke-Wulf Fw 190Fs, was one of the Luftwaffe units sent in during the initial stages of battle. On the morning of D-Day the Gruppe received orders to move from its bases in the south and east of France to forward operating airfields at Laval and Tours. During such combat deployments a mechanic was carried in the rear fuselage of each Focke-Wulf, to assist in the rapid turnaround of the aircraft when it arrived at the new base. Unfortunately for those on board, as the German fighter-bombers were in transit, several of them were intercepted by Mustangs and Thunderbolts. Five of the German planes were shot down and, lacking parachutes, the mechanics had no means of escape. Their pilots refused to bail out and leave them, and of the ten men on board the planes, eight were killed.

Flying from the new bases late on the afternoon of D-Day, the Gruppe mounted three attacks against *Sword* Beach with a total of 13 aircraft. Allied fighters prevented one raiding force from reaching its target, the other two got through to the beachhead but the volume of anti-aircraft fire forced them to make fleeting attacks which caused little damage.

That night there were violent skirmishes at the western end of the English Channel, as U-boats from the bases along the Biscay coast tried to force their way past the *Cork* patrols. The patrol planes obtained contacts on 22 U-boats and converted seven of these into attacks. Two U-boats were sunk and four were damaged to such an extent that they were forced to turn back.

At dawn the surviving U-boats submerged, for a daylight passage was far too dangerous to attempt. After darkness fell on the evening of June 7, the U-boats surfaced and doggedly continued their move eastwards trying to recharge their depleted batteries. The patrol planes were again in action and one of them, a Liberator of No. 224 Squadron RAF commanded by Flying Officer Kenneth Moore, achieved the unique feat of sinking two boats – *U-373* and *U-629* – within a space of 15 minutes.

In the days following the initial landings Allied bombers and fighter-bombers continued their round the clock attack on the road and rail networks leading into Normandy. On the night of June 8/9, 24 Lancasters of No. 617 Squadron RAF carried out a precision attack on the Samur rail tunnel using 12,000lb (5,440 kg) "Tallboy" deep penetration bombs. The exploding bombs collapsed the tunnel and the line was blocked for a considerable period,

Also that night, Luftflotte 3 sent about 130 bombers to attack the concentrations of Allied shipping off the coast. During their approach flights the attackers suffered losses not only from the Allied night fighters, but also from German flak batteries long accustomed to regarding all aircraft as hostile. Those bombers that reached the beachhead area encountered so violent a reception that in many cases they were forced to break off their attacks prematurely. The only Allied losses were the headquarters ship *Bulolo* and the destroyer *Lawford*, both of which were sunk by radio-controlled glider bombs.

■ The story of One Fighter Gruppe

Under the long-prepared Luftwaffe plan, when the Allied landings began, home defense fighter Gruppen were to move from Luftflotte Reich to France to stiffen the defenses there. We shall follow the fortunes of one such unit, IInd Gruppe of Jagdgeschwader 1, which flew its 25 Focke-Wulf Fw 190s from Rheine in western Germany to Le Mans on the afternoon of D-Day. On June 7 the Gruppe mounted three full-strength fighter sweeps over roads along which German reinforcements were moving and, remarkably, encountered no Allied aircraft. On the next day, June 8, the unit was ordered to load bombs on its Fw 190s for an attack on shipping off the coast. The pilots had no previous experience of fighter-bomber operations, and although they reached the invasion area and dropped their bombs, from Allied records we know that no ship was hit. The German pilots described the flak they encountered as "terrific" yet, again, all of the aircraft returned though some had minor damage. A similar operation on the following day was also unsuccessful, but still the unit's run of luck held and there were no losses. On the night of June 10/11 a force of more than a hundred RAF Lancasters and Halifaxes bombed Le Mans airfield. Craters pock-marked the landing ground, but prudently the Gruppe had dispersed its aircraft into the surrounding fields and none was damaged. Lacking mechanical earth moving equipment, however, it took six days of hard work to fill in enough craters by hand to provide a flat strip for take-offs. As soon as the Focke-Wulfs were able to get airborne they moved to Essay, and from there they flew fighting patrols over the battle area for the next four days. Then the unit transfered to a field landing ground near Alençon, where its charmed existence came to an abrupt end. Soon after the German fighters landed, a force of Mustangs swept over the airfield at low altitude and, in a series of coordinated strafing runs, destroyed 15 of the Fw 190s and effectively put the Gruppe out of the battle.

As a result of the continual harassment of Luftwaffe units in France from the Allied air forces, the German ground troops received minimal air support.

■ Headquarters Attack

Allied fighter-bombers and bombers flew large numbers of sorties against German troop positions, and headquarters were priority targets for attack when these could be found. On June 10, RAF aircraft bombed three sites

123

thought to be the locations of major headquarters. Only one of the attacks, that against Château-la-Caine south of Caen, was successful but it brought handsome dividends, for the building housed the headquarters of Panzer Group West. Forty Typhoons of Nos 181, 182, 245 and 247 Squadrons fired rockets into the château then 71 North American Mitchells of Nos 98, 180, 266, and 320 Squadrons carried out a horizontal attack on the area from 12,000 feet (3,600m) dropping large numbers of 500lb (200kg) bombs. The headquarters was wrecked and the Chief of Staff Gen. von Dawans and many of his staff offcers were killed.

By now construction was well advanced on the first landing grounds in the beachhead, and from June 13 Allied fighter and fighter-bomber squadrons used these to refuel between missions. A couple of days later, units took up residence on the new bases.

Off the coast of Normandy the Luftwaffe anti-shipping units continued to suffer heavy losses in their attempts trying to attack the assembled vessels. In the ten days following the invasion, IIIrd Gruppe of Kampfgeschwader 100, a Dornier Do 217 unit equipped with glider bombs, lost ten aircraft and eight crews. During that period only two destroyers and three smaller vessels were lost to direct air attack. Shortly afterwards the Luftwaffe abandoned direct attacks, and sent its bombers to sow mines in the shallow waters off the coast. The newly developed pressure mine was difficult to sweep, but ships were safe provided they kept their speed to a minimum while passing through the shallows. The mines caused considerable inconvenience, but few ships were lost.

■ German "Secret Weapon"

In mid-June the Luftwaffe sent one of its new "secret weapons" to France: the *Mistel*, a Junkers Ju 88 bomber with the crew compartment replaced by a 6,200lb (2,800kg) high explosive warhead and with a Messerschmitt Bf 109 fighter mounted rigidly on top. The Bf 109 pilot was to fly the combination to the target area, align it on the target and lock in the autopilot on the Ju 88. Then he fired explosive bolts to release the fighter, leaving the explosive-laden bomber to continue on and smash into the target. The first *Mistel* unit, Kampfgruppe 101, deployed to St. Dizier near Reims and went into action on the night of June 24/25. Hauptmann Horst Rudat, the commander, led four of the ungainly aircraft into the invasion area and the pilots aimed their explosive Ju 88s at ships off the coast. Hits were claimed but the Allied report of damage that links with this attack was from the headquarters ship HMS *Nith*, which suffered extensive splinter damage when an explosive Ju 88 exploded on the sea nearby.

During that and subsequent *Mistel* operations against shipping off the coast about ten explosive Ju 88s were launched. At least one hit was claimed on a "battleship" but this is not confirmed in Allied records. An explanation that fits the known facts is that the victim was the old French battleship *Courbet*, which had been abandoned and sunk in shallow water to form part of the breakwater for the *Mulberry* artificial harbor.

■ Heavy Bombers Support the Land Battle

Operation *Goodwood*, the powerful thrust past the east of Caen by British and Canadian divisions on July 18, called for the use of large numbers of medium and heavy bombers to blast a path through enemy defenses. In the heaviest and most concentrated air attack yet made in support of a ground action, nearly 2,000 bombers were to lay carpets of bombs across designated target areas ahead of the advancing troops. RAF Bomber Command opened the attack at dawn, when Pathfinder Mosquitoes marked the five target areas which were then bombed by 1,013 Lancasters and Halifaxes. Later that morning, 571 B-24 Liberators of the US 8th Air force attacked five more target areas. Then 318 medium bombers of the US 9th Air Force – A-20 Havocs, B-25 Mitchells and B-26 Marauders – attacked a further five target areas. During these attacks seven heavy bombers were lost, all of them to flak.

The bombs fell across positions manned by the 21st Panzer Division and the 16th Luftwaffe Field Division and caused considerable losses and disruption to their defenses. One company of 21st Panzer, laagered in farm buildings around the village of Guillerville, was hit particularly hard. It had 15 of its tanks put out of action and the area was cratered to such an extent that its surviving vehicles were unable to move. During the hours immediately following the bombing the attacking troops advanced rapidly, but then the defenders recovered and were able to halt their progress.

On July 25/26 in a similar series of attacks in a prelude to Operation *Cobra*, large forces of Flying Fortresses and Liberators of the US 8th Air Force put down a carpet of bombs along the Périers-St. Lô highway and some 1,200 yards (1,000m) in front of troops of the US First Army who were preparing to attack. On this occasion the targets were too close to US forward positions for safety, however, and several sticks of bombs fell across US Army positions causing more than 600 casualties and leaving some units in a dazed condition. As a result the subsequent land attack achieved little. The lesson was clear: when heavy bombers were used to support the land battle, a separation of at least 3,000 yards (2,700m) from the nearest Allied positions was necessary if such losses were to be avoided.

■ Jets Join the Battle

At the end of July the Luftwaffe moved another of its "secret weapons" to France: the revolutionary new Messerschmitt Me 262 jet aircraft. Hitler had insisted that these planes be modified to carry bombs and used to disrupt the Allied seaborne invasion. Due to various problems with the novel engines, the aircraft was not ready in time to combat the initial landings but if the Allies landed in the Pas de Calais area, as the Führer still believed they might, the "Blitzbombers" would be in position to strike, each carrying two 550lb (250kg) bombs. The first jet fighter-bomber unit, part of Kampfgeschwader 51 and equipped with nine Me 262s, began operations from Châteaudun near Paris early in August.

In the event the jet planes achieved little. To minimize the risk of losses their pilots had strict orders not to descend below 13,000ft (4,000m) while over enemy territory, and from that altitude accurate bombing was impossible against small battlefield targets such as bridges or vehicles.

Throughout the Battle of Normandy, Allied field commanders received frequent and comprehensive photographic coverage of the enemy positions in front of their forces. Their German counterparts, in contrast, often knew nothing of Allied movements until the attacking units came within sight or sound of their forward positions. Luftwaffe reconnaissance aircraft attempted to fly low altitude photographic sorties by day, and high altitude photographic missions at night using flares. The powerful Allied fighter defenses covering the beachhead and its approaches took a heavy toll of these planes, and those that survived usually did so by breaking off their missions prematurely.

This lack of effective aerial reconnaissance had serious consequences for the defenders. At the end of July American troops broke out of the western side of the lodgment area and, undetected by the German high command, advanced in force down the western side of the Cherbourg Peninsula. On the 31st the advancing units seized the bridges over the Rivers Sée and Sélune at the southern end of the peninsula intact.

Exploiting his unexpected opportunity, Gen. Patton poured his troops across the bridges and into the undefended countryside beyond.

For the Germans, the road between the two bridges now became a "fighter-bombers' paradise"; mile upon mile of vehicles jammed nose-to-tail and moving slowly along the one narrow road. But by day the German fighter bombers were quite unable to penetrate the thicket of defensive patrols. In a desperate attempt to stop the advance, Dornier Do 217s carrying glider bombs were sent to attack the bridges at night. During these operations one bridge suffered minor damage but it continued in use, and six of the bombers were shot down.

In a move aimed at overcoming the lack of effective aerial reconnaissance over Normandy the Luftwaffe committed another of its "secret weapons": the Arado Ar 234 jet reconnaissance plane. Two of these aircraft, both prototypes, were dispatched to Juvincourt near Paris, and on the morning of August 2 Lt. Erich Sommer took off for the world's first jet reconnaissance mission. Flying at 34,000ft (10,000m) at 460 mph (270 km/h), the German pilot made three long photographic runs over Normandy. The skies were clear, but if any Allied fighter attempted to intercept the Arado the latter's pilot never noticed it. In a flight lasting less than 90 minutes Erich Sommer achieved more than the entire Luftwaffe reconnaissance force in the west had done during the previous eight weeks; he photographed almost the entire Allied lodgment area, from one end to the other. When the films were developed it took a twelve-man team of interpreters more than two days to produce an initial assessment of what the photographs revealed; that is hardly surprising, for by then the Allies had landed more than 1½ million men and 300,000 vehicles. Detailed examination of the prints took several weeks. From then on high-flying Arados flew regular photographic missions over the Allied rear areas. Yet the time had almost passed when such intelligence might play a decisive part in the land battle. By now the US armored units were streaming out from the Cotentin Peninsula, and their spearheads were thrusting east, west and south into the hinterland and meeting little opposition.

On August 7 the German Army launched Operation *Lüttich*, a powerful counterattack by five Panzer divisions and elements of a fourth with the intention of driving west to cut off the American advance. That morning a cloak of mist prevented air operations, allowing the German troops to make good progress. By noon the skies had cleared, however, and for the first time since D-Day Allied fighter-bombers went into action against columns of enemy vehicles moving in the open by day. Nineteen squadrons of rocket-firing Typhoons maintained a shuttle service of attacks against the tank columns. Meanwhile, Spitfires, Mustangs, Thunderbolts, and Lightnings strafed the soft-skinned vehicles and mounted barrier patrols to prevent German fighters from interfering. By the end of the day the German advance had been halted for the loss of more than a hundred tanks. Despite determined attempts to renew the assault, the scale of Allied air power thwarted troop movements during the daylight hours and combined with a stiffening of resistance on the ground, forced the abandonment of *Lüttich*.

Now in an exposed salient and unable to advance, the German Army began to pull back its forces. And again there were lucrative targets for the marauding Allied fighter-bombers. During an armed reconnaissance mission along a road near Carrouges on August 13, for example, a Thunderbolt pilot of the 366th Fighter Group caught sight of a couple of trucks parked under trees. As he pulled round to line himself up for a strafing attack he suddenly noticed what looked like trees growing in the middle of the road. Examination revealed about 30 heavily camouflaged tanker trucks in the area and at least six tanks taking on fuel. The pilot summoned the rest of the Group by radio and the fighter-bombers carried out repeated bombing and strafing runs. When the aircraft departed, having expended their munitions, they left behind a line of blazing vehicles more than a mile (1.6km) long. Elsewhere that day, Thunderbolts of the 36th Fighter Group located a column of several hundred vehicles on the move near Argentan and destroyed a large number of them.

Meanwhile, the American armored thrust plunged deep into France. As other units headed towards Paris and other important cities, the US XV Corps swung north for Argentan. At the same time Canadian and Polish troops advanced on the Falaise area, threatening to envelop the 16 German divisions pulling back from positions to the west of those towns. By August 16 the net was drawing tight and the network of narrow roads leading out of the pocket filled with vehicles of all types moving eastwards. Allied fighter-bombers attacked with bombs, rockets and cannon destroying hundreds of vehicles and creating numerous road blocks, that prevented movement altogether in some areas. The German troops abandoned their vehicles and heavy equipment, and fought their way out of the pocket on foot.

■ Operation *Dragoon*

On August 15 Allied troops launched Operation *Dragoon*, an assault landing on the French Mediterranean coast. The Luftwaffe had about 65 Junkers Ju 88 torpedo bombers and 25 Dornier Do 217s carrying glider bombs based within reach of the landing area, but there were no fighters in the area until a single Gruppe of Messerschmitt Bf 109s was rushed there from Italy. The ships were well protected by land-based and carrier-based fighters, and the German attempts to strike at them had little success. Only one ship, an LST, was sunk by direct air attack, while air-dropped mines accounted for a few small craft. Within a few days of the landings Luftwaffe air activity over southern France ceased altogether.

By mid-August the Luftwaffe units in France were on the brink of collapse. Luftflotte 3 was down to its last 75 single-engined fighters and their number was dwindling rapidly. To cover the withdrawal of ground forces a further four Gruppen of fighters were transfered from Germany. One of the units to arrive at this time was IInd Gruppe of Jagdgeschwader 6, an Fw 190 unit that had been recently formed with pilots from disbanded twin-engined bomber-destroyer units. The Gruppe flew to Herpy near Reims on August 23, and one of its pilots, Feldwebel Fritz Buchholz, recalled: "Our airstrip at Herpy was nothing more than a piece of flat cow pasture surrounded by trees in which our aircraft could be hidden; nearby was our tented accommodation. The Allied fighter-bombers seemed to be everywhere and our survival depended on the strictest attention to camouflage. As part of this we even had a herd of cows which moved on to the airfield when no flying was in progress; as well as giving the place a rustic look, these performed the valuable task of obliterating the tracks made on the grass by the aircraft. Such attention to detail paid off and there were no attacks on Herpy while I was there."

The Gruppe flew its first major operation on August 25, when it mounted an offensive patrol with some 40 aircraft over the St. Quentin area. The Focke-Wulfs surprised a dozen Lightnings of the 367th Fighter Group, 9th Air Force in the act of strafing the airfield at Clastres, and shot down six of them. The American pilots' distress calls summoned the other two squadrons of the Group to the area, and when these joined the fight they quickly turned the tables. Numerically the two forces were almost equal, but the German pilots lacked experience in dogfighting and suffered accordingly. In the resulting mêlée the Gruppe lost 16 aircraft destroyed and several more damaged, and accounted for only one more

Lightning. Fritz Buchholz survived the encounter but on the next day he was bounced by a Mustang, shot down and wounded.

The withdrawal of the Luftwaffe from France quickly disintegrated into a rout. The fighter Gruppen sent from Germany to cover the move all suffered heavy losses, and they made no noticeable difference to the predicament of the German Army units which had to face repeated attacks from the air as they headed east. With the exception of its one small reconnaissance unit, the Luftwaffe played no effective role in this phase of the land battle. One German soldier who took part in the Battle of Normandy and the subsequent retreat later commented with some bitterness: "If the aircraft above us were camouflaged, we knew they were British. If they were silver, we knew they were American. And if they weren't there at all, we knew they were German!" His pungent remark sums up, more effectively than any statistical list of aircraft involved or damage inflicted, the degree of air supremacy achieved by the Allied air forces during the Battle of France.

THE NORMANDY BATTLEGROUND

By June 10, the Allied forces had established and secured a lodgment in Normandy. Four corps were ashore, with their forward elements well inland of the assault beaches, connected by a continuous perimeter. They enjoyed the benefits of safe logistic and administration areas, and mutual support.

The US VII Corps was pressing northwards against Montebourg, westwards to force the line of the River Merderet, and south to invest Carentan. To the southeast of the US VII Corps, the US V Corps, having bounced across the marshy flood plain of the River Aure, was pushing south towards the River Elle. East of their area the British XXX Corps was struggling through the bocage south of Bayeux, British I Corps was deployed astride the River Orne, held to the north of Caen, with the troops east of the river crowded into a shallow bridgehead overlooked by enemy positions. Reinforcements and supplies poured in across the beaches; the minor ports were being cleared, and the two *Mulberry* harbors, one off *Omaha* beach and one near *Gold*, were being assembled.

Rommel's plan to contain the landing forces on the beaches with his fortified positions, and destroy them between the tidelines, had failed. Because of Hitler's belief that the Allied assault on Normandy was a feint, he was reluctant to release the mobile reserve forces that von Rundstedt and Geyr von Schweppenburg wanted to launch in a counterstroke. Those German units that were ordered to Normandy were hindered and delayed by the effects of Operation *Point-blank*, the offensive patrols of the 2nd Tactical Air Force, and disruption caused by the French Resistance. The German forces were unable to mount a major counteroffensive; all they could do was to defend and make local counterattacks. In the American sector, these were directed towards clearing the area around Carentan, in an attempt to force the US VII and V Corps apart. But the fall of Carentan to a pincer attack by both US corps on June 12 frustrated these German efforts. In the British sector, the most dangerous counterattacks were made by 21st Panzer Division, which continuously probed the defences of the bridgehead east of the Orne.

As the Allied buildup continued, the senior commanders considered their plans. Montgomery had expected that once the hard crust of coastal defenses had been penetrated, the Germans would conduct a fighting withdrawal, using counterattacks, ambushes and blocking actions to reduce and delay the Allied armies, until they reached strong positions on the Seine. He had planned to make the whole Allied beachhead absolutely secure, and build up an overwhelming superiority of men and materiel. Once certain of this superiority, he would launch breakout operations on both flanks simultaneously. The Anglo-Canadian armies in the east would pivot on Caen, swing to their left, and drive for the Seine. In the west the American forces were to break out on an axis selected by Gen. Bradley. Once through the enemy lines, they were to send one army southwest-wards to liberate Brittany. Another army was to move to the southeast, and advance parallel to the Anglo-Canadian troops, to the Seine. Once on the Seine, the Allies would have to prepare for a succession of opposed crossing operations.

But it was apparent by June 10 that the Germans would not conform to Montgomery's expectations, and that his plans would have to be changed. Contrary to the conventional military doctrines, the Germans did not conduct a withdrawal after the beach defenses had been overrun. Hitler insisted that his soldiers must defend every inch of ground, and die in position rather than yield. This meant that the Allied armies did not advance as rapidly as intended. In the British sector, operations were particularly inhibited by the failure to take Caen as planned on D-Day. Caen was of critical importance as the most important center of commu-nications in the British area. The Germans proved to be tenacious and very skillful in making the best possible use of the ground they were defending. They were assisted by the weather. Spells of heavy rain deprived the Allies of the benefits of their superiority in air power and in artillery.

Allied plans and actions were modified in accordance with the enemy behavior and adverse circumstances. The British Second Army mounted a series of offensive operations which aimed to take Caen and advance south of the city. An attack eastwards was barred by the inundated valley of the Dives, where the German engineers had worked to extend the flooded area. An attack south to the west of Bayeux would be impeded by a series of steep ridges, and dense bocage country. The British offensives, *Perch*, *Epsom*, *Charnwood*, and *Goodwood*, did not achieve a breakout. But they did maintain pressure on the German Army, so that it was never able to assemble a reserve big enough to make a successful counterattack. The British offensives also drew in German reinforcements. Highly mobile Panzer units were employed in static containment operations, digging in to hold ground. When not involved in making major offensives, the soldiers of the British Second Army kept up the pressure by constant local attacks and aggressive patrolling. These offensive activities were not decisive, but did have a great effect on the Germans. The Panzer reserves were held in waiting in front of the Second Army's sector, because it was closest to Paris and to Germany, and therefore, according to conventional military thinking, the most likely place for the Allies to attempt their decisive attack. This meant that the German Army was never able to seize the initiative, and suffered from a very limited maneuver.

Like Montgomery and Dempsey, Bradley gave top priority to securing his base in Normandy. He felt confident that given a secure beachhead he could build up a local superiority that would guarantee victory, and was in no mood to risk a setback by optimistic and premature offensives. By mid-June he decided that his first aim must be to clear the Cotentin Peninsula and take Cherbourg. If the Cotentin remained in enemy hands, it would be a permanent menace to the rear of the US First Army. Furthermore, the German division in the Channel Islands and other formations located in Brittany might be sent into Cherbourg to reinforce the threat. On the other hand, once captured and cleared, Cherbourg would be a major asset to the Allied logistic infrastructure. Again, the fall of such a strongly fortified and garrisoned port would be bound to damage the morale of the German Army.

Once the Cotentin and Cherbourg were clear, Bradley could choose a suitable place for a breakout to the south. He was intent upon breaking through the German defenders, and conducting a war of maneuver deep in their rear. Pushing back the enemy was bound to be a slow process, and costly in casualties. Bradley wanted a swift, decisive operation to minimize casualties. But it was not easy to pick a good axis for the breakout attack. In the far west of the American sector there were desolate moorlands strewn with rocks, bad going for armor and affording little cover for infantry. Inland of the moors were extensive marshlands, extended by German hydraulic engineers, crossed by long straight causeways, too deep for wading and too shallow and reedy for boats to cross. Beyond the marshes lay the bocage country, hills and deep, narrow streams, the hills one-third woodland and orchard, the rest a patchwork of tiny fields surrounded by hedgerows. In the extreme east of the American sector lay the great Forêt de Cerisy, dense woodland traversed by a few roads and rides which would canalize any large-scale movement.

The key ground to the south of the US First Army was the town of St. Lô, which had been scheduled for capture by June 12. St. Lô was at the center of the major road network in west Normandy, and commanded crossings of the Vire, the most important river in the American sector. The town had been flattened by incessant bombing between June 6 and 12, but remained in German hands. As Bradley was deciding to take Cherbourg before moving south, the German command concluded that St. Lô was more important than the Cotentin. Accordingly, the German plan was to hold St. Lô, not only to retain a center of communication, but also to test the morale and resolution of the American Army and if possible to break its spirit.

Bradley knew that the capture of St. Lô would cost his army bitter fighting and heavy casualties and was reluctant to attack the town directly. But the logic of geography was inexorable. Having attempted to push his troops across the marshes to the west of the Vire, and probed the moorlands beyond, Bradley was eventually driven to the conclusion that there could be no breakout until St. Lô was taken. Thus, just as in the British sector the vital operations were centered on Caen, in the US sector the most important and vicious battle was fought for St. Lô. Once St. Lô fell, on July 18, the way was clear for operation *Cobra* – the decisive breakout attack.

■ Operation *Perch*

The first major British offensive began on June 10. The plan for Operation *Perch* was to make a wide outflanking maneuver to the west of Caen, crossing the River Odon to seize high ground near Evrécy. The XXX Corps was to employ the 50th Division to break defensive positions held by Panzer Lehr in the area of Tilly sur Seulles, Juvigny, Hottot and la Senaudière. Once the way was clear, 7th Armoured Division was to drive through to Evrécy, taking Villers-Bocage on the way. Montgomery arranged for Allied tactical aircraft to provide reconnaissance. The initial attack by 50th Division was also supported by the fire of two cruisers and a battleship.

Despite the lavish support, the attack by 50th Division made little progress. This was due in part to the inherent difficulty of movement through the bocage. But it was also because of the sheer quality of the enemy, the élite Panzer Lehr Division, which was effectively supported by the 12th SS Panzer Division (Hitler Youth) from the east. On June 10 the Germans launched their own preemptive attacks on the forward positions of 50th Division. On the left side of 50th Division, the 8th Durham Light Infantry (DLI), newly in possession of the village of St. Pierre, next to Tilly, were vigorously attacked. From across the River Seulles they were subjected to heavy artillery and mortar bombardment by Panzer Lehr. From the east the 12th SS sent tanks to shell the village, and infantry to infiltrate through the orchards and gardens. These infiltration teams established machine gun posts to pour concentrated fire onto the Durhams. The 24th Lancers were deployed on Point 103, north of St. Pierre, to support the Durhams. But neither they nor the Sherwood Rangers who relieved them for the night of June 10/11 could move forward because the slope south of the hill was covered by the fire of Panzer Lehr's heavy tanks and self-propelled guns, dug in on higher ground west of the Seulles.

The Germans made four strong attacks on St. Pierre and Point 103 on June 11. The most violent occurred in the evening, described by an officer of the 24th Lancers:

"...a number of Tigers penetrated our positions, up to Brigade HQ. Six of our tanks were knocked out in as many seconds. We withdrew to the west of the hill. Hidden in the trees we sighted our guns onto the advancing monster Tigers and Panthers. The Shermans shook with the recoil of their guns. Most of our armour piercing shells were bouncing harmlessly off the enemy … the few remaining tanks were called up, those that mounted the new enormous 17 pounder … An ear-splitting crack, a vivid flash – and whoosh – the leading Tiger stopped, smoked, and then burst into flames. The others began to withdraw. Meanwhile the German infantry were working their way up the left flank of the hill. I could hear the bullets pattering on the outside of my tank. The infantry could hardly lift their heads. The firing became intense… we held. Slowly darkness fell. The enemy withdrew."

Next morning the HQ Squadron of 24th Lancers discovered a whole company of Panzer Grenadiers, lavishly equipped with close-range anti-tank weapons, who had infiltrated into their midst during the night.

On June 12 the enemy attacks abated. The 8th DLI were withdrawn from St. Pierre, having been reduced to half their effective strength.

Further west, 231st Brigade attempted to push south towards Hottot and Longraye, but were held up in the hedgerows. The German defenders had prepared successive defensive positions, and supported them with mobile counterattack groups of armor and infantry. They employed mines and antitank weapons to separate tanks from infantry, and snipers to kill leaders at all levels. The British attackers found it difficult to counter these tactics, and to coordinate their artillery and air support in the close country.

On June 12, the XXX Corps commander, Gen. Bucknall, decided that he must change the plan. Whilst the 50th Division continued to attack to hold Panzer Lehr, the 7th Armoured Division would move further west. Here they would advance through positions held by the German 352nd Division, which had been heavily engaged for six days and was showing signs of demoralization. During the afternoon of June 12, the 22nd Armoured Brigade, followed up by 131st Motorized Infantry Brigade, moved round the western flank of Panzer Lehr, skirting the inter-army boundary beyond which the US V Corps was advancing on Caumont. Enemy resistance was light, and early on the morning of June 13, the 7th Division's leading elements passed through Villers-Bocage unopposed. At Point 103, on the road to Caen, A Squadron of the County of London Yeomary (CLY) and A Company of the 1st Rifle Brigade halted. As the sentries were being deployed, the column was attacked by a detachment of German tanks led by SS-Hauptsturmführer Michael Wittmann, who had driven west from Baron-sur-Odon in search of action. Wittmann's approach had been masked by the bulge of the ridge, and the noise of his tanks' engines muffled by the trees and drowned by the sounds of CLY's own vehicles so he achieved complete surprise. The first round from the 88mm gun on his Tiger destroyed the leading vehicle in the British column, so immobilizing the tanks and halftracks stretching behind it into Villers-Bocage. As his accompanying four Mark IV Panzers engaged the head of the column, Wittmann motored along it, putting a shell into each vehicle as he passed. Wittmann drove through the town, then returned to attack the confused British troops in it again. On his third pass through the town centre, a Sherman Firefly waiting in ambush, using a shop window opposite the square as a mirror, knocked out the Tiger with a hit on the engine. Wittmann and his crew fled on foot, pistols in hand, and got clean away.

Meanwhile, German tanks and infantry began to arrive in small detachments, and attempted to break into Villers-Bocage from the south. By late afternoon the Germans were making well-coordinated attacks with infantry and artillery, and the 22nd Armoured Brigade moved back westwards to occupy a position just east of Amaye-sur-Seulles. Here the brigade set up a box position. This position withstood a series of German attacks: noisy attacks made by armor and infantry with substantial support from mortars and artillery, and silent infiltration by infantry. Meanwhile, the 7th Armoured Division HQ ordered the 131st Brigade to keep open the line of communication to 22nd Armoured Brigade, and hoped that 50th Division could advance to reach the box. However, the corps commander decided that 7th Armoured Division was vulnerable to isolation, and ordered it to withdraw. During the night of June 14/15, with massive support from the corps artillery, 7th Armoured Division withdrew to positions in conformity with the 50th Division's front line. The 2nd Panzer Division attempted a pursuit, but was severely checked by the 7th Division's rearguard. The operation had not reached its objectives, indeed 50th Division did not secure Hottot until June 19, and Villers-Bocage was not taken until early August. However, German plans to insert 2nd Panzer Division along the inter-army boundary had been frustrated.

■ Operation *Epsom*

The next major British offensive, *Epsom*, was carried out by VIII Corps, which was forming up in Normandy. The assembly of the corps, and the offensive, were delayed by the storm of June 19–22. The attack began on June 26. The plan for Epsom had two phases. For Phase I the objectives were Hills 112 and 113 near Evrécy, as in Operation *Perch*. Once this high ground had been taken it was to be the base for Phase II, an advance eastwards across the Orne, to seize key ground south of Caen, so threatening that city with encirclement. The axis of advance for Phase I was east of Tilly-sur-Seulles, and ran across the front held by 3rd Canadian Division, part of I Corps. To the immediate west of the VIII Corps' avenue of attack was the Rauray Spur, a ridge of high ground which dominated ground to the east and south, and covered the road running from Villers-Bocage to Caen. The 49th Division, part of XXX Corps, was ordered to take this feature on June 25. On the other flank, 3rd Canadian Division was to continue its attempts to take the aerodrome at Carpiquet. Before the ground troops moved forward, German positions south of the start line were to be attacked by a mass of strategic bombers. Tactical aircraft based in the theater were to cover the flanks of the VIII Corps sector, and interdict enemy forces moving into the area. Phase I was to commence with a massive artillery barrage fired by 552 field, 112 medium, 48 heavy and 24 heavy anti-aircraft guns drawn from all three corps and Army Troops. The Navy would provide additional support from three cruisers and a monitor. The 15th Scottish Division was to lead the attack for Phase I, with two brigades forward, following a creeping barrage, supported by Churchill tanks of the 31st Tank Brigade. Once the 15th Division had cleared the bottleneck at the village of Cheux, provided all was going well the 11th Armoured Division was to advance through 15th Division on two axes, seize bridges over the Odon, and go on to take Hills 112 and 113. The 43rd Division would consolidate the captured ground whilst 15th Division moved up to support the armored division. If the 15th Division was held up, then 11th Armoured would be held back until an opportunity for exploitation was perceived. The 4th Armoured Brigade was attached to the corps for use as a mobile reserve.

In the event, the enemy and the weather combined to disrupt the plan for *Epsom*. The Germans were acutely aware of the importance of the Rauray Spur, and determined to hold it. The attack by the 49th Division on June 25, made with two brigades forward and an armored brigade in support, was repulsed. The village of Rauray was eventually taken late on June 27, but the Germans continued to contest control of the village and Spur with repeated counterattacks. This meant that throughout *Epsom*, the right flank of the VIII Corps' axis of advance was insecure, and the road from Villers-Bocage via Noyers-Bocage was open for Panzer counterattacks. On the morning of June 26 the weather in England was too bad for the strategic bombers to fly, so they could not bomb ahead of the start line as planned.

The weather in Normandy was wet, but this did not prevent the artillery from preparing the way for the infantry; 240 field guns and 80 medium guns fired a creeping barrage from the start line just south of Bretteville-l'Orgueilleuse and Brouay, whilst the other guns did counter-battery shoots or put concentrations on the flanks and targets in depth. This effort employed the largest concentration of guns used so far on the Allied front. Behind the barrage the infantry advanced, the 46th Brigade, with two battalions leading, heading for Cheux, and the 44th Brigade in similar formation moving on St. Manvieu. They were closely accompanied by Churchill tanks. The ground ahead was held by the Engineer Battalion of 12th SS Panzer.

Initially, the Scots advanced briskly. The Hitler Youth soldiers deployed in the cornfields had been stunned and driven deep into their rifle pits by the bombardment; when they raised their heads they were assailed by furious Scotsmen yelling and hurling grenades. But around le Mesnil-Patry an anti-tank minefield stopped the Churchills accompanying the 46th Brigade, leaving the infantry to press on alone. The going was heavy due to the rain, and south of the River Mue, the infantry fell behind their creeping barrage. The Hitler Youth sappers had thoroughly prepared Cheux and St. Manvieu for defense; the villages had been loop-holed, mined and garnished with booby-traps. By the time the British assaults began, the German defenders had recovered from the effects of the barrage. The 44th Brigade took St. Manvieu by noon, but were then mortared and shelled continuously, except during two counterattacks made from the east by 12th SS Panzer and 21st Panzer in the afternoon. The 46th Brigade had to clear Cheux by close-quarter fighting house to house, in which the 2nd Glasgow Highlanders lost 12 officers and 200 soldiers. It proved impossible to drive the Germans out of le Haut-du-Bosq, a straggling settlement southwest of Cheux, running up the rising ground towards Rauray. The Germans on the Rauray Spur and in le Haut-du-Bosq supported each other very effectively. The official history of the VIII Corps remarked of the situation on the afternoon of June 26 "The wooded areas from the southern slopes of le Haut-du-Bosq to the west and southwest were unsubdued and filled with small parties of infantry, supported by tanks, often dug in, and anti-tank guns which, through their effective concealment and rapid changes of position, gave much trouble."

In the early afternoon the Northamptonshire Yeomanry, reconnoitering for 11th Armoured Division, struggled through the ruins of Cheux. Just south of the village they were attacked by infantry with sticky bombs. On reaching the Ruisseau de Sabley they were fired on by anti-tank guns directly to the south. The 29th Armoured Brigade moved southwards through Cheux with difficulty, but did not attempt to rush the Odon bridges.

On the evening of June 26, the 227th Brigade, the third brigade of the 15th Division, moved forward, but was stopped on the Ruisseau de Sabley. During the night the 43rd Division relieved the 44th and 46th Brigades, which prepared to resume the attack next day. On the morning of June 27 all attempts to move down the western axis to take the bridges at Gavrus were stopped. Indeed, in the morning a German armored force fought its way up the road covered by the Rauray Spur and got into Cheux for an hour. But on the eastern flank the British made progress. German attempts to concentrate forces for counterattacks attracted attacks by RAF 83 Group Typhoons, which broke them up. The 227th Brigade forced its way, in column of battalions, down the road through Colleville and Tourville to seize the bridge at Tourmauville. The battalions of the brigade dug-in and held the road. This was uncomfortable, and dangerous, for the enemy held higher ground south of the Odon in its steep wooded valley. The road, now known as "Scotch Corridor," was fired upon by nebelwerfers, mortars, artillery and anti-tank guns. The soldiers could do nothing but simply had to sit in their foxholes and endure the bombardment. Despite the shelling, 29th Armoured Brigade raced down the road, across the Tourmauville bridge, and on to Hill 112.

Later in the day the 159th Brigade, the motorized infantry of 11th Armoured Division, moved up to form a defensive perimeter around the bridge. This relieved the 2nd Argyll and Sutherland Highlanders, who went off on an adventure of their own. In the late afternoon patrols sent westwards along the banks of the Odon discovered that the bridges at Gavrus were undefended; the Germans had created a strong position on the road to the north. The whole battalion moved to secure the bridges. This was a difficult move; according to Maj. McElwee, a veteran of the action, it was "a nightmare trek through the thick woods lining both banks of the Odon. All-round defence in such country was impossible. The going was vile, and at one place the whole march was held up for over an hour while the anti-tank guns were man-handled over a sticky patch. Any well-planned ambush might have proved fatal." Once at Gavrus the Argylls deployed, and waited for the road north to be opened, but it never was. Instead the battalion was isolated by persistent attacks. Attempts by the 15th Division to force the road through the German positions at le Valtru failed. Indeed, this was the area of the strongest and most frequent German counterattacks. Eventually the battalion withdrew on the night of July 1–2, having been cut off for four days.

Meanwhile, 11th Armoured Division had made the most of the eastern axis. On June 28, the 29th Armoured Brigade, reinforced by 44th Royal Tank Regiment, had cleared and secured the crown of Hill 112. Next day the Germans were driven from their positions on the south slopes of the hill. The 29th Armoured Brigade enjoyed excellent views across the valley of the Orne to the rolling downlands south of Caen.

However, Gen. O'Connor, the commander of VIII Corps, was concerned. The enemy continued active resistance on the western side of his axis. The wooded Odon valley was vulnerable to infiltration by infantry. Scotch Corridor, the only line of communication to Hill 112, was subject to enemy observation and under heavy fire. There was intelligence that the II SS Panzer Corps was moving into the area to deliver a counterstroke. Accordingly, on June 28, O'Connor ordered that there was to be no further advance until the area between Cheux and the Odon had been thoroughly mopped up. On June 29 the Germans showed their strength by preparing five counterattacks. A column of three battalions mixed with armor attacked up the road from Noyers-Bocage and broke into Cheux; an infantry assault pushed eastwards into Grainville; there was a push on Gavrus which forced the Argylls out of the village; 29th Armoured Brigade was forced back up the south slope of Hill 112 and a force of 40 tanks moved westward from Caen. These attacks were all greatly disrupted by British artillery and tactical air power. The Panzers motoring out from Caen were caught in the open near Carpiquet by Typhoons and dispersed. The other attacks were crushed by massive artillery bombardments. The Germans made no serious attacks on June 30, but on July 1 attempted to push along four axes, from east and west, simultaneously. Once again, the artillery broke up these attacks before they could make an effective impact. The sheer volume of high explosive demoralized the German soldiers; the commander of 2nd Panzer Division, von Luttwitz, remarked: "The incredibly heavy artillery and mortar fire of the enemy is something new both for the seasoned veterans of the Eastern Front and new arrivals."

But the German counterattacks on June 29 had been effective, for they persuaded O'Connor that he could not proceed to Phase II of *Epsom*, and should withdraw 29th Armoured Brigade from Hill 112. The 29th Armoured Brigade felt disappointed, but, as Gen. Roberts, the divisional commander, observed, they were "…. out on a limb". The brigade evacuated Hill 112 on the night of June 29. The VIII Corps was reinforced by 53rd Division and 32nd Guards Brigade, and consolidated its gains. *Epsom* had gained about six miles (9.6km) and inflicted serious damage on the enemy, especially during the repeated and unsuccessful counterattacks made by the Panzer formations. Apart from 12th SS Panzer, these included Panzer Lehr, 2nd Panzer, 21st Panzer, 1st SS Panzer, 9th SS Panzer and 10th SS Panzer. All the divisions could have been employed more effectively in the offensive role had they not been drawn to contain the Odon bridgehead. In fact, *Epsom* had forced Rommel to commit his entire strategic reserve in Normandy, and convinced him that the German Seventh Army should make a fighting withdrawal to the Seine. But Hitler absolutely forbade any withdrawal; he argued that in the face of Allied superiority in airpower and artillery the only sensible policy was to dig in deep and defend every inch of ground.

■ Operations *Charnwood* and *Goodwood*

Having failed to take Caen on D-Day, and made two fruitless attempts to compromise the garrison of the city by flanking maneuvers, Montgomery decided that the British Second Army must storm it. He had considered an offensive operation from east of the Odon, but ruled it out because the bridgehead was small, congested with troops, and overlooked by the enemy from three sides. However, there was no doubt the Germans would exact a very high price for Caen. On July 4, the Canadian 3rd Division attacked and took the village of Carpiquet, but were repulsed from the airfield by 12th SS Panzer. The main attack on Caen, Operation *Charnwood*, was made on July 8. The I Corps deployed the 3rd Canadian Division to the west, British 59th Division in the center and the British 3rd Division on the east. In order to overawe the enemy and hearten the attacking troops, Bomber Command devastated the city in a massive raid on the evening of July 7. But the Germans had located most of their defensive positions so close to the British front line that the bombs missed them. In fact, the physical effects of the bombing made the task of clearing Caen much more difficult for I Corps. However, they fought through the German defenses and cleared the city up to the Orne. The Germans, however, retained the industrial quarters east of the river.

Ten days later, Second Army launched Operation *Goodwood*, the last great British attack before the breakout in the west. By mid-July Montgomery was under political pressure to do something decisive, or at least spectacular, to appease the press and public opinion. The success of the landings on June 6 had created a euphoria and expectation of easy victory which had been disappointed. Montgomery's critics at SHAEF, in particular Air Marshal Tedder, claimed that the Allied breakout had been delayed because Montgomery was too cautious. This pressure made Montgomery apprehensive. He was also aware that in the American sector Bradley was having difficulty; his plan to advance down the west side of the Cotentin to Coutances had stalled, and progress towards St. Lô was slow and costly The Germans had reinforced Seventh Army with infantry, and were planning to create a mobile armored reserve with which to make a major countermove in the US sector. But it was difficult to decide where to attack; *Perch* and *Epsom* had tested the possible avenues west of Caen; the city itself was still choked with rubble and partly held by the enemy. Only the Orne bridgehead remained, and this was the area through which *Goodwood* was launched, despite its inherent disadvantages. Chief amongst these was the constricted and crowded nature of the bridgehead; this meant that only one armored brigade of the main attacking force could be assembled there before the offensive began; it also meant that there was no room to deploy extra field artillery behind the start line, so the fire support provided by 25-pounder field guns could cover only the first few miles of the advance from positions west of the Orne. These considerations did not deter Dempsey, commander of the Second Army, who believed that the German army in Normandy had been so worn down by attrition that it was no longer capable of effective resistance. According to his intelligence, the enemy facing I Corps east of the Orne consisted of the 346th Infantry Division, 16th Luftwaffe Field Division and 21st Panzer, all seriously depleted and exhausted, deployed in a defensive position four miles (6km) deep. In fact, Rommel had realised that the open rolling country between the Orne and the Bois de Bavent ridge to the east was good going for tanks, and had taken measures to defend it. The German defenses were actually eight miles (12km) deep, and very well designed.

The forward posts were held by the 16th Luftwaffe Field Division and 346th Infantry Division; behind them, on the slopes of the Bourguébus Ridge was a network of stone-built villages, each held by antitank guns protected by infantry, and with overlapping arcs of fire, under the 21st Panzer Division; along the crest of the Ridge were 78 88mm guns of the II Flak Corps; on the reverse slope of the Ridge three counterattack groups were in waiting, each of some 40 tanks and a battalion of Panzer Grenadiers. The general artillery reserve of guns, mortars and nebelwerfers was concealed in the woods of Garcelles-Secqueville, also on the reverse slope. On the eastern flank, around Emiéville, a detachment of Tigers lurked amongst the copses and manor houses, with excellent views across the open fields towards Caen. In Colombelles, the Germans had observation posts on the chimneys of the steelworks which gave a panorama of the whole area. The 1st and 12th SS Panzer Divisions were ready to reinforce this area if necessary.

The Second Army plan drawn by Dempsey envisaged a massive air raid by 2,000 aircraft to destroy all enemy positions ahead of the start line, then a rolling barrage to work over the first four miles (6km) of the advance. The main attack, from between Ste. Honorine-la-Chardonnerette and Escoville, was to be made by VIII Corps. For *Goodwood,* VIII Corps consisted of 11th Armoured Division, Guards Armoured Division, and 7th Armoured Division, advancing in echelon in that order. The 29th Armoured Brigade was to follow the barrage, leaving the Division's motorized infantry, 159th Brigade, to clear the villages of Demouville and Cuverville on the eastern outskirts of Caen, then race forward southwards over the Bourguébus Ridge, as far as possible towards Falaise. Guards Armoured and 7th Armoured were to follow as swiftly as possible, the armor leaving the infantry brigades behind if they could not keep up once beyond range of the 25-pounders; Typhoons were there to provide any close support required. But Dempsey believed the Germans were demoralized and on the verge of collapse, and that it might be possible to push light forces into Falaise, so cutting the line of retirement of all German forces west of the Orne. Whilst the VIII Corps was racing southwards, the II Canadian Corps was to slog through and clear the industrial suburbs of Caen, on the western flank. On the eastern side of the VIII Corps axis, 3rd Division was to advance along the Bois de Bavent Ridge, taking the villages at the foot, clearing the woods on the crown, and seize Troarn.

Montgomery considered Dempsey's plan far too optimistic, he had a much greater respect for the German defenders. He altered the plan to set VIII Corps objectives just beyond the Bourguébus Ridge; his aims were to tie down, draw, and reduce the German armor, and to expand and make safe the Orne bridgehead. Gen. Roberts, commanding the 11th Armoured Division, had doubts about the plan; he thought it was unsound to push his tanks forward without their infantry. His comments were discounted by O'Connor and Dempsey, who believed that the weight of the aerial bombardment and sheer number of tanks would overwhelm the enemy.

July 18 was a fine day, and the heavy bombers of Bomber Command arrived over the battlefield at 05:45 to attack the villages along the flanks of VIII Corps' sector. They were followed by medium bombers which carpeted the main axis with fragmentation bombs; the intention was to destroy enemy personnel and equipment without cratering the ground. The artillery fired counterbattery missions against German flak during these air raids. At 07:45 the main barrage commenced, as a third wave of aircraft attacked Troarn and Bourguébus.

The heavy bombing on the flanks was effective. Half of the Tigers in the heavy tank unit at Emiéville were knocked out, and the commander, Lt. von Rosen, recalled that under the stress of the bombardment two of his men committed suicide and one went mad. Later in the morning, soldiers of the 3rd Division moving up the eastern flank found "villages that were battered beyond description. Those Germans left conscious were far too dazed to offer any resistance." But by the time the 3rd Division's leading elements reached the outskirts of Troarn and the Caen-Troarn railway, the Germans had recovered, and mounted a stout defense. Despite strenuous efforts, the 3rd Division could not take Troarn or the hamlets around Emiéville.

In the center, the 29th Armoured Brigade advanced through the positions of the 51st Highland Division. They were delayed and disordered by having to pass through a defensive minefield laid by the 51st, but kept moving forward. Until they crossed the Caen–Troarn railway they were opposed only by snipers hiding in the corn. The 159th Motorised Infantry followed, then swung west to clear and secure Demouville and Cuverville. The 29th Armoured Brigade pushed on alone. The armored brigade of Guards Armoured Division was held up by a traffic jam on the approaches to the bridges over the Orne and Orne Canal; the Guards were on time, the leading elements of 7th Armoured Division were ahead of schedule.

The 29th Armoured Brigade was alone, with only its integral battalion of half-track infantry the 29th Armoured Brigade was alone, when it reached the Caen-Vimont railway. The 3rd Royal Tank Regiment were on the right, 2nd Fife and Forfar Yeomanry on the left, with the 23rd Hussars in reserve. As the leading regiments ascended the gentle concave slope of the Bourguébus Ridge they came under concentrated crossfire from anti-tank weapons in the villages, backed up by 88s from the crest of the Ridge.

The tanks of the 29th Armoured Brigade continued to fight, and tried to find ways forward. But they lacked the means to attack the villages, because they were short of infantry and were beyond the range of the field artillery. Their own self-propelled guns were insufficient to suppress the antitank batteries. Above, a "cab rank" of Typhoons flew, but were unable to give close support as planned. This was because the brigade had only one Forward Air Controller with them, at Brigade Tactical HQ, and, according to Gen. Roberts's memoirs, "Only minutes after the armored brigade's Tac HQ had arrived at their 'embankment' position and the RAF had first got contact with the 'cab rank', a shell scored a direct hit on the armoured car, the RAF officer was badly wounded and the armoured car was a write-off." 'When the self-propelled guns attempted to mark enemy targets with pink smoke, the enemy replied in kind. The pilots could not tell friend from foe in the confused mêlée on the Bourguébus Ridge.

Meanwhile, the Guards Armoured Division advanced into battle for the first time. The tanks were delayed by the 51st Division's minefield, and found the Germans recovered from the successive shocks of the bombing and the artillery barrage. Gen. Adair, commanding the division, recalled in his memoirs, "… my tank had two near-misses from a bazooka team lying in a cornfield." Ahead of the general, the 2nd Grenadier Guards led the division, but found that "Every advantage lay with the defenders; the ground haze was thickened by the dust churned up by the armour, and thick hedges and belts of tall trees limited the vision of the tank comman-ders as they peered through their fieldglasses, trying to pick out the enemy guns in the corn and root fields. Three tanks of the leading squadron were hit when they were still over a mile (1.6km) from Cagny, and as it was impossible to escape the fire by maneuvering to left or right the squadron was brought to a standstill." The Grenadiers were engaged from the front, by antitank guns in le Prieuré Farm, and from their left by the Tigers around Emiéville. As the armor of the division shifted westwards to support the 29th Armoured Brigade, Gen. Roberts gave warning that the village of Cagny was highly dangerous and strongly held. He was in error, for Cagny was occupied by only four 88s, one tank and a section of infantry, but the 88s had opened fire suddenly on the Reserve Squadron of the 23rd Hussars and done great damage, and this had impressed the general. The Guards duly took warning, and made formal attacks, with infantry support, on le Prieuré and Cagny.

The fighting on the Bourguébus Ridge continued. On two occasions troops of Shermans managed to reach the crest, using the smoke of burning tanks to cover their movement; but each time they were pushed back by an enemy counterattack group. Late in the morning, the commander of 22nd Armoured Brigade (of 7th Armoured Division) arrive on a recce, and according to Roberts, said: "There are too many bloody tanks here already, I'm not going to bring my tanks down yet." In his view, O'Connor's scheme to rush the enemy defenses with a mass of armor had simply provided the German antitank gunners with a big juicy target. When the 2nd Irish Guards arrived northwest of Cagny they observed, "...a confused mass of tanks shooting in all directions ... the little rises in the ground and occasional hedges, combined with the standing corn, gave excellent cover from which the Tigers and Panthers could shoot up the steady stream of Shermans as they came across open country."

The Guards cleared Cagny and its outposts in the afternoon, and tried to press on southeastwards along the railway to Vimont. But they made little progress, because the Germans had posted tanks and antitank guns protected by infantry in the hedgerows on the rising ground from Emiéville to Frénouville. The approaches to this belt of dense cover were open, and in places the ground was soft. As the Guards closed with the enemy, according to the history of the Irish Guards, the attack lost cohesion, "... dissolved into isolated games of hide and seek among the corn stacks and hedges..." As the day wore on, "In the failing light the tanks were on top of each other before they fired." After nightfall the exhausted tank regiments fell back and went into laager. Infantry came up to consolidate the captured ground, and to mop up pockets of resistance in the rear. Some went forward to explore the enemy positions, and came to close quarters.

By the end of the fighting on July 18, VIII Corps had lost about 220 of the 700 tanks committed to the attack. The Germans had lost some

120 of the 240 tanks they had put into the battle. The corps had gained approximately six miles (9km) of ground. On the western flank the Canadians had fought a bitter battle to annihilate the German defenders of Colombelles and Vaucelles, Caen was now completely in Allied hands.

On July 19, the Guards Armoured, 11th and 7th Armoured Divisions mounted a series of attacks on the villages, along the Bourguébus Ridge, using coordinated groups of tanks, infantry, engineers and artillery. These set-piece attacks succeeded in taking villages from the Panzer Grenadiers of the 1st SS Panzer Division. But the Germans were already rolling back to form a new system of defense in depth on the next suitable ridge to the south. Late on 19th the weather broke and rain stopped play; tanks were bogged in the mire, the infantry were stuck, artillery suffered from reduced visibility. So the battle of *Goodwood* ended.

■ The American Sector

Until the end of June, whilst the British Second Army was concentrating its attention on Caen, the US First Army was occupied in securing the link between the *Utah* and *Omaha* beachheads, clearing the Cotentin, and capturing Cherbourg. In order to connect the two beachheads it was essential to capture and secure Carentan. This was difficult, because the approaches to the town were cut by numerous water obstacles, which were crossed by causeways and bridges. The Germans had demolished bridges and zeroed their artillery and mortars on the causeways. Between the causeways were marshes, within which islands of higher ground were covered with bocage.

The use of armor was extremely hazardous, as German 88s in the town could reach out over the marshes 2,000 yds (1,800m) along the causeways. The town had to be taken by infantry using close-combat techniques, clearing defensive positions with grenade, and bayonet. The Germans delayed the progress of the infantry of the 101st Airborne and 29th Divisions by counterattacks.

Whilst the town was being closely invested, the soldiers of the US VIII and VI Corps also maneuvered to seal off the outer approaches. On June 10 the 327th Glider Infantry advancing across the Lower Douve from the west met the 29th Division's recce troops moving up from the east at Auville-sur-le-Vey.

On June 11 Gen. McAuliffe took command of Task Force F, the 501st and 506th Parachute Infantry, and 327th Glider Infantry. In accordance with his plan, Carentan was heavily bombarded during the night of June 11. Early on the 12th, Task Force F made a double pincer attack on Carentan; two battalions of the 327th advanced into the town from the northeast; battalions of the 506th moved to the southwest to forestall attempts at relief or counterattack. The outer arms of the double-pincer helped to secure Carentan, but did not meet in sufficient time to prevent the retirement of the survivors of the garrison. The Germans reacted violently. On June 12 and 13 they launched counterattacks from the southwest. The second of these was made by the 6th Parachute Regiment and elements of 17th SS Panzer Grenadier Division, and was thrown back by a counterstroke by Combat Command 'A' of the 2nd Armored Division. The US forces consolidated, and pushed outwards from Carentan; the VII and V Corps were firmly in contact. Subsequently, V Corps expanded southwards, obstructed by the extensive marshes south and east of Carentan, and held back by shortages of ammunition. VII Corps was to advance westwards and northwards, to cut off the Cotentin from the south, and to take Cherbourg. Bradley gave priority of supply to formations in the Cotentin. Despite this, the VII Corps, and also – later – the VIII Corps, had much difficulty and delay in the Cotentin. This was primarily because of the inherent difficulties of operating in the peculiar terrain. The German forces in the Cotentin were heavily outnumbered and exhausted, but knew how to use the ground to maximum advantage. They could probably have made the American advance more slow and costly had they not been subjected to detailed and irrational interference by Hitler.

On June 10 VII Corps was held by the Germans on good defensive ground to north and west. The US Army Historical Division, description of the ground to the north remarks, "The ground rises gently giving the defender commanding heights liberally criss-crossed with hedgerows. Fortifications supported the German defense in depth. A back-stop line was anchored to the coast at Quinéville, it stretched inland along a high ridge to Montebourg, and then bent southwest. It was part of VII Corps' D-Day objective, but five infantry regiments took a full week, from June 8–14, to reach and secure it."

The 4th Division had to take this line by close-quarter fighting, hedgerow by hedgerow, with artillery and air support. On the coast, infantry had to rely on cooperation with sappers to take the fortifications. Some of the batteries in the area of Quinéville were still shelling *Utah*

Beach, hindering reinforcement. But by June 14, the 4th Division was through, breaking the Germans' main defensive line in the north.

VII Corps also had difficulty moving west, across the Rivers Merderet and Douve. On June 8 the 325th Infantry had attempted an assault along the causeway at la Fière. The movement was preceded by heavy artillery preparation, and supported by direct fire from tanks. Even so, the attack was too difficult. The Historical Division recorded: "The men had been told that they were to cover the exposed, 500-yard (450m) causeway in one sprint. But the long run in the face of small arms and mortar fire proved to be too much for most only a handful made the initial dash others, who hesitated, were hit; the first casualties induced more hesitation and the causeway became congested with the dead, the wounded and the reluctant."

Next day, Bradley directed VII Corps to cut off the Cotentin. On June 10 attempts to force the Merderet at la Fière and Chef-du-Pont had limited success, because of the inherent difficulties of such assaults. However, the American pressure was relentless, and gradually the Germans were forced back from the west bank of the floodplain. But progress was still very slow; a regimental attack could take all day to push a few hundred yards. Every yard was paid for in blood; the 357th Regiment was losing an average of 150 men a day. The attacking troops had to learn to reapply the basic principles of tactics in combat, if they lived long enough to appreciate the lessons of experience.

On June 15 Gen. Collins, Commander of VII Corps, sent the 82nd Airborne and 9th Infantry Divisions into the drive west of the Merderet. At the same time, the Germans had decided to swing back on to an east–west line in order to reduce their commitments. This meant that the 82nd and 9th met only blocking parties and rearguards, The 82nd seized St. Sauveur-le-Vicomte and bridged the Douve on June 16. At once Collins saw and grasped his opportunity. He ordered the 82nd and 9th to form four regimental columns and charge down the main roads westwards to the coast, and not to worry about flank guards. The speed of this movement took the Germans by surprise; the regiments in columns reached the coast during the night of June 17/18. On the northern side of the axis, the 60th Infantry Regiment (9th Division) set up blocking positions, and intercepted columns of the German 77th Division which had been ordered to evacuate the Cotentin.

The Germans attempted no substantial counterattack: their forces were too weak. On June 15, the German LXXXIV Corps had formed two

Kampfgruppen ("battlegroups") in the Cotentin: "Hellmich," of elements of the 77th and 91st Divisions, which had been ordered to move south but was not trapped in the peninsula; and "Von Schlieben," of the remnants of the 709th and 243rd Divisions, intended to defend Cherbourg. Bradley and Collins realized that the German forces were too weak to hold a line all the way across the Cotentin. On June 16 they decided to advance north on a front of three divisions from west to east the 9th, 79th and 4th, with the 4th Cavalry Group covering the gaps with light patrol forces. The important thing was to close in on the fortress of Cherbourg quickly, to minimize the Germans' chances of reinforcing and strengthening the, defenses.

On June 19 the 4th Division used heavy artillery preparation, followed by an envelopment by armor and infantry to force the German garrison out of Montebourg, and clear the main highway to Cherbourg. Valognes was devastated by heavy air attacks, and was abandoned by the enemy. The advance north by the 4th Division was made in column of route. The 9th and 79th Divisions were impeded only by demolitions; on June 20, the Germans broke contact and moved to occupy the formidable defenses of Cherbourg. They would have done this days earlier had it not been for Hitler's insistence that every inch of ground must be defended. As it was, the line they attempted to hold before Cherbourg was too long for the 21,000 men available, being 30 miles (48km) from St. Vaast-la-Hougue to Vauville.

■ The Attack on Cherbourg

The main defenses of Cherbourg were on an arc of high ground extending four to six miles (6-9km) beyond the center of the port. A deep belt of fortifications covered all lines of approach and provided for mutual support. Anti-tank ditches and steel obstacles supplemented the streams which made natural obstacles to armor. Hedgerows were cut back to clear fields of fire. The actual works were protected by wire. In some areas they were concrete emplacements with machine gun turrets, mortar emplacements, antiaircraft casemated artillery. In other areas they were well-made entrenchments. The VII Corps closed up to the outer works on June 20, and probed the positions in the night. All the patrols were sharply repelled. But Collins was encouraged by reports from prisoners of war who said that the garrison was a motley collection of detachments, exhausted and demoralized, and that the defenders were short of ammunition. Nevertheless, when Collins called on the German commander Gen. von Schlieben to capitulate on June 21, his message was ignored.

All the US divisions attacked the defenses on June 22, but the main assaults were made by 9th and 79th Divisions from the west and southwest. At 12:40, 10 squadrons of Mustangs and Typhoons attacked the defences with bombs and gunfire. They were followed at 13:00 by 562 fighter-bombers, who unfortunately hit friendly troops as well as the enemy, because smoke marking their targets had drifted south. At 14:00, 377 medium bombers attacked 11 major strongpoints. After these air attacks, which forced German infantry into underground shelters, the American infantry, sappers and armor moved up, protected by an artillery barrage. The assault forces proceeded to methodically reduce the German fortifications; intense machine gun and antitank gunfire directed at embrasures suppressed the defenders, and allowed the sappers to move forward. Once at the concrete works, the sappers used shaped charges and bazookas to blow in the steel doors, then hurled in phosphorus grenades and pole-charges until the Germans were finished.

Next day (June 23) the Germans attempted counterattacks, and some in by-passed strongpoints continued active resistance. But they were too weak to stop the progress of VII Corps. As the American forces, learning on the job, improved the coordination of their tactical aircraft, artillery and infantry, the enemy was forced to yield ground. By the end of the 23rd, the 9th Division had seized the key ground of the Bois du Mont Roc southwest of the port. The advance was maintained from the east as well. On the 24th, the 3/12 Battalion from 4th Division attacked a position near Digosville as described in the Historical Division account: "Scouts came within 200 yards (180m) of the German emplacements before machine guns opened fire on them. The four tanks deployed, returned the fire and then overran the first gun positions. The tanks provided a base of fire with both 75mm guns and machineguns, and the platoons worked forward. Twelve P-47s dive-bombed and strafed the German positions, and, as soon as the last bombs fell, tanks and infantry closed in rapidly and destroyed the enemy in a short, sharp fight." On the same day, the German commander of Cherbourg, von Schlieben, complained to Seventh Army HQ that his forces were being crushed by the American artillery. The fire reached a crescendo on June 25, when the US Navy gave extra support from three battleships and four cruisers. With this support the VII Corps broke through into the town. The Germans systematically wrecked the port installations; strong fortifications like the Fort du Roule and the Arsenal were still resisting on June 26, but the Americans were in the town and German activity was uncoordinated. Gen. von Schlieben was discovered in a bunker at St. Sauveur, and surrendered. Some 10,000 German troops became prisoners of war. The Arsenal was persuaded to capitulate by a loudspeaker unit on June 27, and by the 29th the outlying forts of the harbor had been forced to submit.

The fall of Cherbourg had a depressing effect on the morale of the German Army in Normandy. A great port, very strongly fortified, had surrendered, against the express orders of the Führer. The Americans felt euphoria and relief. Bradley could now turn his full attention to organizing the breakout operation.

THE BREAKOUT

In the US sector, while VII Corps advanced to Cherbourg, VIII Corps faced south and struggled towards the northern edge of the Carentan marshes. East of the marshes, the XIX and V Corps made a slow advance south. After the storm of June 19/22 these formations were severely rationed in their use of ammunition, and could not make progress. The Germans, principally the II Parachute Corps under the resourceful Gen. Meindl, made good use of the respite to survey the ground and prepare positions. Meindl's men complained bitterly that all their time was spent digging,

By June 21 Bradley was considering plans for a breakout. He regarded a penetration and mobile exploitation essential, because, as he wrote in his memoirs, "As long as the enemy confined us to the bocage ... where we were forced to match him man for man, he could exact a prohibitive price for the few miserable yards we might gain." The essential thing was to find an area which gave sufficient room for the deployment of large-scale mobile forces. What Bradley wanted to do was find a weak place in the enemy line, concentrate sufficient force to break a hole in the line, then send mobile forces through it to exploit. These requirements entailed getting control of a line of departure south of the Carentan marshes, and finding a system of parallel roads sufficient to support the movement and

154

supply of several divisions of mechanized troops. Bradley's analysis of the terrain led him to select the St. Lô–Coutances road as the ideal line of departure. From that straight highway, two adequate roads ran parallel along elevated ground to the southwest. A few miles south of the line of departure, beyond Marigny and St. Gilles, the whole country tilted so as to give the advantage to an army approaching from the north, and the bocage gave way to more open country.

■ Attacking the St. Lô–Coutances road

The immediate grand tactical question was how to secure control of the St. Lô–Coutances road. Bradley wanted to avoid a direct attack on St. Lô, because it was so strongly held. An advance across the Carentan marshes was uninviting; the use a skillful defender could make of such ground had been demonstrated in the Cotentin. Initially, the moorlands, hills and woods of Normandy's far west seemed an avenue of attack. Accordingly, early in July, Bradley's plan was for V and XIX Corps to hold, whilst VII crossed the marshes and VIII advanced down the west coast. However, the ground, weather, and enemy defeated this plan. Wet weather not only spread the marshes, but made all movement difficult. The VII Corps managed to cross the Vire and numerous other water obstacles and advance southwards, but much more slowly than anticipated. Attempts to boost the advance by pushing the 3rd Armored Division through the 30th Division (of XIX Corps) immediately west of the Vire led to congestion and confusion. The Germans responded to the advance west of the Vire by counterattacking on July 9, with the 17th SS Panzer Grenadier and 2nd SS Panzer Division. On the 11th, they mounted a major counterattack by the Panzer Lehr Division, newly arrived from south of Bayeux. These German attacks ran into exactly the same difficulties of movement, communication, and coordination as the American assaults had, and did not have the desired effect. But they did limit the VII Corps advance, so that by July 17 the forward elements were just by Pont-Hébert, still over 3 miles (6km) from the St. Lô–Coutances road.

Further west VIII Corps also ran into difficulty. The Mont Castre hills, thickly wooded and stoutly defended, could not be penetrated quickly. The advance was slow; by July 14 the corps had gained 12,000 yards (13km) in 12 days, and at a very high cost in life; in the fighting from July 3/10 the 90th Division had taken 5,000 casualties.

By July 10 Bradley had changed his mind, and decided he must grasp the nettle and attack St. Lô. This was partly because VIII and VII Corps were not moving as fast as he had hoped, and also because there was political pressure on him to get on. But it was also due to the realization that he would need the road-net east of the Vire to sustain an advance southwest from his favored line of departure, and St. Lô was the center of that system.

The immediate question for the US First Army was, how to take St. Lô? The enemy in the area consisted of the II Parachute Corps. In the east stood the 3rd Parachute Division, consisting of two strong regiments of parachute infantry (Fallschirmjäger) – élite troops of great skill and determination. To the west of them were Kampfgruppen ("battle groups") of the 353rd, 352nd, and 266th Divisions. In support were the 12th Assault Gun Brigade, a nebelwerfer battalion, two batteries of 88s, plus 105mm and 150mm howitzers, and many heavy mortars. There were very few German soldiers in St. Lô itself, which lies in a depression; the defense of the town was based on the hills to the north and east. The II Parachute Corps could not man a continuous line of defense. Instead they occupied a number of intervisible mutually-supporting strongpoints covering all the approaches to the town. These strongpoints were not always on the higher ground, but were capable of denying such ground to the enemy by use of fire. Such posts were effective and unobtrusive, and extremely difficult for aircraft or artillery spotters to locate. Facing these positions stood the American V and XIX Corps. The 2nd Division of V Corps was on the eastern flank, opposite Hill 192, mistakenly believed to be the highest point in the area. To the west of 2nd Division was the 29th Division.

Gen. Gerhardt, commander of the 29th Division, believed that the key ground was Hill 122, which looms directly to the north of St. Lô, surmounted by the Church of St Georges de Montcoq. But Hill 122 was very strongly held and protected by a strong hedgerow position to the north at le Carillon, and a hilltop strongpoint at le Cauchais to the east. Therefore it would be advantageous to evade an assault on Hill 122, and to make an indirect approach by moving from east to west along the Martinville Ridge. According to Gerhardt, such a maneuver would threaten the line of retreat from Hill 122 and make it untenable. However, an attack on the Martinville Ridge could not succeed whilst Hill 122, to the east, remained in enemy hands. Gen. Corlett, commanding XIX Corps, agreed with Gerhardt's analysis. Accordingly, on July 11 the 2nd Division attacked Hill 192, and 29th Division advanced up onto the Martinville Ridge. Hill 192 had been attacked in regimental strength on July 16 and 19, but was still in enemy hands. The feature was a sugarloaf promontory about 150 feet (45m) higher than its surroundings. Lt-Col. Little recalled: "The Germans had built a tower in the trees on its summit, and from this tower on a clear day, one could see the shipping off *Omaha* Beach, 20 odd miles (32km) to the north." The hill was held by two parachute battalions, who had done much to develop its defensive possibilities: according to the history of the 2nd Division: "The base of Hill 192 was zeroed-in by the Germans at every gap in the hedgerows. In dugouts tunneled under them a handful of men with machine guns could hold off a regiment simply by crossing each field with deadly close-range fire. They cut boxed-in apertures in the hedgerows at ground level through which their 88s and machine guns could sweep the fields, while remaining unobserved." The use of prepared hedgerows in an elastic system of defense in depth was reinforced by the construction of strongpoints in the four hamlets of Cloville, le Soulaire, St. Georges-d'Elle and la Croix-Rouge. The parachutists were very aggressive in defense, patrolling and raiding vigorously, especially at night. American reconnaissance patrols found it difficult to explore the German positions. The men of the 2nd Division felt dominated by the hill and the strong German defenses on it; one man remarked; "Every time I clean my teeth I feel some German is looking down my throat."

■ Hill 192

It was obvious that it would take a special effort to take Hill 192, and V Corps made the effort. The artillery support was exceptional. Besides the four battalions of 105mm howitzers from the division, corps provided two battalions of 155mm and two of self-propelled armored 105s and a company of chemical mortars. There was no limit on the expenditure of shells. The air force was to send four groups of P-47s, each 40 strong, to bomb and strafe the southern side of the hill once the attack had started. The artillery preparation began at 05:00 on July 11. For 50 minutes the medium guns fired on German batteries, command posts, reserve areas and field kitchens whilst the field guns bombarded all known mortar and machine gun posts in the first three hedgerows. From 05:50 until 06:00 all the artillery, and all infantry support weapons in the area, hit the first hedgerow. The medium guns fired shells with impact fuses, to collapse dugouts, the 105s fired air bursts to catch personnel in the open. Promptly at 06:00, the field guns commenced a rolling barrage, moving 100 yards (90m) forward every four minutes. Behind the barrage advanced three battalions of infantry, from the 38th and 23rd Regiments, closely supported by four companies of tanks. Each leading battalion could advance, halt, or reverse the barrage. The medium guns dealt with German artillery, as spotted by air observation posts. The barrage did not destroy the German positions, but did suppress the paratroopers, and screened the American infantry. The village strong points were demolished by direct fire from the tanks and self-propelled 105s. When the enemy retired to tunnel systems, sappers threw in explosive charges, and bulldozed five feet (1.5m) of earth over the entrances. The attack was a complete success, and the enemy proved unable to mount effective counterattacks. However, on arriving on top of the hill the Americans discovered that Hill 101, to the south, surmounted by St. Jean des Baisants, was even higher.

To the west of the 2nd Division, the 116th and 115th Infantry of the 29th Division were due to attack the Martinville Ridge at 05:00 on July 11. But their attack was delayed by enemy action against the 115th. The history of the 115th in World War II remarks that from 22:00 on July 10, German mortars and artillery fired on the regiment and: "For the men crouching in their foxholes this was the heaviest artillery barrage experienced in combat". At about midnight on July 10/11, the fire concentrated on the 1st Battalion of the 115th (1/115) then, "under cover of the barrage a reinforced company of infantry infiltrated through the center and right. As the artillery lifted, the Germans charged upon the dazed men who were in their holes. Flamethrowers and flares lit up the scene and the Germans took advantage of the opportunity to smash through Company A ... cut the company into small isolated groups who resisted with rifle butts, bayonets, hand grenades, and anything else that could be found." The Germans withdrew at dawn, leaving 87 of their men behind; the 1/115 had suffered 150 casualties. The attack on the Martinville Ridge was delayed until late morning, and made very little progress.

To the east, the 116th Infantry had attacked adjacent to the 2nd Division area, at 06:00, in column of battalions up the ridge and then westwards along it, gaining some 3,000 yards (2,700m). The 175th, the third infantry regiment of the 29th Division, moved up east of the 116th, to exploit down the southern slope of the Martinville Ridge, and establish firm contact with the 2nd Division.

On July 12/13 the 29th Division attempted to advance south and west. On the southern slopes of the Martinville Ridge, the 175th was stopped by fire from Hill 101 Ridge, directly south. The 116th made some progress westwards along the Martinville Ridge, but was stopped on the 13th. The 115th closed up to the foot of the western end of the ridge but could not take or by-pass the enemy position at le Cauchais.

By July 12 Gen. Gerhardt had changed his mind; he told Gen. Corlett that it was necessary to take Hill 122, but that 29th Division, with no reserve available, could not make the attack. On July 13 Gen. Corlett produced a new plan; Hill 122 was to be attacked by P-47s whilst the 115th advanced south down the Isigny–St. Lô road, and the 116th and 175th moved west along the Martinville Ridge. The disappointment of his advances on July 13 led Gen. Corlett to revise his plans yet again. The 35th Division was moved into the area on the west of the 29th Division. On July 15th the 134th Regiment would assault Hill 122, supported by tactical aircraft, artillery and tanks. The 137th would slip past Hill 122 to the west, whilst the 320th occupied and masked the enemy at le Carillon. At the same time, the 115th would push down the road into St. Lô, supported by armor; the 116th and 175th would resume their attempts to move westwards.

The 134th Infantry moved forward, supported by a rolling barrage on the morning of July 15, and had reached Emélie by midday. In the afternoon the regiment was joined by 21 tanks and 3 tank destroyers and sappers to form Task Force Sebree. At 20:00 a swarm of P-47s attacked Hill 122. The artillery began to shoot at 20:15 and at 20:50 the Task Force advanced and overran the German positions. At once, the tanks dug in on the north slope of the hill; the sappers helped the infantry dig in on the forward slope, and protected the position with mines and wire. Meindl was acutely aware of the importance of this position, and organized two counterattacks on it on the 16th. The second of these temporarily displaced the 134th back to Emélie, but the regiment regrouped and charged back to secure the hill again.

To the east of the 35th Division, the 115th, supported by tanks, had set off for St. Lô at 05:15. But the ground off the road was soft, which impeded the armor. Further, as the history of the 115th says, "… Germans were still in position in woods to the right and a deep draw to the left". The regiment could not get forward and suffered heavy losses, C Company being reduced to fewer than 35 men. Up on the ridge, and beyond it, the 116th and 175th were also stopped after moving a few hundred yards. But the 116th had better luck in the evening of the 15th, when the attack resumed. The history of the 29th Division records: "It carried the 116th 1st and 2nd Battalions through the enemy's positions with unexpected swiftness. Division Headquarters was reluctant to let the attack progress too far in the dark, and, aware of strong enemy occupying the ridge, ordered the attack halted ..." But this order never reached the 116th's 2nd Battalion, who moved on to take a position at the la Madeleine crossroads, on the outskirts of St. Lô. The Germans closed in behind it, and the battalion was cut off. However, Meindl was deeply anxious, because the Americans had taken Hill 122 and were infiltrating through his defensive positions. On July 16, besides the desperate attempts to recapture Hill 122, he launched two strong counterattacks eastwards along the Martinville Ridge. These attacks were beaten off. A force assembling south of la Madeleine to attack the isolated 2nd Battalion was, by chance, spotted by a group of P-47s which dispersed it.

Developments on July 17 convince Meindl that he could no longer hold St. Lô. The 134th was firmly ensconced on Hill 122, looking down directly into the market place of the town. The 116th and 115th managed to penetrate his defenses by using guile and fieldcraft rather than numbers and firepower. The 29th Division history describes how the 3rd Battalion 116th "... at 04:30, in a quick, silent move unheralded by artillery or small arms fire, slipped through the main German defense line ... relying solely on the grenade and bayonet and the cover of an early morning fog," to join the 2nd Battalion at la Madeleine at 06:00. the 115th too, had realised that the enemy lacked the manpower to patrol the areas between their strong points. Late on the 17th, having made an attempt to storm the la Cauchais feature, the 115th sent its second battalion along a stream around the hill, to reach la Planche du Bois, west of the end of the Martinville Ridge, by the early hours of July 18. By then Gen. Meindl had already issued orders to his units to move south of St. Lô, but be prepared to return to the town if the opportunity arose. The German soldiers evacuated their positions at le Carillon, le Cauchais and Martinville. In the afternoon Gen. Norman Cota, Assistant Commander of the 29th Division, led Task Force C into the town. He was preceded by the 2nd Battalion 116th, carrying the body of their commander, Maj. Howie, on the leading jeep. The "Major of St. Lô" was placed on an improvized bier of rubble on the steps of the cathedral.

The XIX Corps rapidly consolidated the position at St. Lô, relying mainly on the artillery. The infantry were much depleted and very tired. According to the history of the 110 Field Artillery, Lt. Col. Johns, an infantry officer, said, "The infantry occupied St. Lô but … artillery held it. Three rifle companies, each down to 30 or 40 effectives, couldn't have done much in so large a town if the artillery had not kept the Germans out." The 29th Division had suffered particularly from exhaustion and loss; the rifle companies had suffered more than 20 percent casualties, and the division had been in continuous contact with the enemy since D-Day.

■ Operation *Cobra*

On the day St. Lô fell, Bradley's plan for *Cobra* was approved by Montgomery. The attack was scheduled for July 21, but was delayed until the 25th by bad weather. The weather was a key factor because the offensive was to commence with massive air attacks involving 2,246 aircraft. The first wave, 350 fighter-bombers, was to attack just south of the St. Lô–Périers road for 20 minutes. Then 1,500 heavy bombers, each loaded with 40 100lb (45kg) fragmentation bombs, were to saturate an area three and a half miles (5.5km) wide and one and a half miles (2.4km) deep, for one hour. Subsequently, the fighter-bombers were to return to give close support to the advancing ground troops. Then the medium bombers would attack the southern edge of the bombing box for 45 minutes. Bradley was particularly anxious that the bombers should fly laterally *along* the St. Lô–Périers road rather than *across* it, to minimize the risks of bombs falling on his attacking formations. The ground attack was to be made by VII Corps, with the 4th, 9th and 30th Divisions advancing supported by 1,000 guns. Once the infantry had seized the roads leading south and cleared corridors along them, the 2nd and 3rd Armored Divisions and 1st Mechanized Infantry Division would pass through to exploit. Having passed through the enemy positions, 3rd Armored would swing west towards Brittany, the 2nd Armored would move southeast to Canisy and beyond, whilst the 1st Mechanized would make for Coutances.

Bradley was keen to attack as soon as possible, because the German Seventh Army was receiving reinforcements from Fifteenth Army and was planning to move two Panzer divisions across to the west. If the Germans were able to create a reserve opposite US First Army they could spoil his plans for maneuver At the opposite end of the front, the Canadians attacked southeast of Caen to discourage any such development.

The weather seemed favorable very early on July 24, then it deteriorated. This was unfortunate, because one group of heavy bombers took off, and could not be recalled. Over Normandy, they approached the start line from the north, contrary to Bradley's wishes, and also bombed short. This inflicted casualties on the forward elements of VII Corps, and killed Gen. McNair, the most senior officer of the US Army. The incident also alerted the German commanders, who ordered a Kampfgruppe of 2nd SS Panzer Division to move across from the front opposite VIII Corps.

But the Germans had no time for a major redeployment, for on July 25 *Cobra* was unleashed. Once again, the heavy bombers flew in from the north and bombed the 9th and 30th Divisions, inflicting losses and delaying the advance. But the effects on the Germans south of the start line were devastating. The commander of Panzer Lehr, Gen. Bayerlein, had deployed his tanks in depth along the roads leading to St. Gilles and Marigny. After the war, Bayerlein remembered, "My flak batteries received direct hits which knocked out half the guns and silenced the rest. After an hour I had no communication with anybody. By noon nothing was visible but dust and smoke. My front lines looked like the face of the moon and at least 70 percent of my troops were dead, wounded, crazed or numbed. All my forward tanks were knocked out." Some of the German infantry, in deep bunkers, emerged in better condition and fought hard. The US 9th, 4th and 3rd Armored Divisions moved forward, and concentrated on clearing the key roads leading south. By the end of July 25 they had gained two miles (3km).

Gen. Collins studied reports of the action, and concluded that the enemy had no reserves in the area. So, on July 26 medium bombers attacked corridors along the main axis roads, and then the 2nd and 3rd Armored Divisions advanced down them towards St. Gilles and Marigny. German engineers mined and cratered the roads, but American tanks had been fitted with hedgecutters which enabled them to move through hedgerows, and by-pass these blocks. The few German armored vehicles left were still confined to the roads, and were easy targets for the roving bands of P-47s. The American tanks soon outran their artillery support, but each combat command now enjoyed the services of a Forward Air Controller, so coordination with the fighter-bombers was excellent. On the eastern side, 2nd Armored Division passed through St. Gilles unopposed, reached Canisy by dusk, and went on to seize high ground at le Mesnil-Herman, and secure the flank. On the western side, 3rd Armored

Division supported by 1st Mechanized Infantry Division had to fight hard for Marigny, and faced the prospect of a counterattack from the west by 2nd SS Panzer and 17th SS Panzer Grenadier Divisions. But the enemy in the far west was under pressure from the north, as VIII Corps reinforced by 4th Armored Division attacked southwards.

On July 27 the 3rd Armored and 1st Mechanized Divisions swung westwards, threatening the eastern flank and rear of the German LXXXIV Corps. The 2nd SS Panzer and 17th SS Panzer Grenadiers moved to block this advance, so opening the way for VIII Corps. Late on the 28th the 6th and 4th Armored Divisions met at Coutances. The German formations had dissolved into chaos; there was no front and no coordinated resistance.

Gen. Patton took over direction of VIII Corps, which raced south unopposed, seized the bottleneck at Avranches, and advanced into Brittany. The Luftwaffe made desperate efforts to destroy the bridge at Avranches, but failed. By August 4 Patton's forces had captured Vannes on the south coast of Brittany, and Rennes, the capital of the province. The day before, 30th Division had captured Mortain, and Bradley ordered Patton to advance eastwards. By August 7 Patton's forward elements were at Le Mans, deep in the rear of the Seventh Army.

In the east, the Germans and British reacted to the success of *Cobra*. On July 27 Von Kluge sent 2nd and 116th Panzer Divisions westwards; these formations were delayed by air strikes en route and arrived too late to contain the breakout. Immediately east of the Vire, the Germans attempted to hold fast, and resisted the US V and XIX Corps. Between July 26–30, V Corps advanced 3 miles (5km) in the teeth of bitter opposition. XIX Corps also pressed forward, but was unable to advance swiftly. Montgomery's reaction was to send his VIII Corps from the vicinity of Caen to attack through XXX Corps just east of Caumont, to compromise the right flank and rear of any putative German defensive position on the east bank of the Vire. This offensive, *Bluecoat*, began on July 30, hindered by heavy rain, rough bocage terrain and extensive minefields. However, the 15th Division and 6th Guards Tank Brigade gained five miles (8km) on the first day. On July 31 11th Armoured Division, on the right flank, found a gap in the German line, passed through it, and went on to encounter and intercept elements of the II SS Panzer Corps moving westwards. On August 1 and 2 the VIII Corps swung southeast, whilst XXX Corps moved forward to assault Mont Pinçon, the highest hill in

Normandy. These movements confronted the Germans with yet more demands on their inadequate reserves.

■ The Mortain Counterattack

By early August the German commanders in France realized that the game was up and were convinced that only a withdrawal to the Seine could save them from annihilation. The Allies were present in the theater in a great superiority of numbers and material, and could prevent German reserves and supplies from moving into the area. After *Cobra*, the Americans had ample room in which to use these advantages to decisive effect. Once again, Hitler disagreed. He perceived a great opportunity. On August 2 he ordered von Kluge to allow the Americans to pour into Brittany unchecked, then assemble every Panzer unit in Normandy to make a counterattack intended to retake Avranches and cut the lifelines to Patton's forces. In vain the German commanders argued that if they took all the Panzers away from the area south of Caen, they would lose Falaise. Hitler was adamant. Only the battered 12th SS Panzer Division remained facing the British and Canadians before Falaise. In an area east of Mortain the Germans assembled the Fifth Panzer Army, consisting of the 1st, 2nd and 9th SS Panzers, and the 2nd and 116th Panzer Divisions, which, in total, had only 250 tanks. The German forces not involved in the attack on Avranches must, as always, stand firm and not retreat, relying on willpower to resist the enemy when materiel means were insufficient.

The preparations of Fifth Panzer Army were spotted by Allied aircraft, and Bradley reacted. He deployed five infantry divisions between Vire and Mortain, backed up by two armored combat commands and three more divisions around St. Hilaire. Driven by Hitler's insistence, protesting at the lack of time to prepare, and of materiel, the Fifth Panzer Army attacked on August 7. On the northern flanks 116th Panzer was checked by the US VII Corps pushing south from Vire and St. Sever. The 2nd Panzer Division advanced between Sourdeval and Mortain, gaining seven miles (11km) before it was stopped by encountering Combat Command B of the 3rd Armored Division. The 1st and 2nd SS Panzer Divisions to the south made less progress, because the 30th Division, deployed around Mortain, held on to hilltop positions which gave them good observation. The infantry of the SS Panzer divisions made repeated attempts to seize the hilltops, but the 30th Division would not be dislodged.

On August 7 the advance of Fifth Panzer Army had been covered by mist, but on the 8th the weather was clear. Allied tactical aircraft slaughtered the tanks and half-tracks of the Fifth Panzer Army as it struggled to move westwards. The VII Corps applied such pressure from the north that 116th Panzer was unable to advance at all. On the southern flank, Combat Commands of the 2nd and 3rd Armored Divisions moved northeast towards Ger and Domfront, to menace the rear of 1st and 2nd SS Panzer. By dusk on August 8 it was obvious to the German commanders in Normandy that the counteroffensive had failed, and that Fifth Panzer Army was in grave danger. But Hitler insisted on exerting control of his armies, and ordered a renewed attack on Avranches, oblivious of the danger.

Even as Fifth Panzer Army attacked westwards, the jaws of the pocket were developing. Part of Patton's Third Army was moving north on Eisenhower's orders, to advance in the direction of Alençon, the main supply depot of Seventh Army, Argentan and Falaise. By August 9 leading elements of the US XV Corps were only five miles (8km) from Falaise. In the north, the First Canadian Army, south of Caen, made an ingenious attack on the night of August 7. The plan for Operation *Totalize* was drawn by Gen. Simonds, commander of II Canadian Corps. He decided that the attack must be made without any artillery preparation, to gain surprize. The advance would be at night, in order to deprive the enemy of the advantage of the superior range of the 88s. For the first three miles (5km), all movement would be in vehicles, formed up in close columns four tanks wide. The infantry would travel in the hulls of self-propelled guns with the artillery pieces removed; anyone on foot was to be regarded as hostile. After three miles (5km), the infantry would dismount and attack the second line of enemy defenses.

The flanks of the main axis, which ran along the Caen–Falaise road, would be bombed by strategic aircraft of RAF Bomber Command. Tracer fire, star-shells, searchlights and radio beams were to give directional guidance. The 2nd Canadian Division would attack west of the road, and the 51st Highland Division to the east. At dawn American heavy and medium bombers would attack enemy positions to assist a further advance by the 4th Canadian and 1st Polish Armoured Divisions. Facing the attack were the 272nd Division, the 89th Division, recently arrived from Norway, and, in reserve, the 12th SS Panzer Division. The advance began at 00:30 on August 8, and, inevitably, there was apprehension and confusion, as described by Ian Hammerton, who was there commanding a troop of flail tanks: "To say that we were apprehensive is an understatement. Tanks are almost blind at night ... there were more dry mouths and butterfly stomachs than at any time previously including D-Day. We trundled forward, all eyes straining to see. As we reached the near edge of the German positions, our visibility was reduced to zero – so much smoke and dust that it was impossible to see even the pin-point red rear lights of the tank in front. We proceeded by fits and starts, the radio filled with messages of bewilderment. I found there were no tanks in front of me. The next moment we plunged into a giant crater."

But despite the obvious difficulties, the tempo of the advance was maintained. The German position was broken, the 272nd and 89th Divisions had collapsed. The 12th SS Panzer sent forward two Kampfgruppen which delayed the 4th Canadian and 1st Polish Divisions, whilst their comrades fell back to a new line on the River Laison, seven miles (11km) north of Falaise.

The Canadians forced the Laison on August 14. On this occasion they used smoke to blind the German anti-tank guns, and attacked in phalanxes of tanks and tracked infantry carriers. Strong tactical air support. helped them close in to within 3 miles (5km) of Falaise.

To the west of the Canadian sector, the British Second Army was pushing southeastwards through the tangled hills of the Suisse Normande. The pocket was forming. By August 16 when the Canadians captured Falaise, most of the Seventh Army was still west of the Orne. On the following day Hitler authorized a withdrawal to a new defensive line on the east bank of the Orne, but it was too late. On the same day the 4th Canadian and 1st Polish Divisions swung wide to the eastern flank and crossed the Dives. The US V Corps moved north through the XV and attacked towards Chambois and Trun on the Dives. The German Seventh Army and Fifth Panzer Army were trapped in a pocket 20 miles by 20 miles (32km x 32km), surrounded by higher ground: 100,000 soldiers, the remains of 20 divisions, were caught in an arena overlooked from all sides.

The Germans did not give up easily. To the south they used the Forêt de la Grande Gouffern to delay the advance north of the Americans. They attempted to break out of the pocket eastwards by forcing a way across the Dives and through the Auge Hills beyond. The II SS Panzer Corps made two attempts to break into the pocket from Vimoutiers, to establish a safe exit. But the 4th Canadian Division had seized the crossing over the Dives. The Poles had occupied high ground on Mont Ormel, and could not be driven off it, even when reduced to fighting armor with bayonets and bare hands because they were out of ammunition. South of the Poles, near Exmes, were the tanks of the Tactical Group de Langlade, part of the French 2nd Division. They too enjoyed commanding views of the pocket, its exits and the retreating German forces.

Eventually only one ford and narrow track was still open to the Germans evacuating the area, and it was under concentrated artillery and air attack. By August 19 this route was so choked with wrecked vehicles, corpses and dead horses that it was impassable. Ever since that day it has been known as the "Couloir de Mort", the corridor of death. In the evening of the 19th the Poles, Americans and Canadians met in Chambois. For three more days the Germans inside and outside the pocket continued the fight, then they gave up. On August 22 the II SS Panzer Corps was ordered to join a general retirement towards the Seine. By that time the leading elements of US Third Army had already crossed that river in two places.

The Falaise pocket completed the ruin of the German Army in Normandy. The Allies took 50,000 prisoners and estimated they had destroyed 5,000 armored vehicles and tanks in the area. The German Army had lost 400,000 men in the campaign, and was in full retreat. They did not stop running until they reached the Vosges hills in the east and the canals east of Antwerp in the north.

THE INVASION OF SOUTHERN FRANCE

The invasion of southern France underwent several changes between concept and execution. President Roosevelt and his military leaders – notably Gen. George C. Marshall, and Gen. Dwight D. Eisenhower, who had commanded the Allied invasion of northwest Africa – believed in a knockout blow across the English Channel against the center of Germany's strength. In contrast, British Prime Minister Churchill and his advisors preferred to jab away at weak spots on the perimeter of Nazi-occupied Europe. After the conquest of North Africa, the Allies had to choose between the two strategies, a decision complicated by the fact that a battle-tested Anglo-American army stood on the shores of the Mediterranean, whereas the buildup in the United Kingdom had just begun. Although hard-pressed Soviet forces had checked the Nazi invaders at Stalingrad, the issue on the Eastern Front remained in doubt. The two western Allies could not ignore the danger to the Soviet Union, rein in their forces, and prepare for a cross-channel attack. Churchill's peripheral strategy, though it might delay the decisive blow from the west, would force Hitler to divert forces from the east and also sustain the momentum the Anglo-American Allies had gained in North Africa. Consequently, the Americans and British conquered Sicily, secured in August 1943, and invaded Italy in September.

In May 1943, before the western Allies invaded Sicily and Italy, the Anglo-American *Trident* conference in Washington committed the two nations to a cross-channel attack in the spring of the following year, but during the *Quadrant* meeting at Quebec in August, the British success-fully resisted an American proposal to assign this operation, *Overlord,* an "overriding" priority. The possibility of further peripheral jabs in Mediter-ranean area thus survived, and Churchill's strategy received a further boost when Josef Stalin, the Soviet dictator, indicated that he would accept a postponement of *Overlord* so that the western Allies could attack imme-diately in the Mediterranean or the Balkans. Stalin, however, changed his mind by the time he conferred with Roosevelt and Churchill at Tehran, Persia, in November 1943. The Red Army had defeated the Germans at Kursk in July of that year, recaptured Kharkov in August, and advanced westward. Stalin still wanted an Anglo-American invasion, but on the Channel coast of France, definitely not in the Balkans, where western troops might interfere with his plans to dominate the region after the war.

■ Operation *Anvil*

Stalin's endorsement of *Overlord* ensured that the western Allies would try for a knockout blow in France. The initial concept of operations there called for a pincers movement to crush German resistance. Simultaneously with *Overlord,* the cross-channel assault, the Allies would invade the French Riviera in Operation *Anvil.* Although he accepted *Overlord,* Churchill hoped to replace *Anvil* with an advance into the Balkans. He preferred to seize a beachhead in Yugoslavia, strike through the Ljubljana Gap, capture Vienna and establish a British presence in the path of the Soviet juggernaut already gathering momentum far to the east. Britain, however, lacked the resources to undertake such a venture without Amer-ican collaboration. While planning went ahead for *Overlord* and *Anvil* Churchill won two American converts to his Balkan strategy – Lt. Gen. Mark W. Clark, commander of the Fifth Army in Italy, and Gen. Ira Eaker, who headed the Mediterranean Allied Air Forces – and arranged for one of his own commanders, Field Marshal Sir Henry Maitland Wilson, the Supreme Allied Commander, Mediterranean, to begin planning for a possible thrust across the Adriatic.

While Churchill looked to the Balkans, Allied planners in London realized they could not muster enough landing craft to invade Normandy and the Riviera at the same time. The Allies decided to launch *Overlord* early in June, knowing they could not shift the necessary amphibious shipping to the Mediterranean before mid-August. Although the delay gave Churchill another chance to argue for the Balkan alternative, his eloquence could not overcome strategic and geographic reality. Ill served by ports, highways, and railroads, the Ljubljana Gap wound through mountains where a defender could readily contain the Allied advance, as had happened in Italy, in an area too far to the east to support the post-*Overlord* liberation of France. In contrast, *Anvil*, even though delayed, could attract German strength from elsewhere in France. Moreover, the Riviera beaches provided access to two generally parallel routes to north-eastern France or Germany. The invasion force might advance up the Rhône Valley to Lyon and then continue to Nancy or pass through the Belfort Gap to the Rhine and Germany, depending on Allied progress eastward from Normandy, or follow the Route Napoléon from Cannes, by way of Grenoble, to Lyon, thence to Nancy or the Belfort Gap. *Anvil* had other advantages over a Balkan operation, among them: the opportunity to use the Free (Fighting) French troops now fighting in Italy for the liberation of their homeland; a chance to take advantage of the French FFI, the Resistance – strong in southern France; and access to the ports of Marseilles and Toulon as conduits for supplies and reinforcements. The American arguments in favor of *Anvil* prevailed; the operation, redesignated *Dragoon* because the original name might have been compromised, would go ahead despite predictions of disaster from Churchill. Indeed, the Prime Minister's opposition gave rise to the legend that he insisted on the new name of *Dragoon* because he had been dragooned into going along with the plan.

Aware that an invasion was drawing near, Field Marshal Rommel, responsible for the defense of France, inspected the Mediterranean coast in May 1944 and found a shockingly thin shell of coastal fortifications backed by a fairly sizeable mobile force. The task of shoring up the beach defenses that Rommel found so weak fell to two veteran officers, Generaloberst Johannes von Blaskowitz and General der Infanterie Friedrich Wiese. Blaskowitz, a thoroughly competent soldier whose zeal for the offensive and for the Nazi cause Hitler sometimes doubted, commanded Army Group G, which stood guard over the entire region from the Pyrenees to the Italian border. Wiese led the Nineteenth Army, the principal combat force in southern France. They assigned the highest priority to the coastal fortifications, dispatching some 14,000 laborers – members of the

Todt Organization, supplemented by French civilians impressed into the work force – to build almost 600 camouflaged gun positions covering likely invasion beaches. Some of the steel-reinforced concrete structures resembled bath houses or waterfront cafes. Inland of the beaches, level areas where gliders or paratroops might be expected to land sprouted stakes of Rommel's asparagus, supplemented by heavy wire strung among trees and poles to trip the gliders.

The defenses of the beaches and the inland obstacles grew more formidable, but after the invasion of Normandy, troop strength declined as Rommel shifted forces northward. By August 15, D-Day for *Dragoon*, Wiese's Nineteenth Army had one division at Toulon, the former French naval base, another at the port of Marseilles, a third near the Riviera beaches, and four other combat divisions and one reserve division between the Rhône River and the Spanish border, Finally, the 11th Panzer Division, commanded by Generaloberst Wend von Wietersheim, had refitted after fighting in the Soviet Union and was moving from Bordeaux on the west coast toward the mouth of the Rhône. Some 30,000 troops stood guard on the Riviera, with another 200,000 within easy reach.

While the Germans improved their fortifications along the Riviera, planning for *Dragoon* neared completion. Vice Adm. H. Kent Hewitt, USN, commanded the Western Naval Task Force, which would conduct the preliminary naval bombardment and land the assault force. The US Seventh Army, commanded by Lt. Gen. Alexander M. "Sandy" Patch Jr., who had fought the Japanese on Guadalcanal, faced the task of seizing three beachheads along 45 miles (72km) of coastline from the Golfe de Napoule, southwest of Cannes, to the Baie de Cavalaire, southwest of St. Tropez. Three American divisions in Italy underwent hurried training on the Salerno beaches, where one of them, the 36th Infantry Division, had stormed ashore in September 1943, and another, the 45th Infantry Division, in reserve initially, had taken part in the subsequent fighting. The other, the 3rd Infantry Division, had landed in northwest Africa, Sicily, and in January 1944 at Anzio in Italy.

The *Dragoon* plan called for major landings over the *Camel* beaches at Fréjus in the north, the *Delta* beaches near Ste. Maxime in the center, and the *Alpha* beaches between St. Tropez and Cavalaire in the south. The *Camel* Force under Rear Adm. Don P. Moon, USN, a veteran of *Utah* Beach in *Overlord*, had the assignment of landing Maj. Gen. John E. Dahlquist's 36th Infantry Division. Rear Adm. Frank J. Lowry, USN, a participant in the Anzio invasion, commanded the *Delta* Force, carrying the 45th Infantry Division under Maj. Gen. William W. Eagles. Rear Adm. Bertram J. Rodgers, USN, and his *Alpha* Force would put ashore John W. "Iron Mike" O'Daniel's 3rd Infantry Division. The three assault divisions, plus their supporting units comprised the US VI Corps, under Lt. Gen. Lucian K. Truscott, Jr., who, while commanding the 3rd Infantry Division, had trained his men in the Truscott Trot, a forced march that in eight hours covered 30 miles (48km) instead of the usual 20 miles (32km). Subsidiary landings on Truscott's flanks would distract the defenders and capture coastal defenses. In advance of the assault, 41 eleven-man underwater demolition teams would clear lanes to the various beaches.

Throughout the planning process, French representatives, headed by Col. Jean L. Pettit, tried to insert Army B, commanded by Général d'Armée Jean de Lattre de Tassigny, into the *Dragoon* assault force with the mission of seizing a beachhead of its own. Patch however, lacked the amphibious shipping and supporting aircraft to oblige, even if de Lattre's force had been fully trained to make assault landings, which it was not. As a result, French Army B would follow the Americans ashore and function as a component of Patch's Seventh Army. The first French troops ashore, II Corps of de Lattre's army, would land in the wake of O'Daniel's 3rd Infantry Division and seize Toulon and Marseilles; I Corps would not see action until early September.

Air power formed a critical element of Operation *Dragoon*. After heavy bombers of the American 15th Air Force, which normally hit industrial targets from southern Germany to Romania, had hammered the coastal defenses, squadrons of the Mediterranean. Allied Air Forces and carrier aircraft would. join Brig. Gen. Gordon P. Saville's XII Tactical Air Command in supporting the operation. During the assault, fighter-bombers supporting *Dragoon* got their orders from controllers in the command ship USS *Catoctin*, who monitored air traffic, issued air raid warnings, and backed up the radar-equipped LST that directed the fighter defenses. Once VI Corps had established a beachhead, Saville's airmen would support the advance inland.

Dragoon, like *Overlord*, called for pre-dawn airborne landings beyond the invasion beaches to cut off reinforcements and confuse the defenders. Preparations for the airborne attack typified the hectic effort to launch *Dragoon*. Assigned to carry the airborne troops into battle, the American

1st Provisional Troop Carrier Division, led by Brig. Gen. Paul L. Williams, had to borrow 416 C-47s, their crews, and 225 glider pilots from units in the United Kingdom. Maj. Gen. Robert T. Frederick assembled his 1st Airborne Task Force, which would board the transports and gliders, from the airborne units available in the theater. Short of a dozen staff officers, he obtained them from the 13th Airborne Division, still training in the United States. Frederick's command consisted of one American parachute infantry regiment, a British parachute brigade group, and four American battalions – two of parachute infantry, one of parachute field artillery, and one of glider infantry. Some of the fragile gliders would carry volunteers from line infantry units like the Japanese-American 442nd Infantry. Airborne troops began hurried training after the fall of Rome on June 4, two days before *Overlord*, but the available aircraft and crews did not permit more than a handful of men at a time to make practice jumps.

The rapidly approaching deadline of August 15 also complicated the training of the amphibious forces. Three American heavy cruisers and three old battleships, plus the French battleship *Lorraine* and the British *Ramillies*, joined Adm. Hewitt's naval forces, while nine carriers, seven from the Royal Navy, prepared to help land-based aircraft in maintaining control of the skies over the Riviera beaches, After a disappointing rehearsal by his *Camel* Force, Adm. Moon decided that the amphibious forces could not be ready in time. He urged Hewitt to postpone D-Day, but the naval commander, even if he had shared Moon's concerns could scarcely have delayed the impending invasion. Hewitt tried to reassure his subordinate, on the verge of nervous collapse after the strain of *Overlord*, and thought he had succeeded, but on the morning of August 5, Moon killed himself, a victim of the intense pressure generated by two successive amphibious operations. Another American, Rear Adm, Spencer S. Lewis, took over the *Camel* Force. In the aftermath of Moon's suicide, Churchill, still fascinated with the Ljubljana Gap, argued one last time for canceling *Dragoon*, but Eisenhower would not hear of it.

Although pressed for time and resources, the planners of *Dragoon* benefited from excellent intelligence. Indeed, Allied intelligence officers maintained a huge map that covered the Riviera coast from Cannes to Toulon, showing bunkers, artillery positions and their fields of fire, entrenchments, obstacles to airborne and amphibious landings, and in some instances the number of German defenders at a particular place and the names of their officers. Aerial photography revealed much about the defenses, but *Ultra* provided an even clearer insight into plans as well as troop dispositions. The results of the *Ultra* intercepts went to special liaison units reporting to commanders like Patch. Many of the details about names, numbers, and individual strongpoints came from the Resistance, which also engaged in sabotage and harassment, its activity sustained and coordinated by the Special Operations Executive (SOE) in London.

The SOE arranged to drop supplies to the FFI, which included such disparate elements of the Resistance as Communists loyal to Moscow and conservative followers of Charles de Gaulle. In the south of France, the Resistance sabotaged coastal guns, crippling two of the 340mm weapons taken from the French battleship *La Provence* at Toulon and mounted ashore, and ambushed road and rail traffic. Lt. Col. Francis C. A. Cammaerts, a British officer of the SOE, who had parachuted into France, coordinated, albeit loosely, the activity of some 10,000 irregulars, lightly armed but able to materialize suddenly, make deadly use of explosives or automatic weapons, and then vanish into the countryside.

A series of successful ambushes, the Normandy landings, and a premature call for an armed uprising issued by mistake from de Gaulle's headquarters in London encouraged bolder action that had tragic consequences. On June 10, 1944, four days after *Overlord* began, de Gaulle's staff realized the wrong message had gone out and, too late, issued orders to revert to guerrilla warfare. Already, Resistance forces near the village of Oradour-sur-Glane in southwestern France were attacking the 2nd SS Panzer Division, "Das Reich" as it deployed to help defend Normandy. As an example to those who dared resist, German soldiers of this Waffen-SS division herded the populace of Oradour into buildings, opened fire through the wooden walls, and set the structures ablaze. A few people escaped, but 642 men, women and children perished in the village that afternoon.

On the Vercors, an elevated plateau stretching from Grenoble southward to Die, the Resistance forces, protected by the surrounding mountains and encouraged by a supply drop from American aircraft, celebrated Bastille Day, July 14, as their day of liberation, but freedom lasted little more than a week. On July 21, the Germans attacked with aircraft and armor, rapidly overwhelming the lightly-armed irregulars. The Waffen-SS troops who spearheaded the assault burned entire villages, slaughtered the inhabitants, and tracked down and executed many of the surviving members of the Resistance. Those who escaped the Nazi vengeance fled into the forest to await the Allied invasion of the Mediterranean coast.

■ The *Dragoon* Landings

Dragoon began on August 15 with an airborne assault. While a handful of aircraft jettisoned hundreds of dummy parachutists into the early morning darkness west of Toulon to confuse the defenders, 396 C-47s, launched from ten different airfields in Italy, thundered toward the fog-shrouded vineyards and meadows near the town of le Muy, where the first stick of paratroopers jumped at 04:30. The low-lying fog proved disconcerting to the parachutists, some of whom cast aside weapons and equipment under the impression they were coming down at sea, and it may also have contributed to a navigational error that dropped one battalion more than 20 miles (32km) from the assigned drop zone. Save for this one unit, the vanguard of the 1st Airborne Task Force landed as planned.

Almost five hours later, the first of the gliders arrived near le Muy. En route, while over the Mediterranean, a tow rope parted, but the glider pilot ditched his Waco CG-4 near one of the lifeguard ships posted along the route, and all on board the aircraft survived. Shortly afterward, the right wing of another glider snapped off; the craft rolled sharply, broke the tow rope, and disintegrated, sending men and equipment tumbling into the sea. This time no-one survived. At 09:20, the first of the 71 remaining gliders hurtled out of the sky, plunging to earth at speeds approaching 90 miles (125km) per hour to deliver troops, jeeps, artillery pieces, and anti-tank guns. Some of the gliders slammed into trees or man made obstacles, even though the earlier wave of parachutists had thinned the crop of Rommel's asparagus. As dusk approached, another 332 gliders landed, so that at day's end some 9,000 American and British airborne soldiers, 221 jeeps, 213 artillery pieces, and miscellaneous other weapons and items of equipment stood ready to attack the Germans at le Muy. Thus far, airborne casualties totaled 434 killed and 292 injured.

Between the time the dummy parachutists plunged earthward and the real paratroopers arrived, Allied amphibious forces undertook a series of operations in preparation for the three main landings. On the left of the invasion beaches, a few vessels, trailing radar-reflecting balloons to multiply their numbers, created the illusion of a seaborne assault in conjunction with the airborne demonstration near Toulon. On the opposite flank, Lt. Cdr. Douglas Fairbanks, Jr., the hero, of many an adventure film, landed a team of French commandos to cut the highway that hugged the coast. The commandos came ashore in an undetected minefield, causing explosions that drew German fire; the landing force then scrambled back into the boats, which Allied aircraft mistakenly strafed. The enemy captured the surviving commandos, who swam ashore, but within 24 hours, assault troops of the 36th Infantry Division freed the prisoners.

To the left of the invasion beaches, while French commandos cut the road to Toulon, the 1st Special Service Force, made up of Canadians and Americans, attacked the Iles d'Hyères to silence German guns that dominated the *Alpha* beaches. Early on the morning of D-Day, the force overran the batteries and discovered only dummy weapons. Elsewhere on the islands, this so-called "Devil's Brigade," commanded by Col. Edwin A. Walker, overcame stiff resistance with the help of naval gunfire, including 15-inch salvoes from HMS *Ramillies*, and seized Port Cros for landing supplies.

The minefields and obstacles off the Riviera beaches presented a challenge to the planners of *Dragoon*, who sent minesweepers as close to shore as the depth of water would permit and followed up with explosives-laden, radio-controlled boats designed to blast lanes for the assault craft. Underwater demolition teams dealt with the least accessible of the obstacles, many of them booby-trapped with mines.

While the battleships, cruisers, and destroyers bombarded the German defenses, rocket-firing landing craft accompanied the assault waves along the cleared lanes. The 3rd Infantry Division seized the *Alpha* beaches, where aerial and naval bombardment had neutralized the strong defenses, and the 45th Infantry Division benefited from the most powerful of the gunfire support flotillas – built around the American battleships *Texas* and *Nevada* – in rapidly overrunning the *Delta* beachhead. On the *Camel* beaches, the 36th Infantry Division encountered formidable minefields and, off *Camel Red* Beach, savage enemy fire that not even repeated shelling by the battleship USS *Arkansas* could suppress. As H-Hour for storming *Camel Red* approached, Adm. Lewis, Moon's replacement, diverted the assault force to *Camel Green*, where it landed in the wake of other elements of Dahlquist's division.

On August 16, D+1, the Allies consolidated their grip on the Riviera beachhead. As on the previous day, Gen. Dahlquist's 36th Infantry Division, which wore the T patch of the Texas National Guard, had the hardest fight, attacking *Camel Red* from the flank to avoid an anti-tank barrier disguised as a row of beachfront houses. Meanwhile, the airborne force captured its assigned objectives. British and American paratroops and American glider infantry took le Muy, and the American 551st Parachute Infantry Battalion, assisted by irregulars of the Resistance, captured Draguignan, freed the French guerrillas held there, and made prisoners of Generalleutnant Ludwig Bieringer, a corps commander, and his staff. Late in the afternoon, the battalion that had parachuted far from its intended drop zone – the 3rd Battalion, 517th Parachute Infantry, under Lt. Col. Melvin Zais – rejoined its regiment and helped push the enemy beyond les Arcs. At dusk, tanks from the beachhead made contact with the airborne force, and the invasion entered a new phase.

The buildup of the Seventh Army proceeded rapidly. By midnight on August 17, more than 86,500 American and French troops had landed, along with 12,500 vehicles and 46,100 tons of cargo. During the month, 380,000 men crossed the *Dragoon* beaches, as did 69,000 vehicles, 306,000 tons of supplies, and 18,000 tons of fuel. As Patch's forces gained strength, Truscott's VI Corps set out in pursuit of the retreating Germans, and the French II Corps attacked Toulon and Marseilles.

Patch, in planning to exploit the beachhead, had three powerful advantages: *Ultra*, aerial domination, and the French Resistance. Of these, *Ultra* proved the most important, for it revealed Blaskowitz's intentions. On August 17, the German commander received orders to withdraw his mobile forces, leaving the garrison troops to hold Toulon and Marseilles for as long as possible. Bletchley Park decoded the message on the 18th, and by the 20th, Patch had received the information and, without indicating the true source, passed it to his subordinate commanders. Once *Ultra* had revealed that von Blaskowitz would withdraw, Patch pursued with his most mobile forces – the three infantry divisions of Truscott's VI Corps. The Seventh Army commander sent Frederick's airborne task force, which had fewer vehicles available than the "leg" divisions, to liberate Cannes and Nice and then secure the eastern flank, even though *Ultra* revealed no immediate threat from the German divisions in northern Italy

The Allies controlled the skies over the invasion beaches, and only briefly could the Luftwaffe challenge this mastery. Between August 16 and 18, the Germans launched 141 sorties by Junkers Ju 88 and Dornier Do 217 bombers, some of the latter carrying glider bombs, and rushed fighters to the area. Aerial attacks sank an LST, and in the fading twilight of August 18, five Ju 88s bombed !he command ship USS *Catoctin*, killing six and wounding 42 but causing only minor damage. After this parting shot, the Luftwaffe withdrew its squadrons from southern France.

For ten days after the landings, Saville's light and medium bombers and fighter-bombers tried to destroy the bridges across the Durance and Rhône rivers in the hope of isolating von Wietersheim's 11th Panzer Division from von Blaskowitz's main body. The Germans succeeded, however, in massing the available bridging equipment and bringing the armored troops across both streams. Von Wietersheim could shuttle his tanks between Route N7 on the eastern bank of the Rhône and the Route Napoléon, as the American threat dictated and the road network permitted. Patch soon realized that he needed the bridges to pursue the Germans almost as desperately as von Blaskowitz. After August 25, therefore, Allied airmen spared the bridges on which Patch depended to conduct and supply the pursuit, concentrating instead on strafing road and rail traffic. Reflecting the important change in priorities, Saville claimed the destruction of 1,400 vehicles, 30 locomotives and 263 railroad cars between August 23 and 29.

The Resistance, including survivors of the disaster on the Vercors, gave Patch another advantage by providing him a source of both firepower and intelligence. The exploits of these men and women ranged from reporting German movements to ambushing retreating columns. On one occasion, Christine Granville, a Polish-born agent dispatched to southern France by the SOE, singlehandedly prevented the Germans from using an important pass through the mountains near Digne. Scrambling alone up steep and heavily forest slopes, she called out to the Polish conscripts in their own language and persuaded them to desert to the resistance.

■ **The Liberation of Toulon and Marseilles**
While the pursuit of von Blaskowitz got under way, fighting raged at Toulon and Marseilles. The II Corps of de Lattre's army followed O'Daniel's 3rd Infantry Division ashore on August 16 and advanced on the two ports, expecting to capture them in 40 days. Toulon presented a formidable challenge to the French, lightly armed by American standards. Three fortified heights barred the way, backed up by minefields, barbed wire, trenches, and pillboxes. French shock troops scaled the hills and routed the defenders with flamethrowers and fire from rifles and

mortars. By August 23, the attackers had captured the three objectives and begun probing Toulon itself, where some 1,800 Germans, commanded by Adm. Heinrich Rufus, manned the fortifications that dominated the harbor. The undamaged pair of 340mm guns taken from the battleship *La Provence* formed the backbone of the harbor defenses, which exchanged salvoes with an Allied fleet that included *Lorraine*, a sister ship of *La Provence*, and two other battleships, USS *Nevada* and HMS *Ramillies*. The hammering of the fortifications took a toll among the German guns, enabling the attacking warships to steam past the batteries on August 26 and enter Toulon harbor. Acknowledging the futility of further resistance, Rufus promptly agreed to surrender; he formally capitulated on August 28.

Instead of seizing Toulon before attacking Marseilles, the French II Corps moved simultaneously against both ports. Marseilles lacked Toulon's powerful hilltop defenses, and the Resistance provided information on the minefields and batteries the Germans had prepared. With the hour of liberation apparently at hand, the FFI inside Marseilles attacked German strongpoints, which proved too rugged for the irregulars. A call went out for help, and II Corps responded. With the assistance of air strikes and naval gunfire, French troops overran the enemy defenses, sometimes in a building-by-building struggle. After brief negotiations, the Marseilles garrison surrendered, also on August 28.

While one corps of de Lattre's Army B seized the ports to which Eisenhower attached such importance – the French I Corps had not yet landed – Truscott set out to trap the German forces withdrawing northward. Von Blaskowitz had two first-rate divisions to screen this risky maneuver, the 388th Infantry Division and the 11th Panzer Division. The armored unit had reorganized and refitted after serving in the Soviet Union, where its mobility earned it the nickname "Ghost Division." Again and again, the Ghost Division had materialized at the critical moment on the Eastern Front, and it would continue to do so as Army Group G retreated.

Truscott planned to harry and delay the German retreat toward the Belfort Gap so that the 36th Infantry Division, spearheaded by Brig. Gen. Frederick B. Butler's Provisional Armored Group, known as Task Force Butler, could speed northward up the Route Napoléon in the direction of Grenoble. The Resistance might be able to seal the Rhône Valley; if not, Butler could veer westward to sever Route N7 on the river's east bank. Butler's objective would be the narrow gorge at Montélimar, through which road and river passed. While O'Daniel's 3rd Infantry Division, advancing at a Truscott Trot, pursued the Germans up Route N7, Butler led the 36th Infantry Division up the Route Napoléon and established a blocking position at the Gap. On August 20, when he realized that the FFI could not contain the retreating Germans, Truscott ordered Butler to head west, generally along the Drôme River valley, to cut Route N7 and slam shut the so-called Montélimar Gate. En route, Butler established a series of outposts to protect the road he had followed.

■ Battle for the Montélimar Gate

Elsewhere in the VI Corps zone, the rest of Dahlquist's 36th Infantry Division spread itself thin, capturing Grenoble on August 22 and holding the town until relieved by a regiment from the 45th Infantry Division, replacing the elements of Task Force Butler on the Drôme River outpost line, and reinforcing Butler's thrust toward the Rhône. Meanwhile, the 45th Infantry Division crossed the Durance River, mopped up east of Avignon, and advanced northward on the right flank of O'Daniel's division. If the Texas Division could seize and hold the high ground dominating Montélimar, Truscott could destroy Army Group G.

Task Force Butler – consisting of one battalion each of tanks, field artillery, and infantry, plus a reconnaissance squadron, and companies of tank destroyers and engineers – reached Route N7 late in the afternoon of August 21, but reinforcements from the parent division lagged behind, delayed by the threat of a German counterattack in the vicinity of Grenoble. Until additional troops arrived, Task Force Butler could only dig in and establish a roadblock north of Montélimar; the German force in the town proved too strong for Butler to dislodge, but help was on the way, following the same route the task force had used. During the night infantry and artillery units from the 36th Infantry Division joined Butler, and the gunners laid their 105mm howitzers to shell German road traffic on both banks of the Rhône.

The battle for the Montélimar Gate became a race between Dahlquist's infantry division and von Wietersheim's Ghost Division, and the Panzer unit got there first with the heaviest firepower. Despite a scourging from American artillery, the Germans held Montélimar, and from the town they could fight their way up Route N7 or take advantage of the roads that converge in the town to outflank Task Force Butler. Actually, they did both, with tanks leading each of the attacks, Dahlquist recognized that his divisional spearhead, Task Force Butler could be bypassed and cut off, so he jury-rigged a defensive line generally along the Roubion river, using troops that otherwise might have helped block Route N7. German armor crashed through the Roubion position on the night of August 25–26, even as the bulk of the 11th Panzer Division held open the Montélimar Gate.

To close the highway north of Montélimar, Dahlquist's Texans had to hold a dominant ridge line that rose some 300ft (91m) above the river valley. On August 25, Dahlquist reported from his command post near Grenoble, where an expected counterattack had yet to materialize, that his troops held the critical ridge, passing along information he had received from subordinates there. When he arrived on the scene, however, he discovered that his men held the wrong objective; the officers there had mistaken one ridge for another. The key terrain remained in German hands long enough for von Blaskowitz to escape. Although Army Group G survived to fight another day, it would do so without some 2,000 or more trucks, 80 artillery pieces, and five railroad guns destroyed at Montélimar by air strikes and artillery fire or overrun by Truscott's soldiers,

Furious at Dahlquist's erroneous report, Truscott's first impulse was to relieve the division commander, who realized all too well the consequences of the failure, but the corps commander relented. He accepted Dahlquist's explanation that hard-pressed subordinates had made an honest mistake at a time when he was distracted by the possible danger from the direction of Grenoble and the real threat to his supply line when the Germans broke through the makeshift Roubion line.

Dahlquist may have remained in command because Truscott realized that a shortage of ammunition prevented the Texas Division from using its field artillery to deadliest effect, and in the US Army of World War II artillery proved the most effective of weapons. True, a concentration fired by the 133rd Field Artillery Battalion savaged a 55-car railroad train on the west bank of the Rhône, but Dahlquist's gunners had to prioritize targets to make the best use of a dwindling ammunition supply. Truscott, moreover, was carefully doling out gasoline, which hampered the movement of trucks carrying shells, and troops throughout VI Corps subsisted for a time on two-thirds rations. The crisis in logistics resulted from the distance that truck convoys had to travel in avoiding bridges that American airmen or German demolition teams had dropped into stream beds. Whether influenced by the supply shortage or not, Truscott kept

Dahlquist in command, though he could easily have turned to Gen. Frederick of the 1st Airborne Task Force, who took over the 45th Infantry Division later in the war.

Once von Blaskowitz had skillfully extricated his forces through the Montélimar Gate, Truscott looked ahead to a new objective, Lyon, which he assigned to Dahlquist and the 36th Infantry Division. While the 45th Infantry Division under Eagles, cut the escape route eastward from Lyon, the 3rd Infantry Division would mop up around Montélimar, and the II Corps of de Lattre's army, the victor at Toulon and Marseilles, would advance on the west bank of the Rhône. The French I Corps was to close the gap between VI Corps and the Swiss border and provide security for Patch's right flank.

Eagles and his 45th Infantry Division, wearing the Thunderbird shoulder patch of the Oklahoma National Guard, moved swiftly to sever the roads east of Lyon, but on September 1, von Wietersheim's tanks pushed past a key strongpoint at Meximieux on the Lyon–Geneva highway. Meanwhile, Dahlquist's Texans reached the hills overlooking Lyon only to learn from documents captured by the Resistance that the Germans intended to abandon the city. After reconnaissance patrols verified the enemy's departure, the 36th Infantry Division waited on the outskirts so that the French II Corps could formally liberate the city.

Although the Germans had eluded them at Montélimar and again at Lyon, Patch and Truscott still hoped to trap Blaskowitz short of the Belfort Gap. The pursuit resumed with VI Corps in the center, the French II Corps on the left, and the French I Corps moving up on the right. The 11th Panzer Division succeeded in holding the Thunderbird Division at bay, but the 177th Cavalry Reconnaissance Squadron – a part of Task Force Butler until that organization disbanded on August 30 – got ahead of the Germans and set up a roadblock at Bourg-en-Bresse on September 3, the same day that French troops took possession of Lyon. As had happened at Montélimar and Meximieux, the forces mobile enough to outpace the Germans lacked the firepower to stop them. Elements of von Wietersheim's Ghost Division all but destroyed the cavalry squadron, though suffering heavy casualties in doing so.

Blaskowitz next chose to fight a delaying action at Besançon to gain time for the final withdrawal through the Belfort Gap. Fortified in succession by Romans, the French monarchy, and finally the republic, Besançon seemed an ideal place to slow the American pursuit, and some 3,000

German troops massed there. On September 7, after a two-day fight, O'Daniel's 3rd Infantry Division captured the city, but the pursuit rapidly lost momentum. While O'Daniel's troops struggled for control of Besançon, the 45th Infantry Division became involved in a prolonged slugging match, as German resistance grew fiercer.

On the left of VI Corps, the French II Corps advanced from Lyon, liberating Dijon on September 10 and taking tens of thousands of prisoners, mostly second-line troops, East European volunteers like the battalion of Ukrainians that killed its officers and went over to the Allies. The best of the German units facing the French corps retreated in good order and conducted a stubborn defense of Langres that put an end to the pursuit in that region. On September 12, however, de Lattre's force made contact near Dijon with advance elements of Maj. Gen. Leclerc's French Armored Division, which had fought its way from Normandy. The Allies thus established a single front from the English Channel to Switzerland as they closed in on Germany.

PURSUIT TO THE SEINE

■ The Strategic Setting

Cobra began the end of the Normandy campaign. When Bradley turned his *Cobra* breakthrough into a breakout, rushing his forces southward, he began the second phase of the *Overlord* plan, introducing new forces and changing the command structure. The activation of the US 12th Army Group on August 1, gave Bradley a field command equal to Montgomery's 21st Army Group and brought Lt. Gen. George S. Patton's Third Army into the field. Though Monty would retain temporary "coordinating authority" over both Army Groups then totaling some 38 divisions, American commanders eagerly awaited the day Eisenhower's SHAEF headquarters established itself on the continent, enabling Ike to assume control of the Allied armies.

The original forecast of operations designated Brittany and its key ports, St. Malo, Brest, and St. Nazaire plus the Quiberon Bay area, as Bradley's objective. Along with the entire area from the Brittany Peninsula to the perimeter formed by the River Loire in the south, and the Seine outside Paris in the north, this area constituted the American sector of the crucial "lodgment" required to begin the liberation of Western Europe. With 21 St Army Group taking up the area from their boundary west of the Seine outside Paris to Le Havre, the planners forecast that the entire "lodgment area" would be occupied by D + 90.

While the Allies paused to build up forces, the US 12th Army Group would switch to using Brittany's sea ports when available, to deploy America's armies directly from across the Atlantic. Then the 21st Army Group would take over Cherbourg for its supplies and then capture the Channel ports along the coast to mount the long drive towards Germany.

Cobra's success promised a change to that concept. With the German front collapsing without an established defense in depth, the total defeat of the German armies in the west appeared possible. Attacking east, the American First, British Second, and Canadian First Armies ground up the German main defense head on, while Bradley activated Patton's Third Army to take command of the forces breaking out of the Normandy perimeter both to seize Brittany and to position itself for its move towards the Seine.

Hitler's defense had surprised the Allies. Their estimates indicated that the Germans would fight on successive defense lines rather than attempting to form a tight cordon close to the water's edge. Though the defenders had held the attackers for 40 days in an area they had hoped to have captured within the first nine, fighting forward on a solid line had been costly. Heavy losses and the necessity to match the growing Allied force stripped the Germans of reserves, thus preventing any shift to subsequent defense lines on favorable terrain or major river lines, while off-balancing their force, leaving most German armor in the east between Bayeux and Caen. When Bradley broke out, German forces weren't positioned to both hold the line and eliminate the breakthrough.

Breaking the ground deadlock would eventually reveal that there was a significant long term effect for the Allies in failing to gain the ground marked on 21st Army Group's phase line map, beyond the perception of being slow or being behind schedule. The effect was a predictable shortfall in logistical support.

The Allied armies were limited in stockpiling supplies in their rear areas, which were being filled by reinforcing units. Bradley's sudden success created a problem. As divisions quickly advanced, the long-term forward "dumping" of supplies behind the lines became impossible, with all available transportation being used to supply the rapidly-moving forces. Trucks brought food, ammunition, and most critically gasoline, directly to fighting units. Every mile forward doubled the distances for the supply vehicles. Every new division committed added hundreds of tons to the supplies.

■ Patton's Command

The VIII Corps' drive through Avranches was taken over by Patton, who now commanded nine of Bradley's 21 divisions. The 12th Army Group's first battle directive ordered Patton to drive south to take the area between Rennes and Fougères and then turn westward to take St. Malo, Quiberon Bay, Brest, and clear the Brittany Peninsula.

The plan was bold. Rennes was 25 miles (40km) south of VIII Corps' lead elements; it was nearly 90 miles (144km) to the peninsula's base and a further 135 miles (216km) to the western tip. Patton would have to race his divisions through the narrow gap at Avranches, and then form a rapidly expanding front, deploying his divisions towards every point of the compass to overrun the defenders while ensuring his northern, eastern, and southern flanks were not counterattacked.

Patton was ideal for the job. His genius was in seizing the moment. His boldness and skill in operational maneuver, particularly pursuit, was unmatched by anyone in the Allied camp. Holding open a narrow movement corridor through Avranches as his divisions moved south, Patton planned to introduce three new corps into the battle behind Middleton's veteran VIII. First to follow would be Haislip's XV, and eventually Cook's XII, and Walker's XX, which initially were held back in reserve. Coming south through Avranches, the follow-on corps would begin pushing outward both to the south and east.

First into the peninsula's neck were his two armored divisions. Maj. Gen. John "P" Wood's 4th Armored reached Rennes' outskirts the first day and rapidly encircled the city, while Robert W. Gerow's 6th Armored moved to the north towards St. Malo and west towards Brest. The 79th and 8th Divisions moved southeast and south to seal the peninsula.

Tension was high and the early command scuffles were predictable. Bradley had engineered his breakout with careful planning. His deputy and successor at First Army, Hodges, and the VIII Corps commander, Middleton, were methodical, professional infantrymen.

Bradley intentionally kept Third Army out of the attack, waiting instead to hand off the battle after the breakthrough when the pursuit began, wishing, his aide's diary explains, to maintain "finger tip control." Within hours, Bradley showed his ire at Patton's tactics.

The methodical Bradley chased after Patton whom he wrongly believed to have ignored orders to protect the vital corridor. Soon afterwards, Patton chastised Middleton for being too slow and concerned with flanks, and for temporarily stopping Gerow's advance. With Haislip's XV Corps finishing its passage, Bradley still gripped control like an army commander, ordering Patton to form a front facing east from the corridor's mouth down to Rennes, before developing operations towards Brest.

Patton pushed Middleton west; Haislip formed the flank protection by moving eastward. Patton had seven divisions committed within two days, with individual columns moving rapidly under wide-ranging air cover provided by the XIX Tactical Air Command as the only flank protection.

As Patton's force began its drive against an enemy unable to form any cohesive front throughout Third Army's area, decisive opportunity presented itself. Eisenhower, Montgomery, and Bradley all independently stared at their maps and concluded the same: the German flank for their entire Army Group lay wide open. Montgomery and his planners decided earlier that the campaign should be modified to send a single corps westward, which he confirmed with orders on the morning of August 1. Ike's periodic appreciation to the Combined Chiefs now spoke of using minimum forces in Brittany and pressing their advantage eastward. Bradley soon agreed.

Brittany no longer held significant forces and didn't require Patton's entire force for its capture; Patton would therefore drive east and north encircling the Germans using XV, XII, and XX Corps. For both army groups Montgomery defined the focus: "the main business lies east."

Other considerations intruded. Hitler's attempts to cobble together a last counterthrust loomed in *Ultra*'s decrypts, but initially German capability and intent didn't betray the location. Hitler wanted a counteroffensive to split the breakout corridor at Avranches to restore the Normandy front. While von Kluge scraped together forces to counterattack, army commanders Crerar, Dempsey, Hodges, and Patton struggled with tactical control of a fast developing situation.

By August 7 Patton had wheeled three corps towards the Seine. Brittany, meanwhile, had been completely overrun. But with the essential ports holding out and under siege, four of Patton's divisions, including his best armored formations, the 4th and 6th Armored, were out of the pursuit eastward. Wood, whose 4th Armored had just finished road-marching throughout the peninsula, making impressive gains against no opposition, railed at his corps "commander ... we're winning the war the wrong way, we ought to be going towards Paris."

With Hodges's First Army grinding ahead and Patton's three maneuvering corps heading both east to the Seine and south towards the Loire, Bradley looked at the narrow neck connecting First and Third Armies. Worried about a counterthrust cutting across Patton's lines of communications at Avranches, he correctly forecast what intelligence later predicted, an attack designed to drive to the sea and split the Allied line.

Patton, too, looked briefly to his north at the hinge that connected his army with the main front. With his army aiming towards Le Mans and beyond, he had uncharacteristically held out three divisions from the battle, his diary noting "a secret source" predicting an attack from Mortain to Avranches.

The Mortain attack (Operation *Lüttich*) sealed the fate of France. Von Kluge's force was too small to effect an immediate decision and with American forces poised to block their advance and attack their flank, the pattern for German defeat was set. Bradley snatched one of Patton's three uncommitted divisions to hold Mortain's southern flank, while the remaining two moved east with Patton whose forces were moving to the Seine.

Von Kluge's Mortain failure sparked differing solutions from Allied commanders each seeing opportunities to defeat the enemy. Montgomery looked to the Seine and beyond, seeing Patton as the right flank moving on Paris while paratroops blocked the escape between Chartres and Orléans.

While fending off the Mortain counterattack, Bradley sought immediate battlefield destruction of the enemy, planning a short envelopment to encircle the German Seventh Army at Falaise if Monty would send one of his armies south. Patton already had been converted to Wood's view, which a week before he had called "bull headed." He wanted a deeper drive towards Chartres or Dreux to ensure entrapping the Germans nearer the Seine, not the immediate turn to the north that Bradley directed for Haislip's XV Corps.

Bradley's Falaise encirclement was never consummated, but Patton didn't brood long over being held near Argentan and from closing the Falaise gap. He soon convinced Bradley to widen Third Army's move to the east, with the XX Corps moving towards Chartres, and the XII towards Orléans, while a temporary headquarters held the Argentan shoulder with three divisions and Haislip's XV Corps with two divisions moved east to Dreux. Despite the coordination problems of switching divisions from corps to corps or rapidly changing axes of advance, Patton kept his forces moving to overrun terrain before the Germans could form a defense on it.

While the rest of Third Army continued east, Middleton's VIII Corps continued its Brittany campaigning. Though the peninsula was generally under Middleton's control, the critical port objectives were still under siege. After more than two weeks, the peninsula held five of Patton's dozen divisions, a force that would remain constant through the end of the month. The capture of the ports proved disappointing. St. Malo held out until August 17, Brest to September 19, and Lorient and St. Nazaire managed to hold out until the war's end.

Third Army sent its divisions in four directions in its first two weeks of operations: west to capture the entire Brittany Peninsula and besiege its hold-out port fortresses, south to reach the Loire running west from St. Nazaire to northeast of Tours, east past Le Mans and Alençon, and around to the north to Argentan. In 15 days, Patton had filled out the planners' lines from the D + 20 line to approximately the D + 60 line. Third Army now held down Brittany as planned, plus a significant area originally designated for First Army's operations.

From a personal perspective, the night of August 15 brought personal vindication for one Allied general. With the blue arrows of Third Army marking the most impressive gains on SHAEF's maps, the world was finally told whose army was "touring France." Patton, whose presence was kept secret to account for his alleged command of the Calais invasion as part of the *Bodyguard* deception, was announced as commanding the army racing towards the Seine, Paris, and Germany. Patton was again in the news, not as the general slapping a soldier or politically embarrassing his country, but as the spearhead of the pursuit across France. The Third Army commander was proving what German intelligence had long since decided, that Patton was the most formidable field commander in the Allied camp.

While the newspaper maps showed sketches of Allied arrows moving across France, command decisions had to be made. Montgomery did send Crerar's Canadian First Army south to link with Hodges as Bradley desired. His real interest, however, appeared to be in a wider envelopment to destroy the Germans trapped in front of the bridgeless Seine, possibly an explanation for his lack of detailed interest in Crerar's linkup with Bradley's Army Group at Argentan. The wider focus caused Monty to send Dempsey east, while wanting Patton's forces to continue a wide envelopment south of Paris.

With von Kluge's forces trying to escape, issues appeared to distract the command. Churchill raised the first, again arguing against the impending invasion of southern France at the expense of the Mediterranean campaign. Neither Eisenhower nor Roosevelt would hear of it, and the subsequent landing not only added an indefensible front to Germany's problems, it added the significant port of Marseilles, which would eventually support an entire Allied army group holding down the southern German front.

The second was a new plan of campaign. Montgomery now called for an operational maneuver outstripping Bradley's battle plan. By mid-August, Monty introduced a new concept for campaigning beyond the Seine. While the plan percolated and the generals conferred, the eyes of the world turned towards the capital of France.

■ The Freedom of Paris

With the Germans encircled at Falaise and Third Army in full cry and about to cross the Seine, Paris loomed as a major strategic problem. The Press, the French populace, the Germans, and probably every soldier in the Allied armies thought the invasion was aimed to liberate Paris, the symbolic heart of France.

In fact the opposite was true. The planners had wanted a firm campaign win and logistical buildup before taking the city, and had carefully declared the "lodgment area" to the east of the Seine. Now, with the D + 90 line on the Seine no longer an objective but something to be ignored in passing, Patton's rampaging columns made the city appear within reach.

To the Allies, the mathematics of supply spelled out the problem. The planners believed that Paris would consume at least 4,000 tons of supplies daily, roughly three days' marching and fighting supply for an army. The rapid moves of Patton's pursuit plus the advances of the other three armies, strained the logistical system. To Bradley, the Siegfried Line was reachable with a week's more campaigning; moving on Paris could end that.

French feelings were understandable. For more than 1,500 days, Parisians had borne the shame, terror, and despair, that had come with occupation at the hands of the Germans. More than 1,500 times, a battalion of troops led by a military band had circled the Arc de Triomphe and marched down the Champs Elysées to the Place de la Concorde.

For them, and for all of France, the success of the invasion meant not destroying the German army in the field; it meant freeing the city of Paris. Events would show that the French people, not the Allied command, would decide when and how Paris would be freed.

On August 10, French railwaymen launched a strike calling for wages and better food in Paris; the first real strike of the occupation. The Metro stopped and gas and electric power became sporadic within the city. Three days later, the Germans began disarming Paris's 20,000 policemen. To counter this move, police resistance groups decided to strike, calling upon policemen to put aside their uniforms and retain their weapons. When word leaked to the Germans, the city's Resistance factions met issuing a proclamation telling the police to stand with the Resistance or be considered traitors and collaborators: "The hour of liberation has come."

What had begun on August 10 grew, and inevitably the Germans reacted. When shots were fired, SS elements responded quickly. Thirty-five French youths were machine-gunned on the night of the 16th at the Carrefour des Cascades, and the city's new commandant, Lt. Gen. Dietrich von Choltitz, received orders confirming Hitler's intent to destroy Paris. Firing was heard near the Gare du Nord and the Gare de l'Est on the 17th. The city that had made popular uprisings famous was now on the verge of another.

Resistance elements within the city prepared to seize the city. To the Resistance, freeing the City of Light meant freeing France. To the competing political factions – the Communists, Gaullists, and others, it also meant establishing an invaluable base within liberated and post-war France. Charles de Gaulle's headquarters in Algiers sent word on August 11 outlining a plan for seizing government buildings by his supporters with the regular FFI occupying less symbolic structures.

Gen. Jacques Chaban-Delmas arrived in Paris with directions from FFI chief, Gen. Pierre Koenig, in London ordering a halt to uprising plans, at least until the Allies were outside the city's gates when de Gaulle's plan could be implemented. Chaban-Delmas, however, was too late and could only send a message to London that the city was on the verge of insurrection.

The Germans prepared to meet an Allied attack and didn't wish to engage in stopping insurrections. Hitler, however, had decided that Paris would not fall into Allied hands unscathed. City commandant von

Choltitz had first received orders to destroy Paris's significant industrial capabilities, the city's 45 bridges over the Seine, and eventually, her monuments. The list of buildings mined for demolition could replicate the best tourist guide. Only lack of orders from von Choltitz prevented the destruction from beginning.

When the rail strike began, some political prisoners were evacuated from prisons, most to die later in Buchenwald or Ravensbruck although the 1,500 Jews scheduled for a predawn move from one prison found their transporting buses had been sabotaged and they had been granted a short reprieve. With the Allies close by, Vichy officials suddenly disappeared. It was inevitable that shots would be fired. When German soldiers were ambushed, the German commander threatened to retaliate by razing whole city blocks and killing inhabitants in reprisal.

The Swedish Consul Gen. Raoul Nordling met von Choltitz hoping to alleviate the inevitable destruction. He struck a deal freeing the remaining political prisoners based on a five to one exchange of Germans to Frenchmen, both sides ignoring the fact that the French prisoners would be released immediately, while the Germans would be released in the future.

Von Choltitz seemed content to meet, negotiate, and attempt to defuze the inevitable. For a veteran of the Eastern Front who had participated in Sevastopol's destruction, he appeared remarkably slow to follow his orders. Two weeks earlier, Warsaw's populace had risen and the Germans had rushed eight fresh divisions to reduce resistance house by house. The battle still raged there. Von Choltitz clearly didn't want that sort of battle with his enemy so close.

Unwittingly, von Kluge's replacement, Field Marshal Model, helped the French cause when he gave the city commandant permission to delay destroying the Seine River bridges, when von Choltitz reasoned that beginning any destruction at that time would further inflame the populace and hamper his efforts for defense.

On August 19, the Resistance planned to rise under the leadership of the French Communist, Henri Tanguy, whose nom de guerre was "Colonel Rol." Alexandre Parodi, heading the Gaullist Resistance group, learned of the Communist plan and decided to seize the Préfecture de Police near Notre Dame with striking policemen before the Communists could act. Other factions soon joined.

Two thousand police in civilian clothes assembled at the Préfecture, near Notre Dame, hoisting the Tricolor and singing the Marseillaise. Soon they took the Palais de Justice nearby, converting the connecting Boulevard du Palais into a fire-swept zone when German tanks and troops appeared.

The Hôtel de Ville fell the next day (August 20) and while Nordling worked to gain a truce, the Germans withdrew into strongholds in the city's center, leaving only to patrol with tanks and masses of infantry. Nordling met von Choltitz on the 20th, obtaining for the Resistance fighters combatant status and recognition from the Germans. Von Choltitz also agreed that the Préfecture and Hôtel de Ville could remain occupied if the FFI would not attack German strongholds.

Neither the Resistance leaders nor elements of the German forces such as the SS wanted such an agreement. Despite efforts both to publicize the truce and limit bloodshed, sporadic firing continued. Resistance leaders met on the 21st and decided to denounce the truce the following day. Rather than Nordling's truce, the famous cry "Aux Barricades" resounded.

In the Latin Quarter and to a lesser extent in other parts of the city uncontrolled by the Germans, hundreds of barricades appeared, Torn up street stones, trees, overturned carts and automobiles soon blocked streets and were manned by street fighters sporting homemade armbands, World War I poilu headgear or occasionally, German helmets.

The first battles set the tone. Tanks machinegunned windows or occasionally fired armor-piercing shot, but no high explosive rounds were used. The Germans never pressed attacks. Resistants used small arms, Molotov cocktails, and captured machineguns. Soft-skinned vehicles by the score were destroyed the first day, after which tanks became the primary accompanying vehicle for German troops. The French took prisoners; SS elements within the city shot theirs.

In ordering the city's defense, Hitler's orders were clear. "Paris must not fall into the hands of the enemy, or, if it does, he must find there nothing but a field of ruins." Von Choltitz's garrison had some 22,000 troops including an estimated 50 tanks. Another division was promised to make Fortress Paris a costly objective for the Allies to take.

By August 22, Paris was an open battlefield with three dozen miniature war zones. Emissaries to both Patton and Bradley pleaded for immediate assistance. Late on the 22nd, Eisenhower ordered Bradley to move on Paris. If von Choltitz decided to fight the Resistance with the tanks and aircraft he had available, thousands would die and the city would be ravaged.

Some German elements did fight. The Grand Palais was set ablaze by incendiary rounds on the 23rd and by nightfall, the 500th Parisian fell in battle. Fighting increased. Resistants seized the mairies, the borough halls that represented local government. Several were now attacked by machine gunning tanks. By the 24th, three-quarters of the city seemed occupied by freedom fighters with the inner city still a German stronghold.

Eisenhower had already directed that the 2nd French Armored Division under Maj. Gen. Philippe Leclerc would be the first Allied division to enter Paris when that day came. Previously directed north from Patton's command to Hodges's to facilitate that move, Leclerc now had the orders he had waited for. Leclerc sent a Piper Cub aircraft to fly low over the Préfecture to drop a message to the police occupying the building, "Hold on. We are coming."

Seeing Leclerc's initial concentration as a confused start by the French, V Corps commander Leonard Gerow asked Bradley for permission to send his US 4th Infantry Division, which had landed on *Utah*, to join the rush to Paris. Bradley's reply reflected his chagrin at Allied politics ruining his advance, "To hell with prestige, tell the 4th to slam on in and take the liberation."

Leclerc's march was not unopposed. His three armored combat commands lost 40 tanks and selfpropelled guns, more than a hundred other vehicles, and over 300 men during their first day's advance to the city.

While he reorganized for the next day's advance, Leclerc infiltrated a small armored force into the city on the night of the 24th. With the column of three tanks and six half-tracks wending its way to the Hôtel de Ville, church bells announced their arrival at 21:22 hours. Choltitz reportedly called Army Group B Headquarters, and holding the phone at arm's length for Model's chief of staff to hear, told him that the bells of Paris were telling the city that the Allies had arrived.

Early on the 25th, Leclerc's 2nd Armored and Barton's 4th Infantry Divisions made their final push. Leclerc's Fighting French entered from the west and south, amid hysterical crowds and occasional gunfire. Maj. Gen. Barton's veteran 4th came in from the south to clear the eastern part of the city.

By 10:00 hours, both divisions were in the city where only strongpoints remained as pockets of German resistance. Despite some street fighting, von Choltitz appeared to do nothing to inspire the city's defense. No orders were given to fire the demolitions. When Hitler received news that the Allies had entered Paris he raged. The negative reply to his question, "Is Paris burning?" marked von Choltitz as a criminal in his own army but made him the unacknowledged savior of Paris.

Von Choltitz signed documents surrendering the city to Maj. Gen. Leclerc and then jointly to Leclerc and the Resistance. By noon on August 25 Tricolors flew over the Eiffel Tower and then Napoleon's Arc. Approximately 10,000 Germans were taken, along with three dozen tanks. Approximately a thousand freedom fighters died, and over 1,500 were wounded.

Charles de Gaulle entered the city on August 26, to proclaim his government without Allied sponsorship. That night, German bombers droned overhead attempting to do what von Choltitz refused to do: destroy Paris. Five hundred houses burned and 50 dead and 500 injured were added to the war's toll. It was the worst raid suffered during the war.

On August 27 Eisenhower and Bradley arrived in the city, and on August 29, the US 28th Division made a triumphal march through Paris, both to soothe French fears and to position itself for battle outside the city the next day. For Paris, the nightmare was over. For the men of the 28th marching towards battles in the Hurtgen, the Ardennes, and the Colmar Pocket, the nightmare would continue.

■ The Strategic Argument

Allied intelligence reports reflected the euphoria that seemed to fill the Allied command. France was rapidly being overrun. The invasion of southern France had succeeded and Marseilles was in Allied hands. The Luftwaffe appeared to be shot out of the sky and only made intermittent appearances over German cities, not over the battlefields. SHAEF's estimate for the week ending August 19 summed up what many commanders believed true: "The enemy has lost the war and the defeat of Seven(th) Army and Panzer-gruppe West will hasten the end."

But how would it end? Eisenhower approved a general campaign plan shortly before the Normandy landings, based on a gradual advance to the Seine, a strong buildup, and a series of major actions that would bring the Allied forces to the German border by D + 330, linking up with the Allied forces in southern France, and clearing France, Holland, Belgium, and Luxembourg.

Four avenues existed for entering Germany: Flanders, Maubeuge–Liège–Aachen, the Ardennes, and Metz–Saarbrücken. The SHAEF "broad front" plan called for advancing on all four, with the main Allied attack being made north of the Ardennes through Aachen, and with a secondary effort going towards the Saar through Metz.

Forces would shift to meet opportunities and concentrate for major attacks, but the intent was to keep the entire front active. When the German Army was destroyed west of the Rhine, a massive double envelopment of the Ruhr would end the war. Using available resources, freeing allies, and tying in with an ongoing aerial campaign against Germany's economy and population, it was a sound plan. The generals closest to the battlefield, however, developed other plans.

Before the Falaise battle played out, Montgomery designed a campaign plan, which if it could not end the war, at least would restructure strategy for 1944. Briefing Bradley on August 17, he mistakenly believed that his American counterpart was still willing to follow his lead.

Montgomery's campaign plan focused on the final *Overlord* objective, the industrial Ruhr, and used all the Allied armies in France, which would go through Belgium entering Germany north of the Ardennes. He planned to keep both Army Groups together, his own 21st clearing the Channel coast, Flanders, and seizing Antwerp, while Bradley's 12th Army Group moved on the prime invasion route into the Ruhr: the Liège–Aachen–Cologne avenue of approach.

Montgomery's plan was attractive because if it succeeded, it would clear the coast of the V-2 rocket sites, obtain the Channel ports and Antwerp to solve the logistics problem, and place the Allies at the front door of Germany's industry and population.

Montgomery, however, tied the plan to the issue of command. He demanded total ground command for himself, which the Americans found both irritating and unsupportable as Montgomery began to cannibalize some divisions to replace losses in others. With up to four American divisions arriving monthly, and the planned final American force outnumbering the total British and Canadian divisions by four to one, the Americans no longer saw a need to serve under Montgomery.

Monty's stock had fallen in many circles, and the American public demanded a change, a feeling also universally held by American generals in Europe. US Chief of Staff, Gen. Marshall, urged Eisenhower to take control. When Eisenhower assumed the ground command at the end of August, Bradley, whose Army Group already was larger than Montgomery's own, would be fully independent.

By August 20, Bradley's planners published his "Operation Plan Normandy To The Rhine" His succinct mission statement defied Monty's ideas: "Twelfth Army Group upon completion of present operation will regroup and resume its advance to the northeast in zone, cross the SEINE, encircle PARIS, and continue the advance to seize the crossings of the RHINE River from STRASBOURG to MAINZ inclusive."

Eisenhower sought to define the next objectives before assuming the ground command in September by meeting Bradley on August 19, and then Montgomery and Bradley separately on the 23rd. Ike still accepted the "broad front" plan advanced in May as the most reasonable course of action for the Allies and with it, granting priority to the Liège–Aachen–Cologne approach with a secondary advance through the Metz approach towards the Saar.

Additionally, he followed the logic of both the size and importance of the avenues of approach, plus their logistical supportability in giving priorities to the Army Groups. Eisenhower ordered Montgomery to take Brussels and Antwerp while clearing the Channel ports along the way. Realizing this would require both Montgomery's armies, he authorized Montgomery to "coordinate" Hodges's First Army's advance to cover his left, Hodges therefore to go to Aachen.

Though this decision kept Hodges under Bradley's command and gave Bradley responsibility for the key avenue of approach to Germany, Bradley viewed the decision as losing an army to Montgomery, and attempted to get Eisenhower to limit Montgomery's "coordinating" to a single corps, calling Montgomery "cautious."

As theater commander, Eisenhower realized that any future plans rode on logistics. He therefore directed Bradley to clear the Brittany ports, his real lifeline until Antwerp and Marseilles could be fully developed and the European rail net rebuilt. Eisenhower authorized Bradley to buildup east of Paris, which Bradley interpreted as tacit approval to continue Patton's advance. But in every guidance message to the army groups or summary to the Combined Chiefs, nowhere did Eisenhower place a priority on Patton's lunge to the Saar as anything but behind Montgomery's clearing the Channel coast and taking Antwerp and Bradley's opening the Brittany ports.

Eisenhower's decision was hotly decried by both his Army Group commanders, each believing that victory was within grasp if all the priorities for advance were to be given to his Army Group. The loudest protests came from the army commander on what Eisenhower, essentially, had designated the least decisive avenue of approach for the immediate future.

Patton fumed, claiming that given the gas and supplies, he could be in Germany with his Third Army in ten days. With one corps tied to capturing the Brittany ports, his other three corps mustered only seven divisions, which even if they made the Rhine at Mannheim, would suddenly find themselves stranded without gas, and minus the airfields needed to maintain essential close air support. Finally, Mannheim is about 175 miles (280km) south of the Ruhr and double that distance from Berlin.

Patton's plan of attack held a problem which summarized the draw-back of every offensive plan advanced during that late August. Momentum was admirable, but a decisive-sized force able to fight the remainder of the German Army in a critical area with adequate supplies was a necessity, not a toehold or a force stranded from its own supplies.

The Allied front was too large for the forces available, even when logistically supported. This fact explains why Eisenhower's original plans concentrated forces in the north, leaving the southern flank thinly held. Until the Channel ports, Brittany ports, or Antwerp opened to ease the logistics problem, and rail and pipe lines were built to carry the required tonnages, supporting unlimited advances on all fronts was not possible.

The race to the Rhine, however, was still not over. Montgomery strained to drag every mile of advance before the predicted gasoline famine halted his forces.

Not able to move with "40 divisions," Montgomery still aimed to have a bridgehead across the Rhine before the German defense solidified, which would require a future river crossing to be an over-water assault approaching a miniature invasion. Spurred on by increasingly optimistic intelligence reports, Montgomery among others, might have hoped that with the Allies at the front door, perhaps German resolve would crumble as it did in 1918, sparing Britain another war winter.

Nor was Bradley convinced he should curb his advance to support Monty's left. He gave Patton equal gasoline rations and directed one of First Army's corps south to maintain linkage with Patton and to support Third Army's advance.

The advance continued with September promising ground gains for perhaps two weeks – gains which could complete France and Belgium's liberation while tightening the grip on Hitler's borders. With no apparent operational decision obtainable, Eisenhower approved Montgomery's thrust to the Rhine, but realistically did not see the move as being able to topple Germany or even reach Berlin.

Yet Monty's Rhine thrust did serve critical needs that Bradley's favored Saar line of operations neglected. Most importantly, it would end the immediate V-weapon threat to England, a threat that if turned against her ports instead of her cities could have severely curbed Allied supplies and disrupted the Allies' logistics.

Antwerp was a key and an obvious objective, but if 21st Army Group were to continue beyond, the Netherlands could be freed and the entire German Fifteenth Army could be bagged like the Seventh had been at Falaise. In the fall of 1944, geography, logistics, and politics ensured that Montgomery's advance would be supported.

■ The Final Days of August

While Monty was discussing his new campaign plan with Bradley on August 17, Patton was pushing reconnaissance east of Orléans and Dreux, which fell the day before. Three divisions were attached to First Army to close the Falaise Gap, but within the shift, Patton acquired two more divisions for his Brittany reduction. He pushed Haislip's XV Corps to the northeast to seize crossings on the Seine as part of the wide envelopment to interdict any German withdrawals from the Falaise area.

Within a day he had forces on the Seine and by the 19th, while Eisenhower and Bradley met, Patton had a bridgehead at Mantes Gassicourt northwest of Paris. First Army and the Canadians closed the "Gap" on the 20th at Chambois. XII Corps, now commanded by Manton S. Eddy who replaced the ill Gen. Cook, added Seine bridgeheads to Patton's eastern drive.

Patton, whose success spurred Bradley to propose a two-army advance to Metz and Germany by the 12th Army Group, proposed two alternative plans to his boss.

"Plan A" would swing Third Army north pivoting on the Seine to take the enemy's rear east of the Seine and in front of the other three Allied armies; "Plan B" sent Third Army east to Germany and the Rhine.

Having already sold Eisenhower on an advance to the Saar, Bradley immediately rejected Plan A. Patton's orders, however, included the statement, "… be prepared to change direction and execute Plan A on Army order." That order never came.

The Seine was the point of no return in the "great argument." Plan B ended the last chance at an even-handed approach to a "single thrust." Had Patton swung north, Eisenhower could still have modified the thrust to send Patton towards Aachen from the south, and the full body of two army groups towards the Ruhr, with Eisenhower in command.

But with Patton racing east, every day made Eisenhower's "broad front" decision more irreversible. Montgomery continued to argue for his plan but now demanded Patton's halt, an unfortunately necessary requirement to consolidate logistical support behind his own advance. Refusing to abandon his plan, Ike permitted Patton's advance and held against Montgomery's demand for total ground command.

By August 25 when Paris surrendered to Leclerc, Patton's six divisions were angled to the southeast from Paris all along the Seine with "P" Wood's 4th Armored characteristically 30 miles (48km) further out in front at the city of Troyes. He still had five divisions in Brittany and, despite having lost XV Corps to First Army as the result of closing the "Gap," Patton still looked east towards Germany.

His columns were being fed, fueled and rearmed by the "Red Ball Express," an ad hoc grouping of more than 130 truck companies, making up to a 600-mile (960km) round trip to carry essential supplies direct to the advancing divisions.

Bradley stopped Third Army for a day in accordance with Eisenhower's priorities to build up, but then unleashed Patton who was determined to drain his tanks and trucks of gas going east and then continue his army's advance on foot. Mesmerized by getting his two corps on the Rhine, Patton headed for the World War I battlefields where he had first commanded tanks in battle.

August's final days brought further spectacular successes, seemingly belying predictions of a future halt in operations. Montgomery's British and Canadian forces, whose hard-bought advances against the bulk of the German armor in the west brought them to the Seine about a week after Hodges's and Patton's armies, now readied their grand advance. They began crossing the Seine as part of the general Allied attack on the 26th, Dempsey's British Second Army with Horrocks's XXX Corps in the lead began its pursuit to the Belgian–Dutch border, and within days would match Patton's best time by covering 250 miles (400km) in six days, freeing Brussels by September 3.

Crerar's Canadians moved to take the vital Channel ports. Hodges's First Army pivoted on Paris with "Lightning Joe" Collins's US VII Corps racing north encircling a further 25,600 Germans in the "Mons Gap."

When Eisenhower took command of the Allied Force on September 1, 21st Army Group's 14 divisions had a bridgehead on the Somme and within ten days would overrun the Channel coast; investing the key ports, freeing Brussels, capturing Antwerp, and would be sitting on the Dutch border.

Hodges's First Army raced 100 miles (160km) to the Belgian border and by the time logistics stopped Monty, most of Belgium and all of Luxembourg would be liberated, and patrols would be probing across into Germany. First Army prepared to attack the Siegfried Line, using Collins's VII Corps in the Aachen corridor. Patton crossed the Meuse at Verdun by the 1st, and with only six divisions pressed rapidly east reaching the Mosel from Metz to Nancy. But even Patton could be stopped by a supply famine.

Finally, logistics halted the general advance while limited attacks tried to strain forward. Eisenhower's four armies were no longer tightly joined presenting a powerful front, but holding a front of approximately 300 miles (480km). By September 10, the pursuit was over, and the war in northwest Europe entered an entirely new stage.

■ Normandy: The Final Account

Overlord's objectives were met on August 24 – D + 79 – when the line outlining the "lodgment area" was reached, although historians normally consider Eisenhower's assumption of command on September 1 as the logical end of the campaign.

By September, the Allies had suffered nearly 210,000 casualties, including almost 37,000 dead. Thirty-eight Allied divisions were on the continent facing 51 German "divisions" whose actual combat strength SHAEF computed at 33 divisions. German losses have been variously estimated between 400,000 and 500,000, with at least 1,500 tanks and 3,500 guns destroyed.

With an Allied force rapidly growing to eight divisions moving up from southern France, most of France was free. Belgium, Luxembourg, and the Netherlands were days away from freedom for some of their populations. The war, however, was far from over. Neither Holland nor France would be totally freed until the end of the Rhineland campaign the following spring. Luxembourg and Belgium would be liberated and then fought over again during the bloody Ardennes campaign in December and January.

Normandy, however, was the essential starting-point on the road to liberation. The "Second Front" long awaited by the Soviets and the "Cross-Channel Attack" that was the center piece of America's direct approach strategy to destroy Hitler, spelt doom for the Third Reich.

Neither the strategic bombing offensive that contributed so much, the essential efforts of the Allied navies and merchant marine, nor the valiant campaigns fought in the Mediterranean, North Africa, nor even the Eastern Front, could have brought victory by 1945 without *Overlord*. Within a year of the invasion, Nazi Germany was smashed, and Western Europe was free.

History's judgements on *Overlord*, its contributions, and its personalities will long continue. Historical research never ends; each generation seems to have the need to reevaluate and assess in the light of its values. Perhaps *Overlord*'s epitaph should follow the symbolism represented on the shoulder sleeve insignia of the Supreme Headquarters Allied Expeditionary Force.

The insignia featured a crusader's sword of liberation representing avenging justice to break Nazi power in Europe, on a sable shield representing the oppression that had fallen over Europe. Atop the shield is a rainbow representing the colors of the Allied national flags, under an azure field representing the peace and tranquility that the United Nations would attempt to restore to Europe's people,

The accomplishments of the Allied Force that marched, flew, or sailed under SHAEF's command matched in deeds what the symbolism of SHAEF's insignia represented. So many years after the event, history has to record that SHAEF's objectives were met.

INDEX